Leadership Secrets
from the Proverbs

Leadership Secrets
from the Proverbs

An Examination of Leadership Principles
from the Book of Proverbs

Robert A. Yost

Foreword by
Ray L. Parker

WIPF & STOCK · Eugene, Oregon

LEADERSHIP SECRETS FROM THE PROVERBS
An Examination of Leadership Principles from The Book of Proverbs

Copyright © 2013 Robert A. Yost. All rights reserved. Except for brief quotations in critical publications or reviews, no part of this book may be reproduced in any manner without prior written permission from the publisher. Write: Permissions, Wipf and Stock Publishers, 199 W. 8th Ave., Suite 3, Eugene, OR 97401.

Wipf & Stock
An Imprint of Wipf and Stock Publishers
199 W. 8th Ave., Suite 3
Eugene, OR 97401
www.wipfandstock.com

ISBN 13: 978-1-62564-069-7

Manufactured in the U.S.A.

Unless otherwise noted, the quotations from the Greek NT are taken from the BibleWorks, v.8 database (BGT/BNT) of the United Bible Society 4th edition/ Nestle-Al- and 27th edition of the *Greek New Testament*, edited by Barbara Aland, Kurt Aland, Johannes Karavidopoulos, Carlo M. Martini, and Bruce M. Metzger in cooperation with the Institute for New Testament Textual Research, Münster/Westphalia. Copyright © 1993 Deutsche Bibelgesellschaft, Stuttgart. Copyright © 1998–2008 *BibleWorks*, LLC. BibleWorks, v.8.

Citations from the Hebrew Bible are taken from the Groves-Wheeler Westminster Morphology and Lemma Database. Copyright © 2008 (release 4.10) by the Westminster Theological Seminary, and used by arrangement with Westminster Theological Seminary, Glenside, Pennsylvania. The Hebrew text has been corrected to the latest available facsimiles of Codex Leningradensis. Copyright © 1998–2008 BibleWorks, LLC.

Unless otherwise noted, the quotations from the Septuagint, the Greek Translation of the OT, are taken from the database of Rahlfs' Septuagint (Copyright © 1935 by the Württembergische Bibelanstalt/Deutsche Bibelgesellschaft, Stuttgart). Copyright © 1998–2008 BibleWorks, LLC.

Quotations designated NIV/NIB are from THE HOLY BIBLE: NEW INTERNATIONAL VERSION®. NIV®. Copyright © 1973, 1978, 1984 by International Bible Society, www.ibs.org. All rights reserved worldwide.

All emphases in Scripture quotations have been added by the author.

To my wife Tessie Ann Yost, my dream girl, lover, best friend, beloved partner in life, and encourager *par excellence*. I am truly the most blessed man in the world.

Special thanks is extended to the faculty and staff of New Life Theological Seminary for their encouragement and many helpful comments during the writing of this book. I am particularly indebted to Dr. Eddie Grigg, President of New Life Theological Seminary, who encouraged me to pursue this book project and gently pushed me to seek publication.

I also wish to extend special thanks to Dr. Ray Parker, Vice President of Trinity Theological Seminary, who planted the idea of marrying the book of Proverbs to leadership principles and who acted as my adviser during the writing of my thesis for the Ph.D. degree. He was always a tremendous encouragement and cheerleader when I was bogged down in the minutiae and tedium of the research and actual writing of numerous drafts. I am honored that he consented to write the forward for this book.

Finally, I owe a debt of gratitude to Dr. Stephen O. Stout, my colleague and dear friend of thirty years who went well beyond the call of duty in spending many hours proofreading and formatting several drafts and who offered many helpful suggestions for clarity of reading. He also spared me the embarrassment of seeing a glaring error or two make its way into print. Thank you again, Steve.

Contents

Foreword by Ray L. Parker | ix
Preface | xi
List Of Abbreviations | xiii

1. Introduction and Overview of the Study: Why Study Proverbs in Connection with Leadership? | 1
2. The Leader's Priorities | 12
3. The Leader's Plans | 23
4. The Leader's Speech: The Proper Use of the Tongue | 31
5. The Leader's Speech: The Improper Use of the Tongue | 69
6. Summary and Conclusions | 126

Appendices

1. *Classification of the Proverbs of Solomon, the Sayings of the Wise and of Agur, Son of Jakeh Pertaining to the Tongue by Chapter* | 129
2. *Classification of the Proverbs of Solomon, the Sayings of the Wise and of Agur, Son of Jakeh Pertaining to the Tongue by Category* | 138
3. *Table 2.1: Characteristics of Admired Leaders* | 143
4. *Table 2.2: Cross-Cultural Comparisons of the Characteristics of Admired Leaders* | 145

Bibliography | 147
Scripture Index | 155
Subject Index | 161

Foreword

FOR CENTURIES BELIEVERS HAVE identified the Old Testament book of Proverbs as the book of practical wisdom. Some find such value in the book; they suggest that one study a chapter each day and thus ponder these truths monthly. Biblical counselors often guide their clients into the book for sensible answers to life's problems. Church youth leaders encourage their teens to apply the principles of life and success found in Proverbs. Motivational speakers often quote the proverbial sayings of the book to inspire their listeners.

Dr. Robert Yost now adds to the depth of application for this Old Testament masterpiece. Dr. Yost explores the book through the eyes of the leader. Valid leadership principles and priorities abound in Proverbs. All who aspire to successful leadership will benefit from a study of this scholarly, interpretive, well-planned journey into the proverbial wisdom of this Old Testament book.

According to Dr. Yost, all successful leaders establish priorities. At the top of this list are God and family. If these two realities are askew, leadership achievement is hindered. These two priorities establish the solid foundation for leadership success. It is vital that the leader make wise decisions in these areas.

Another universal challenge for the leader is communication. Most researchers in leadership theory mention communication as a major leadership ability to master. Dr. Yost in this current volume crafts for us sound communicative principles as taught within Proverbs. All in leadership positions and any aspiring to leadership positions will benefit from a mastery of these biblical techniques.

As you read this scholarly work, you will find encouragement, information, clarity, inspiration, and sound biblical principles of wisdom for the

Foreword

leadership task. You will find yourself coming back to this volume often; it is that kind of book.

Ray L. Parker, Ed.D., Ph.D.
Vice President
Trinity College of the Bible and Theological Seminary

Preface

Title: Leadership Principles in the Book of Proverbs

This book is a revision of my Ph.D. dissertation submitted to the Trinity Theological Seminary in Newburgh, IN, in 2012, under the able guidance of Dr. Ray Parker, under the title "An Examination of Leadership Principles from the Book of Proverbs." The dissertation studied the book of Proverbs, but especially the "sayings" sections in an attempt to discover leadership principles embedded therein. This project actually began as a paper in Dr. Parker's "Leadership and Management Theory" class at Trinity. A 12-15 page paper turned into a 36 page one so intrigued was I by the topic. When it came time to choose a topic about which to write for a dissertation in Biblical Studies, I found myself coming back to the richness of the Proverbs. The leadership angle was a natural one to pursue in that in recent years many popular writers such as Bill Hybels and Andy Stanley were beginning to publish books which featured the very real connections between leadership and the book of Proverbs. However, as I discovered when I wrote my paper for Dr. Parker's class, there were no books of a scholarly nature developing this connection. Hence, my dissertation was born.

Thesis

The thesis of this work is that there are some foundational leadership principles embedded in the book of Proverbs. Whereas this book barely scratches the surface of attempting to delineate those principles, a foundation is laid, I believe, by applying them to the leader's priorities, plans, and speech. The Thesis of this book is that *A godly leader orders his priorities, plans, and tongue by the wisdom contained in the Proverbs.* It is obvious that the principles contained in the book of Proverbs are of value not only to the

Preface

Christian leader, but to the secular leader as well and to all Christians, indeed all people. All leaders and all people, whether Christian or not, would be better for heeding the principles contained therein.

The meat of the book is found in Chapters 3 through 5. Therefore, this book will begin in Chapter 2 with an examination of the leader's priorities. His relationship to God is paramount. This is the foundation upon which godly ministry is built. Then comes the godly leader's relationship to his family. Within the family sphere, the husband and wife relationship is of primary importance. After that, comes the parent and child relationship.

Chapter 3 outlines how the godly leader makes plans for the future. If we consider the planning process to be a partnership, then the godly leader makes his plans primarily in partnership with God. After seeking God's guidance in the planning process, he then makes his plans in partnership with others. In other words, he does not eschew the wise counsel of others.

Chapter 4 begins to examine the speech of the leader. This chapter outlines the proper use of the tongue. Proper uses of the tongue include imparting knowledge and wisdom, encouragement, protection, nurture, healing, telling the truth, pleasant speech, praise, advice, confessing sin, discretion, and rebuke.

Chapter 5 examines the other side of the coin of the leader's speech. Topics covered under the improper use of the tongue include lying, gossip, foolish talk, slander, quarreling, speaking rashly, boasting, flattery, mockery, and perverse talk. It is readily apparent from even a cursory examination of the book of Proverbs that the speech of the leader is important. What is said or not said and how it is said are of no small importance in the eyes of God.

A unique feature of this book is my attempt in Appendix A and Appendix B to classify the sayings proverbs of Solomon, the sayings of the wise and of Agur, son of Jakeh, first by chapter as they occur in the book of Proverbs and second by category. This is by no means a completed task, but rather a work in progress. However, it is an attempt, no matter how feeble, to classify most of the proverbs pertaining to the tongue or to speech. This, to my knowledge, has never been done before.

It is my hope and prayer that this book will stimulate the reading and study of this most unique book of sacred Scripture. And may God grant us better leaders. To God be the glory! "The fear of the Lord is the beginning of knowledge."

Abbreviations

Reference Works
(Full Information Included in Bibliography)

BDAG	*Greek-English Lexicon of the New Testament and Other Early Christian Literature*
BDB	*Hebrew-Aramaic and English Lexicon of the Old Testament*
ESV	*The English Standard Version*
HB	*The Hebrew Bible*
KJV	*The King James Version of the English Bible*
LXX	*The Septuagint, the Greek Translation of the OT*
MT	*Masoretic Text of the Hebrew Bible (see HB and OT)*
NASB	*The New American Standard Bible*
NICOT	*The New International Commentary on the Old Testament*
NIDB	*The New International Dictionary of the Bible: Pictorial Edition*
NIV	*The New International Version of the Bible*
NJB	*New Jerusalem Bible*
NOAA	*The New Oxford Annotated Apocrypha*
RSV	*The Revised Standard Version*
NT	*The New Testament of the Christian Scriptures*
OT	*The Old Testament of the Hebrew Bible (HB)*
SOTI	*Survey of Old Testament Introduction*
TWOT	*Theological Wordbook of the Old Testament*

Chapter 1

Introduction and Overview of the Study

Why Study Proverbs in Connection with Leadership?

THE BIBLE SPEAKS ON a plethora of subjects and is a repository of information on a multiplicity of topics not limited to religious and theological ones. It has been revered for millennia for its religious teaching and guidance, its timeless wisdom, and its literary grandeur and majesty. Although the Bible is known primarily as a religious and theological work with elements of law, history, poetry, gospel, epistle, and apocalyptic incorporated, it also has much to say on the subject of leadership. Lorin Woolfe, a leadership consultant who formerly was a leadership specialist at the American Management Association, writes of the Bible, "Read carefully and with another perspective, it is also the greatest collection of leadership case studies ever written, with tremendously useful and insightful lessons for today's leaders and managers."[1]

The book of Proverbs has increasingly become the focus of attention for Christians in recent years. Tremper Longman III and Raymond Dillard write of this phenomenon, "Our age has become increasingly absorbed with interest in ourselves and how we relate to others, and many feel that this book provides divinely given help in understanding human personality and behavior."[2] In like fashion, interest in leadership studies has increased almost exponentially over the past several decades. Christian thinkers have begun to correlate biblical principles with the study of effective leadership. Like grapes of gold set in silver, the book is Proverbs is ripe for plucking.

---

1. Woolfe, *Leadership Secrets From the Bible*, ix.
2. Longman and Dillard, *An Introduction to the Old Testament*, 265.

A Statement of the Problem

As important as the book of Proverbs is in the area of leadership studies, it is noteworthy that there is a lamentable dearth of scholarly resources on this subject. There are a multitude of scholarly materials available on the Proverbs (e.g., books, commentaries, monographs, journal articles), and even more has been published in recent decades on the subject of leadership. There are also many works that seek to discern leadership principles from the Bible as a whole (e.g., Woolfe's *Leadership Secrets from the Bible*[3] and Manyika's *The Challenge of Leadership*[4]). However, on the subject of leadership principles derived from the book of Proverbs, the landscape is decidedly barren. In recent years, there have been a number of works published on this subject, but these materials have been primarily devotional in nature, not research based. When materials have been published in this area, they have tended to deal primarily with how the book of Proverbs should impact managerial practices (e.g., Zigarelli's *Management By Proverbs*[5]), not leadership, which is an entirely different function. Therefore, there is a definite need for scholarly research to be explored in this very specific area of leadership principles derived from the book of Proverbs and to develop applications that are not just philosophical in nature. This study will critically examine the leadership principles crafted in the book of Proverbs, to discover how the inspired author(s) dealt with leadership issues.

Importance of the Study

Since little has been published in the area of leadership studies in the book of Proverbs, this study will add to the body of literature in this field. The hope is that its findings will assist the contemporary church, para-church, and even Christian and secular business leaders to understand clearly and effectively utilize the inspired proverbial wisdom of the ever current biblical text. This study should result in present day Christian leaders being better able to create a paradigm of effectiveness, efficiency, and edification springing from the font of God's wisdom.

---

3. Ibid.
4. Manyika, *The Challenge of Leadership*.
5. Zigarelli, *Management by Proverbs*.

Organization of the Study

This paper will begin with an Introduction and Overview of the Study, which will outline such introductory elements as Methodology, Delimitations, Definitions, and a brief overview of previous studies. The second chapter will develop The Leader's Priorities, which are primarily twofold: (1) Relationship to God, and (2) Relationship to Family.

The third chapter will develop The Leader's Plans, which are also twofold: (1) Partnership with God, and (2) Partnership with Others. The fourth chapter will outline The Leader's Speech and how it should be used. The chapter is subtitled The Proper Use of the Tongue. This chapter will develop twelve areas: (1) Imparting Knowledge and Wisdom, (2) Encouragement, (3) Protection, (4) Nurture, (5) Healing, (6) Telling the Truth, (7) Pleasant Speech, (8) Praise, (9) Advice, (10) Confessing Sin, (11) Discretion, and (12) Rebuke. The fifth chapter will continue the theme of Chapter 4, The Leader's Speech, this time focusing on the Improper Use of the Tongue. This chapter will develop ten areas under this heading: (1) Lying, (2) Gossip, (3) Foolish Talk, (4) Slander, (5) Quarreling, (6) Speaking Rashly, (7) Boasting, (8) Flattery, (9) Mockery, and (10) Perverse Talk.

Finally, the sixth chapter will be Summary and Conclusions. This chapter will attempt to summarize the major findings of the paper and offer any conclusions that are suggested by the research.

Methodology

This paper will examine the Old Testament book of Proverbs to attempt to discover the leadership principles that are contained therein. Although many other books of the Bible deal with the subject of leadership, this study will limit itself to the book of Proverbs and allude to other portions of Scripture only as they reinforce the arguments presented from that wisdom book. Furthermore, although some of the apocryphal books may have spiritual and practical value (e.g., *The Wisdom of Solomon* and *Sirach*), their non-canonical status precludes them from consideration in this study except as their inclusion may reinforce or supplement its findings. This investigation will follow the organizational pattern as previously outlined. The outline will follow the format of a content model. All Scripture quotations will come from the *New International Version*[6] unless otherwise stated. All

---

6. New International Version, 1978.

references from the Hebrew Bible will come from *Biblia Hebraica Stuttgartensia*[7] unless otherwise stated. All references from the *Apocrypha* will come from *The New Oxford Annotated Apocrypha* Revised Fourth Edition.[8]

Delimitations

The vast literature in the field of leadership studies is a relatively new phenomenon. The subject has been the focus of serious and systematic study for only the past century or so. The endeavor of applying biblical principles to the leadership task is even more recent. It is only in recent decades that this field has begun to produce a literature, and as has already been stated, most of that material has been devotional and less than scholarly. Furthermore, attempts to apply biblical principles to this field of study have not been systematic and have barely touched on the subject.

Although the Bible as a whole has much to say on the subject of leadership, the focus of this study will be confined to one of the Wisdom Books, the book of Proverbs. It will further limit itself to an examination of how the godly leader orders his life with respect to five topics developed in the Proverbs. They are the leader's priorities, the leader's plans, and the leader's use of the tongue.

Thesis Stated: *A godly leader orders his priorities, plans, and tongue by the wisdom contained in the Proverbs.*

Definitions

It is necessary to define a few terms that will be used or presupposed in this paper.

The first is the word *leadership*. The difficulty in defining this word can be seen from the multitudinous attempts to define it. Eugene Peterson and Daniel Southern comment on this difficulty, "Leadership springs from within us and is difficult to fully explain. It is almost easier to define leadership by what it is not, than by what it is. Leaders are *not* passive, they do *not* give up easily, and they are not easily intimidated by circumstances. In untying some of the 'nots' of leadership, I have come to believe

---

7. Kahle, ed., *Biblia Hebraica Stuttgartensia*, 1983.

8. Coogan, ed., *The New Oxford Annotated Apocrypha, Fully Revised Fourth Edition*, 2010.

Introduction and Overview of the Study

that leadership *is* primarily a state of mind."[9] One essential component of leadership is followers. In other words, if nobody is following, is leadership being manifested? The logical answer to that is an emphatic NO! For the purposes of this book, the following definition of leadership from a doctoral class on Advanced Management and Leadership will be utilized: Leadership is the discovery and disclosure of group goals together with the delegation of authority and responsibility to the proper group members and the direction of group activity by an individual who has the ability to guide the group to the accomplishment of the task.

Another term that needs to be defined is the word *inerrancy*. This book proceeds on the assumption that the Bible is the inerrant Word of God, actually God-breathed (2 Tim 3:16) and free from error down to the very words. It is the opinion of this writer that the Chicago Statement on Biblical Inerrancy formulated in 1978 by approximately 200 conservative biblical scholars at a conference sponsored by the International Council on Biblical Inerrancy (ICBI) is an accurate summarization of the biblical doctrine of inerrancy and the position presupposed in this book.

While it is not within the scope of this book to examine the authorship question of Proverbs or the complex hermeneutical issues related to interpreting Hebrew parallelism in the context of extended wisdom discourses and short pithy aphorisms, it would be helpful to address these issues at least briefly.

Some Preliminary Considerations

It is beyond the scope of this study to consider the authorship question in great depth. It is sufficient to say that Proverbs opens with a superscription as is common with wisdom and prophetic books, which as Tremper Longman concludes, "functions something like a title page in a modern book."[10] The superscription reads: "The proverbs of Solomon son of David, king of Israel." Standing at the head of the book, this superscription would lead to the conclusion that Proverbs was, if not authored by Solomon, at least compiled under his direction.[11] Robert Alden writes that it is an oversimplification to conclude that Solomon is the author relying only on

---

9. Peterson and Southern, *The Message of Leadership*, 9.
10. Longman, *Proverbs*, 23.
11. Ibid.

Leadership Secrets from the Proverbs

the superscription.[12] However, on the other hand, there is no reason to jettison the historical, conservative position of Solomonic authorship of the book simply because, as Roland Murphy concludes, "There is now almost universal agreement that he (Solomon) cannot be considered the author."[13] Otto Eissfeldt, the extremely liberal form critic, echoes Murphy's position in dating the book approximately 600 years after the time of Solomon. He writes of the book of Proverbs, "It cannot have come into being before the fourth century."[14] The radical critic and commentator, C. H. Toy, argued that no material in the book of Proverbs can be dated previous to 350 B.C.E. and that the later chapters were written during the second century.[15] There are basically two extreme positions on the authorship question. One position is that Solomon wrote the entire book. The other is that he had no connection at all with it.

It is likely that the authorship question lies somewhere in the middle of two extremes. There is a strong Hebrew tradition associating Solomon with wisdom (1 Kgs 3:1–15) and with the proverb form (1 Kgs 4:29–34) as well as to the authorship of Song of Songs, Proverbs, and Ecclesiastes. According to the *Midrash*, Solomon composed Song of Songs in his youth, Proverbs in his middle age, and Ecclesiastes in his old age. Therefore, it is likely that Solomon was the primary author of Proverbs, which allows for later compilation and editing by the men of King Hezekiah (Prov 25:1) and the sayings of Agur and Lemuel being added as an appendix (Proverbs 30 and 31). Longman and Dillard take a mediating position on the issue. They write, "As usual, the hard evidence of the book leads to something between the two extremes, and this is the position of the majority of conservative and some present-day critical scholars. . . . Thus, it is certainly appropriate for the first verse to identify Solomon as the main contributor and initiator of the anthology."[16] Even a bedrock conservative scholar such as Edward J. Young concedes that "the book does not claim in its entirety to be the work of Solomon."[17] However, he concludes, "On the other hand, there is no reason for doubting the trustworthiness of these titles and not assuming that

---

12. Alden, *Proverbs*, 10.
13. Murphy, *Proverbs*, xx.
14. Eissfeldt, *The Old Testament: An Introduction*, 473.
15. Toy, *Proverbs*, xix–xxxi.
16. Ibid., 267.
17. Young, *An Introduction to the Old Testament*, 311.

Introduction and Overview of the Study

the bulk of the book is indeed from Solomon."[18] The position of this writer is that Solomon initiated the writing of the book of Proverbs, he wrote the greater portion of it, the work of other writers was added to it, and it was finally edited under the sponsorship of King Hezekiah.

The question this debate leads to is this: What does Solomon and his proverbs have to do with the subject of leadership? As mentioned previously, Solomon was noted for his writings of proverbs and great wisdom, in addition to being King of Israel and an author of Scripture. In addition, Solomon achieved notoriety and fame for his marriage and political alliances, his geographic expansion of Israel, and the construction of the Temple in Jerusalem to name just a few. John Bright, the noted Old Testament historian, writes, "Solomon's true genius, however, lay in the realm of industry and trade."[19] His managerial proficiency in commercial ventures comprises a large part of what makes him so attractive to modern writers in the field of management and leadership. However, Michael Zigarelli's warning about generalization and misapplication of Solomon's leadership principles is timely. He writes, "Despite Solomon's managerial proficiency, the business environment of 900 B.C. was so incongruent with our own that applying his advice might not even seem responsible, much less sagacious. Common sense would suggest, then, that the king's time-and-culture-specific 'wisdom' would not generalize across the millennia."[20]

Despite Zigarelli's warning, the wisdom from Proverbs does not represent simply the human writings of a worldly king and author, no matter how brilliant. Rather, they are inspired Scripture relating to mankind the very thoughts and words of God. Therefore, Solomon's words are very current and applicable to the leadership question today.

Again, Zigarelli demonstrates just how up-to-date Proverbs is. He argues,

> And despite the cultural differences three thousand years later, this divine advice informs us today with comparable force. This is because the central problem which Proverbs seeks to correct– a human nature that is bent on doing things its own way rather than God's way–is one that transcends generations, cultures, and circumstances. People remain prone to the greed, envy, dishonesty, arrogance and sharp tongues that typified those living in

18. Ibid.
19. Bright, *A History of Israel*, 214.
20. Zigarelli, *Management by Proverbs*, 14.

Solomon's day.... Proverbs affords us insight into our shortcoming of self-reliance and all of its manifestations, and provides a road map to traverse the less traveled paths of righteous behavior.[21]

The reader of Proverbs is frequently addressed as "my son," leading some scholars to interpret the entire focus of the book as being for the specific purpose of training young men.[22] David Hubbard even goes so far as to suggest that these young men from Israel's society were being "groomed for positions of leadership."[23] Although the specific audience being addressed in proverbs cannot be fixed with absolute certainty, there is no doubt that the emphasis is on the exercise of practical wisdom in daily life, which extends beyond a particular time period and specific application. Thus, the leadership advice offered by Solomon in Proverbs is timeless.

Some Hermeneutical Considerations

The Book of Proverbs is not simply thirty-one chapters of pithy statements on moral matters communicated within the format of Hebrew poetry. As R. Laird Harris cautions, "Damage has been done by some who find in the book merely a collection of ancient maxims for success–a kind of 'Poor Richard's Almanac.' Actually the book is a compendium of moral instruction. It deals with sin and holiness. And the vehicle of instruction is a favorite Semitic device–teaching by contrast."[24]

The prominent feature of Hebrew poetry is parallelism, the balancing of one thought against another. The main contrast in Proverbs is that of the life of wisdom and the life of folly. Because proverbs are by their very nature pithy and general, they are less likely to be universally applicable and totally precise. Douglas Stuart, an Old Testament scholar writing in conjunction with Gordon Fee, suggests several hermeneutical guidelines in interpreting Proverbs. He writes that they are not legal guarantees from God, worded to be memorable and not theoretically accurate, and should not be read in isolation, but in comparison with other proverbs and the rest of Scripture.[25] He states, "What Proverbs does say is that, all things being

---

21. Ibid., 14–15.
22. Estes, *Handbook on the Wisdom Books and Psalms*, 218.
23. Hubbard, *Proverbs*, 26.
24. Harris, "The Book of Proverbs," *NIDB* 830.
25. Fee and Stuart, *How To Read the Bible For All Its Worth*, 198–202.

equal, there *are* basic attitudes and patterns of behavior that will help a person grow into responsible adulthood."²⁶ Thus, as Duane Garrett argues, "The Book of Proverbs does not simply attach the caboose of Yahwism to the train of secular, international wisdom."²⁷ In fact, Proverbs is quite the opposite. It provides the locus of godly wisdom, not worldly and secular wisdom. It outlines the rules, regulations, and attitudes one must follow to lead a responsible, successful, and godly life. As Longman and Dillard observe, "It is a book of practical advice, but it is advice given in the context of the 'fear of the Lord.'"²⁸ Garrett aptly summarizes the hermeneutics of wisdom literature:

> By its very nature and purpose, wisdom emphasizes the general truth over some specific cases and, being a work of instruction, frames its teachings in short, pithy statements without excessive qualification. It is not that the wisdom writers did not know that life was complex and full of exceptions, but dwelling on those cases would have distracted attention from their didactic purposes. It is general truth that those who fear God and live with diligence and integrity will have lives that are prosperous and peaceful but that those who are lazy and untrustworthy ultimately destroy themselves. And general truths are the stock in trade of Proverbs.²⁹

There are four basic themes that run throughout the book of Proverbs. James Williams identifies four "basic motifs constituting the aphoristic wisdom of the biblical period." They are "retribution and divine justice, wise utterance, tradition and the fathers, and individual self-discipline."³⁰ All of these motifs are rooted in the fear of the Lord (Prov 1:7), which provides the way of wisdom. Williams writes, "There is now a consensus in biblical studies that a concept of order is at the very center of wisdom thinking, and this concept of order is usually linked to an understanding of divine rule and divine justice. The order of things manifests itself in a retributive principle of justice."³¹ It teaches one how to live the life of wisdom. If one does thus and so, all other things being equal, this outcome will usually occur. As

---

26. Ibid., 195.
27. Garrett, *Proverbs*, 54.
28. Longman and Dillard, *Introduction to the Old Testament*, 265.
29. Garrett, *Proverbs*, 57.
30. Williams, *Those Who Ponder Proverbs: Aphoristic Thinking and Biblical Literature*, 17.
31. Ibid.

Andreas Köstenberger and Richard Patterson observe, "Where these principles are taught as keys to godly living, they belong to the genre of wisdom literature. All wisdom literature is basically instructional in nature, with the author attempting to impart wise observations on the meaning of life and the proper conduct necessary to enjoy life to the fullest."[32]

Previous Studies

As previously mentioned, the body of literature related to the study of leadership principles from the book of Proverbs is indeed sparse. There are many excellent books on leadership principles from the Bible, but in many the references to passages in the Proverbs are either few or nonexistent. For example, in Henry and Richard Blackaby's excellent book, *Spiritual Leadership*,[33] a quick scan of the contents revealed that in 289 pages of text, there were only two mentions of verses from the book of Proverbs. Another exceptional book, *Transforming Leadership*,[34] does not mention the Proverbs at all. Of course, Leighton Ford's stated purpose is to demonstrate "Jesus' way of creating vision, shaping values, and empowering change,"[35] which would explain the exclusion. John Maxwell is perhaps the best-known of the Christian writers on leadership. Although he mentions verses from the book of Proverbs in his books, he has not yet written a book specifically on that subject.

Numerous books have been written that deal specifically with leadership principles from the book of Proverbs. However, many of them are devotional in nature and not research-based. Two recent examples of this are Peterson and Southern's *The Message of Leadership*[36] and Bill Hybels' *Axiom: Powerful Leadership Proverbs*.[37] These works may be very popular and easy to read, but they are the literary equivalent of "fast food" and hardly of enduring scholarly value with the exception being Peterson's excellent translation of the Hebrew text. Larry Burkett's classic work, *Business By the Book: The Complete Guide of Biblical Principles for the Workplace*, successfully integrates passages from the book of Proverbs into his biblical ap-

---

32. Köstenberger and Patterson, *Invitation to Biblical Interpretation*, 292.
33. Henry and Richard Blackaby, *Spiritual Leadership*.
34. Ford, *Transforming Leadership*.
35. Ibid., 1.
36. Peterson and Southern, *The Message of Leadership*.
37. Hybels, Axiom: *Powerful Leadership Proverbs*.

Introduction and Overview of the Study

proach to management and leadership.[38] His book is much more enduring and substantial than those of Hybels and Peterson/Southern. However, his approach is not simply limited to the book of Proverbs, but to the entirety of Scripture.

One book that does attempt to deal with the leadership question exclusively from the book of Proverbs in a scholarly and systematic way is Zigarelli's exceptional book, *Management by Proverbs*.[39] The main limitation of this book is that it deals more with employee management theory than with leadership theory. With that in mind, Zigarelli's contribution is substantial and very helpful. Without his contribution, this book could not have been written.

38. Burkett, *Business By The Book*.
39. Zigarelli, *Management by Proverbs*.

Chapter 2

The Leader's Priorities

THERE ARE MANY TOPICS that are important relating to the life of the leader in Proverbs. Three foundational ones are the leader's priorities, the leader's plans, and the leader's use of the tongue. This section will outline what his priorities should be.

There are two priorities, which comprise the foundation for the Christian leader: his relationship to God and his relationship to his family. Upon this foundation lie his aspirations for effective spiritual leadership.

Relationship to God

Oswald Chambers, in his devotional classic *My Utmost For His Highest*, writes, "Your priorities must be God first, God second, and God third, until your life is continually face to face with God and no one else is taken into account whatsoever."[1] A Christian leader's relationship to God is the primary and most important priority in his life. If he fails to recognize this fundamental truth, his ministry will be fruitless and a sham. Henry and Richard Blackaby argue the impossibility of being a true Christian leader apart from a vibrant relationship with God. They write, "People do not choose to become spiritual leaders. Spiritual leadership flows out of a person's vibrant, intimate relationship with God. You cannot be a spiritual leader if you are not meeting God in profound, life-changing ways."[2]

Solomon stated this proposition in what is considered by many scholars to be the theme of Proverbs, "The fear of the Lord is the beginning of

---

1. Chambers, *My Utmost for His Highest*, 7/13.
2. Blackaby and Blackaby, *Spiritual Leadership*, 100.

The Leader's Priorities

knowledge, but fools despise wisdom and discipline" (Prov 1:7). This verse employs Hebrew antithetic parallelism to set in antithesis the two opposite philosophies of life investigated in Proverbs. The nineteenth century commentator, William Arnot, writes eloquently of this antithesis:

> The fear of the Lord is the beginning of knowledge: the meaning is, he who does not reverentially trust in God, knows nothing yet as he ought to know. His knowledge is partial and distorted. Whatever acquisitions in science he may attain, if his heart depart from the living God, he abides an ignorant man. He who in his heart says "No God," is a fool, however wise he may be in the estimation of the world, and his own.... These men possess some fragments of the superstructure of knowledge, but they have not the foundation; they possess some of the branches, but they have missed the root.[3]

In other words, if one follows the teachings of the Proverbs, he is considered to be a wise man; if he fails to do so, he is a fool. The most common of the three words translated "fool" in Proverbs is כְּסִיל (*kesil*),[4] which occurs nearly fifty times and by derivation means not only "stupid fellow, dullard, fool," but also seems to imply obstinacy in his belief, "delights not in understanding."[5] He clearly revels in his ignorance and godlessness. Derek Kidner writes of such a person, "The root of his trouble is spiritual, not mental. He *likes* his folly going back to it 'like a dog that returns to his vomit.'"[6]

Such is not the attitude or practice of the wise leader. His first priority is his relationship to God. It is this reverential awe (fear) of God in Prov 1:7 that leads to this wisdom. Daniel Estes writes of this contrast, "Throughout the book of Proverbs, two paths of life are contrasted. On the one hand, there is the path of wisdom, which leads to life in all of its dimensions; on the other hand, the path of folly leads to death in all its aspects."[7]

Another passage that speaks with forceful clarity on this subject is Prov 3:5–7. It too sets in contrast the true path to wisdom against the false path.

> Trust in the Lord with all your heart
> and lean not on your own understanding;
> in all your ways acknowledge him,

---

3. Arnot, *Studies in Proverbs*, 21.
4. Kidner, *Proverbs*, 40.
5. *BDB* § 4575.
6. Kidner, *Proverbs*, 40.
7. Estes, *Handbook on the Wisdom Books and Psalms*, 222.

> and he will make your paths straight.
> Do not be wise in your own eyes;
> fear the Lord and shun evil.

Charles Bridges writes of these verses: "This is the polar-star of a child of God–faith in his Father's providence, promises, and grace."[8] True trust in God means a total abandonment to the Lord and a complete repudiation of trust in one's own wisdom. Such trusting the Lord, as Alden writes, "... means becoming well acquainted with him through his Word, spending time in his presence in prayer, and seeking the counsel of others in the faith."[9] Complete trust in God is the Christian believer's absolute priority. Garrett explains, "The commitment of the heart to God means that all the beliefs and decisions of life are to be submitted to Yahweh."[10]

Relationship to Family

There are two separate components or pairings that comprise the family unit and must be considered in any examination of the family: the husband and wife is the first, followed by parents and children. Both sets of relationships are priorities upon which attention must be focused by the spiritual leader.

Husband and Wife

It is conceded that the spiritual leader in a church, para-church organization, or business may, in fact, be a woman. However, for the purposes of this study, the treatment of a leader's priorities will be examined from the perspective of the man, the husband, and his relationship to his wife, as well as to his children.

Proverbs speaks in several places about the wife and her importance, both positively and negatively.

> He who finds a wife finds what is good
> and receives favor from the lord (Prov 18:22);
> Houses and wealth are inherited from parents,
> but a prudent wife is from the Lord (Prov 19:14);
> A foolish son is his father's ruin,

---

8. Bridges, *Proverbs*, 23.
9. Alden, *Proverbs*, 37.
10. Garrett, *Proverbs*, 81.

The Leader's Priorities

and a quarrelsome wife is like a constant dripping (Prov 19:13);
Better to live in a desert
than with a quarrelsome and ill-tempered wife.(Prov 21:19).

Arnot aptly summarizes the teaching of these verses, which he maintains "contain three distinct but connected propositions."[11] He writes,

> The *first* intimates that the marriage relation as the appointment of God, and without particular reference to the character of the persons, is good for man. The *second*, that when a man, upon entering that relation, obtains a wife who is in her individual character a prudent woman, he has obtained a blessing above all price. The *third*, that when the object chosen to occupy a relation so tender and close is personally unworthy, the calamity to the man is great in proportion to the preciousness of the divine institute which in this case has been perverted.[12]

Under the Sayings of King Lemuel, the writer of Proverbs speaks further of the value of the wife: "A wife of noble character who can find? She is worth far more than rubies" (Prov 31:10).

It is clear from these passages and without qualification that a wife is a gracious gift from God and good for the husband. Thus, it is important that he make his relationship to her a priority so that her character more closely resembles the wife described in Prov 18:22, 19:14, and 31:10 than the one described in Prov 19:13 and 21:19. It has been said that a marriage can provide a taste of heaven or hell upon the earth. This outcome is determined, in large part, upon the value the man, as spiritual leader, places upon the relationship.

It is obvious that Proverbs places a premium on fidelity to one's spouse. References to illicit sexual relations and loose women far outweigh those of any other single subject in the book.[13] Chapter five is representative of the teaching on this subject found throughout the book. The dynamic of this chapter is that of a father instructing his son, as it is in much of the book (cf. "Listen my son, to your father's instruction," Prov 1:8). He prohibits his son to engage in intimate sexual relations with women outside of the marriage relationship.

> My son, pay attention to my wisdom,
> listen well to my words of insight,

---

11. Arnot, *Studies in Proverbs*, 389.
12. Ibid.
13. Peterson and Southern, *The Message of Leadership*, 25.

> that you may maintain discretion
> and your lips may preserve knowledge.
> For the lips of an adulteress drip honey,
> and her speech is smoother than oil;
> but in the end she is bitter as gall,
> sharp as a double-edged sword.
> Her feet go down to death;
> her steps lead straight to the grave (Prov 5:1–5);
> Drink water from your own cistern,
> running water from your own well.
> Should your springs overflow in the streets,
> your streams in the public squares?
> Let them be yours alone,
> never to be shared with strangers.
> May your fountain be blessed,
> and may you rejoice in the wife of your youth (Prov 5:15–18).

Here the writer warns in graphic terms of the adulterous woman. He uses figures of speech to paint a picture of her and her wiles. Her lips drip honey and her speech is smoother than oil. Conversely, that idyllic picture is contrasted with another unpleasant one in the metaphor of the bitterness of gall and also the one of the pain of a sword. The warning also suggests that the adulterous relationship can lead to death. Garrett warns of the bitter outcome of verses one through five, "Anguish and disillusionment and emotional and even physical death all come from this illicit pleasure."[14]

He then admonishes his son to stay within the confines of the marital relationship. It is obvious from Prov 5:15–18 that the writer intends that a man have sexual relations only with his wife. He uses the obvious metaphors of water, cistern, well, and springs to encourage sexual fidelity. He urges his son to drink water only from his own cistern and well, both metaphors for the wife of his youth. These images are quite erotic and obviously refer to the young man's wife. Longman sees this terminology as referring to the wife's vagina (cf. Song of Sol 4:10–15) from comparisons to ancient Near Eastern love poetry.[15] In the ancient Near East, water was at a premium, and wells and springs were extremely valuable and carefully protected. Estes writes, "It is not surprising, then, that a guarded well would be used as a metaphor for sexual intimacy."[16] Alden takes the metaphor a step further.

---

14. Garrett, *Proverbs*, 91.
15. Longman, *Proverbs*, 161.
16. Estes, *Handbook on the Wisdom Books and Psalms*, 229.

He concludes, "The semitic image here is someone who throws water from his wells into the street, a foolish and wasteful gesture. In the east water is so scarce that this picture of waste is even more meaningful, illustrating the activity of an oversexed male who fathers children all over town."[17]

In any event, the conclusion is inescapable that a man's wife is his first priority after his relationship with God. In view of the blessing and delight that a good wife provides, why would any man go outside the boundary of marriage to seek sexual pleasure with another? The clear admonition is to "rejoice in the wife of your youth" (Prov 5:15). Eugene Peterson and Daniel Southern write from a pastoral perspective explaining why sexual fidelity is so important to the spiritual leader. They explain, "What a person does in his private life is a strong indication of what is going on in his heart. And what could be more private than the sexual relationship you have with your spouse? If a leader is unfaithful to his spouse, he is unfaithful to all who would follow him. This is so because the marriage relationship is the foundation for all other relationships we form in society and it mirrors our character."[18]

The spiritual leader who strays outside the marriage has a serious credibility issue with all who are under his care. Warren Bennis and Burt Nanus compiled a survey of sixty successful CEOs, roughly half of whom were from *Fortune's* top-200 list. One surprising finding is that almost all were married to their first spouse.[19] They also concluded, "And not only that: They were also indefatigably enthusiastic about marriage as an institution."[20] Successful leaders, whether they are Christians or not, value their commitments. Blackaby and Blackaby ask the question:

> Why is a leader's personal life so important? Some people claim leaders who commit adultery can still lead their organizations effectively. They argue that one matter does not affect the other. The issue, however, is integrity. If a man can deceive his wife and children, break a vow he made to God in the presence of witnesses, and knowingly betray the trust of those who love him, what guarantee does his organization have that he will be honest in his dealings with them? People who prove themselves deceitful in one area of life are equally capable of being deceitful in other areas.[21]

---

17 Alden, *Proverbs*, 52.
18. Peterson and Southern, *The Message of Leadership*, 21.
19. Bennis and Nanus, *Leaders: Strategies for Taking Charge*, 24.
20. Ibid.
21. Blackaby and Blackaby, *Spiritual Leadership*, 106.

He must make his wife a priority and his marriage the foundation of his ministry. The sad destiny of one who fails to do so is found at the end of Proverbs chapter five:

> For a man's way are in full view of the Lord,
> and he examines all his paths.
> The evil deeds of a wicked man ensnare him;
> the cords of his sin hold him fast.
> He will die for lack of discipline,
> led astray by his own great folly (Prov 5:21–23).

Parents and Children

Parenting skills are needed as much today as in any age. Unfortunately, the principles set forth in the book of Proverbs are not in fashion today. Yet, the message of Proverbs is astonishingly contemporary. The reason is that Proverbs presents God as the model or pattern for parenting, as in 3:11–12, "My son, do not despise the Lord's discipline and do not resent his rebuke, because the Lord disciplines those he loves, as a father the son he delights in." The phrase in verse twelve, יְהוָה יוֹכִיחַ (*yhwh akah*), means "Yahweh reproves" or "Yahweh disciplines" from יָכַח (*yakah*), which carries the meanings "to correct, reprove, chide, or rebuke."[22] While this "discipline" certainly carries with it the threat of punishment, Garrett points out that it ". . . primarily involves teaching or training rather than punishment for wrongdoing. It is analogous to military training, in which, although the threat of punishment is present, even stern discipline is not necessarily retribution for offences. Hardship and correction are involved, which are always hard to accept."[23] Thus, the godly leader as parent must exercise loving discipline to his children as does God to His children. God's *modus operandi* presents a divine pattern for relating to one's children. Bill Hybels, writing pastorally, says, "Leadership's first test is the test of the family."[24] The Apostle Paul echoes this thought in 1 Tim 3:4–5, where he delineates the qualifications for an elder in the Church of Jesus Christ. He writes, "He must manage his own family well and see that his children obey him with

---

22. *BDB* § 3927.
23. Garrett, *Proverbs*, 81.
24. Hybels, *Axiom*, 212.

proper respect. (If anyone does not know how to manage his own family, how can he take care of God's church?)."

A familiar verse that outlines parental responsibility is Prov 22:6, which reads, "Train a child in the way he should go, and when he is old he will not turn from it." Clearly, the verse admonishes parents to train a child so that when he is older, he will not deviate from the correct path; however, beyond the obvious, the verse has lent itself to varying interpretations. Longman concludes, "It has some built in ambiguities, and these should be acknowledged to prevent too dogmatic an application of the principles enunciated here."[25] For example, Derek Kidner argues that the verse is advocating that the parent train a child "'according to his (the child's) way,' implying, it seems, respect for his individuality and vocation."[26] This interpretation would seem to suggest that the teacher should take into account the individualized learning styles of the child and customize his educational plan accordingly. From a pedagogical perspective, such an approach may have merit; however, that is probably not the best way to interpret the verse.

Franz Delitzsch contends that Prov 22:6 should be understood in a developmental sense. He translates the verse accordingly, "Give to the child instruction conformably to his way; So he will not, when he becomes old, depart from it."[27] He argues, "The instruction of youth, the education of youth, ought to be conformed to the nature of youth; the matter of instruction, ought to regulate itself according to the stage of life, and its peculiarities; the method ought to be arranged according to the degree of development which the mental and bodily life of the youth has arrived at."[28] This sounds eerily like Jean Piaget's developmental theory, but it was written by a biblical scholar, not a developmental psychologist, more than fifty years before Piaget put his theories on paper. Piaget was a Swiss developmental psychologist who postulated that children are able to learn different skills and concepts during different stages of cognitive development. His theory of cognitive development and epistemological view, taken together, are identified by the term, "genetic epistemology." Garrett seems to favor the view of Delitzsch. He writes, "In other words, one should train a child using vocabulary, concepts, and illustrations a child can understand. It does not mean that instruction should be tailor-made for each individual child

25. Longman, *Proverbs*, 404.
26. Kidner, *Proverbs*, 147.
27. Delitzsch, *Proverbs*, 86.
28. Ibid., 86–87.

(however valid that concept may be) but that one should begin instructing a child in elementary principles of right and wrong as soon as possible."[29]

A better way to interpret Prov 22:6 is the way the NIV translators rendered the admittedly obscure Hebrew of the verse to read that parents should "train a child in the way he should go." According to Roland Murphy, the latter part of the first line of the verse actually reads, "according to the mouth of his way."[30] He contends that the NIV rendering, "the way he should go," is a superior translation reinforced by the meaning of the second line, "and when he is old he will not turn from it."[31] Therefore, it is the job of godly parents to train the child when he is young in God's pattern of wisdom. The expectation is that when the child grows to adulthood, he will continue to walk in that godly pattern. This is precisely what the godly leader must do.

Educational theories today presume the essential goodness of the child and promote self-esteem as a pedagogical tool. However, Scripture is clear that children are born with imputed sin and with an inherited sin nature. That is why corporal punishment, so out of favor in modern society and today's academic circles, is so essential, as shown in Prov 22:15, "Folly is bound up in the heart of a child, but the rod of discipline will drive it far from him." Firm parental discipline includes corporal punishment. Garrett's analysis of this verse is important. He writes, "Proverbs is realistic in teaching that parenting must seek to counteract the inborn perversity of humans. . . . Discipline provides hope that a child may be turned away from the deadly consequences of folly toward the path of life, but a parent who does not discipline has in effect become a willing party to the death of the child."[32] There are numerous verses in Proverbs that reinforce the necessity of parental discipline, including Prov 29:15, "The rod of correction imparts wisdom, but a child left to itself disgraces his mother;" 19:18 ("Discipline your son, for in that there is hope; but do not be a willing party to his death"); and 13:24, "He who spares the rod hates his son, but he who loves him is careful to discipline him." These verses suggest that a failure to exercise discipline brings disgrace, stems from a lack of love for the child, and actually can lead to his death. Certainly, a failure to exercise discipline is a

---

29. Garrett, *Proverbs*, 188.
30. Murphy, *Proverbs*, 165.
31. Ibid.
32. Garrett, *Proverbs*, 250.

very serious matter. It is a grave wrong and injustice to withhold discipline from a child. The consequences are not inconsequential.

Although Proverbs is clear that corporal discipline should be used when necessary, "the more typical approach of instruction is reproof."[33] Reproof is verbal instruction that does not resort to either verbal abuse or physical punishment. Reproof is a form of discipline, too. One qualification must be kept in mind: there are no guarantees or magic formula for how a child will turn out. However, the general principles that Proverbs teach would suggest that parents have a tremendous capacity to influence a child in the right direction, as in Prov 29:17, "Discipline your son, and he will give you peace; he will bring delight to your soul."

Proverbs 4:1 mandates the parental responsibility of a father to teach his children: "Listen, my son, to a father's instruction; pay attention and gain understanding." Louis Goldberg writes of this verse and the ones following: "These verses describe what is a lost art in our generation. Wisdom provides the picture of a devout home where the father sits in the midst of his children and teaches them the ways of God."[34]

The family of the godly leader, his wife and children, must be the major priority, only after God, in his life. The Proverbs would seem to mandate that.

Summary

The first priority of the Christian leader is not himself. This precedence is antithetical to the prevailing philosophy of this world. The Christian leader's ultimate and foremost priority is God. His primary commitment is to follow his Lord and Savior, Jesus Christ. Without this foundation, his life and ministry is built upon shifting sand and will not endure.

The next priority of the Christian leader is his family. His wife and children are next in order of priority after God himself. No matter what a man accomplishes outside of his home, he is basically a failure if he is a failure as a husband and father. Much has been written about the subject of Christian leadership, but this is a topic that has been sorely neglected. Larry Michael deplores this lack of emphasis on the leader's relationship to his family when he writes:

---

33. Ibid.
34. Goldberg, *Savoring the Wisdom of Proverbs*, 68.

> Unfortunately, many current books on Christian leadership offer little counsel regarding specific ways a leader should relate to his family. What seems to be omitted or assumed is the essential role that a leader has in his home. The manner in which a man leads in his home has direct implications on how he will lead in his work. If he succeeds at home first, that success will undergird his work at the office or on the job. If he fails with his family, he ultimately will fail in his all-encompassing role as a leader. All of the success in the world cannot replace what a leader loses when he fails in the primary responsibility of leading his family.[35]

Therefore, the Christian leader's priorities are two pronged: first to God and then to his family. Any other placement confuses the divine order of God's requirements for the leader. He must get that right or all else will turn out wrong.

---

35. Michael, *Spurgeon on Leadership*, 121.

Chapter 3

The Leader's Plans

A GODLY LEADER ALSO orders his plans by the wisdom contained in the Proverbs. He emulates God, who is portrayed in Scripture as the eternal and ultimate planner. The prophet Jeremiah quotes God in affirming this portrayal, "For I know the plans I have for you, plans to prosper you and not to harm you, plans to give you a hope and a future" (Jer 29:11). Jesus also stressed the necessity of careful planning. In his discussion of the cost of discipleship in Luke's Gospel, He says:

> Suppose one of you wants to build a tower. Will he not first sit down and estimate the cost to see if he has enough money to complete it? For if he lays the foundation and is not able to finish it, everyone who sees it will ridicule him, saying, "This fellow began to build and was not able to finish it." Or suppose a king is about to go to war against another king. Will he not first sit down and consider whether he is able with ten thousand men to oppose the one coming against him with twenty thousand? If he is not able, he will send a delegation while the other is still a long way off and ask for terms of peace (Luke 14:28–32).

Zigarelli concludes, "Since the imitation of God glorifies God, we are to be planners, too."[1] The book of Proverbs provides a blueprint for such planning. It assists the wise planner to find the straight path that has few obstacles; "The way of the sluggard is blocked with thorns, but the path of the upright is a highway" (Prov 15:19); "Folly delights a man who lacks judgment, but a man of understanding keeps a straight course" (Prov 15:21); "There is a way that seems right to a man, but in the end it leads to death" (Prov 16:25).

---

1. Zigarelli, *Management by Proverbs*, 71.

Leadership Secrets from the Proverbs

At the risk of oversimplification, there are at least two elements of wise planning outlined in the book of Proverbs, partnership with God and partnership with others.

Partnership with God

A wise and godly leader plans in partnership with God. It is sheer foolishness and arrogance to believe that plans can be made apart from or in opposition to God. As Prov 21:30 notes, "There is no wisdom, no insight, no plan that can succeed against the Lord." Garrett analyzes this verse, "In Proverbs 'wisdom' almost always includes true piety (that is, the fear of Yahweh). It seldom recognizes or deals with the phenomenon of intellectual antipathy to devotion to God. Here, however, it speaks of a kind of human 'wisdom' that seeks understanding without first submitting to Yahweh and declares that such efforts are futile."[2] Alden notes the peculiar structure of this verse, which includes three negatives ("no wisdom, no insight, no plan"). He concludes, "Another way to say this verse is that no one is wise, bright, or clever who is opposed to the Lord. Wise men, by definition, are on the Lord's side."[3] The verse following provides a concrete example of what Prov 21:30 describes generally, "The horse is made ready for the day of battle, but victory rests with the Lord" (Prov 21:31). Scripture is replete with examples of superior armed force being defeated because "victory rests with the Lord" (cf. 1 Sam 17:1–58, David and Goliath; 2 Kgs 19:20–36, Sennacherib's defeat).

Another passage that reinforces the truth that plans must be made in partnership with God in order to succeed is Prov 16:1–5, 9.

> To man belong the plans of the heart,
> but from the Lord comes the reply of the tongue. (1)
> All a man's ways seem innocent to him,
> but motives are weighed by the Lord. (2)
> Commit to the Lord whatever you do,
> and your plans will succeed. (3)
> The Lord works out everything for his own ends–
> even the wicked for a day of disaster. (4)
> The Lord detests all the proud of heart.
> Be sure of this: They will not go unpunished. (5)

2. Garrett, *Proverbs*, 185.
3. Alden, *Proverbs*, 159.

> In his heart a man plans his course,
> but the Lord determines his steps. (9)

These verses affirm the sovereign control of God over the plans of mankind. As Longman comments on verse one, "This proverb makes it clear that, though humans can legitimately make plans, God's will is definitive as to what will actually happen."[4] Longman also sees verse nine as forming a conclusion to verses one through nine.[5] He concludes, "The idea is that human beings can plan, but plans do not get put into operation and do not find success unless Yahweh so decrees it."[6] R. C. Van Leeuwen, in writing on verses one through nine, represents the consensus of most commentators in seeing the section as forming "an envelope around the theological themes of divine sovereignty and freedom in this passage."[7] People have the freedom and responsibility to plan as godly leaders, but those plans must be made in partnership with God recognizing that God is sovereign. As the writer of Proverbs states, "Many are the plans in a man's heart, but it is the Lord's purpose that prevails" (Prov 19:21). Zigarelli aptly summarizes this teaching, "This is an essential point about planning for anyone who claims a Christian worldview. As with every other area of our life, we are to be dependent upon God and seek His counsel. We are to make Him a full partner, leaning heavily on His Word and on His personal revelation as we chart our course from today until tomorrow.... Bottom line? Plan in partnership with God and plan in pencil."[8] The old Yiddish proverb certainly applies, "Man plans, God laughs."

Partnership With Others

A wise and godly leader plans in partnership with God, but he also plans in partnership with others. He solicits and heeds the advice and counsel of other godly people. He wisely realizes that God can speak through other people. Andy Stanley writes, "*Wisdom seeks counsel. The wise man knows his limitation. It is the fool who believes he has none.*"[9] The book of Prov-

---

4. Longman, *Proverbs*, 327.
5. Ibid., 331.
6. Ibid.
7. Van Leeuwen, "Proverbs," in *The Interpreter's Bible* 5: 159.
8. Zigarelli, *Management by Proverbs*, 77–78.
9. Stanley, *The Next Generation Leader*, 111.

erbs has much to say about listening to instruction in a general sense: "The way of a fool seems right to him, but a wise man listens to advice" (Prov 12:15); "A wise son heeds his father's instruction, but a mocker does not listen to rebuke" (Prov 13:1); "He who scorns instruction will pay for it, but he who respects a command is rewarded. The teaching of the wise is a fountain of life, turning a man from the snares of death" (Prov 13:13–14); and, "Listen to advice and accept instruction, and in the end you will be wise" (Prov 19:20). It also speaks pointedly to seeking counsel when making plans for the future: "Let the wise listen and add to their learning, and let the discerning get guidance" (Prov 1:5); "Plans fail for lack of counsel, but with many advisers they succeed" (Prov 15:22).

Scripture provides many examples of the proud and obdurate who failed to listen to God's voice spoken through others. Solomon was a king who was noted for his wisdom and his proverbs instructing about wisdom. Many consider him to be the wisest man who ever lived. Yet, he failed to follow his own advice in many instances, and he failed to pass along his wisdom to his son, Rehoboam. Leon Wood contrasts King Solomon with his father, David. He writes, "More significant, David maintained a vibrant faith in God as a 'man after God's own heart,' while Solomon, though beginning well in spiritual devotion, failed to hold this basic relationship before God, fell into sinful ways, and finally came under God's censure."[10] Rehoboam's failure to follow the advice of his father and of his elders cost him the kingship over ten tribes of Israel and caused a rift in the kingdom (1 Kgs 12:1–19). Jehoiakim, the king of Judah, failed to heed the timely counsel of Jeremiah, advice that would have saved his country. The results were disastrous (Jer 36:23–24). Another example from Scripture is Balaam, who received a warning from an unlikely source, his donkey (Numbers 22). Woolfe writes about this incident, "The Bible tells us that we should be alert to messages from *any* source that warn us that we are going down the wrong path."[11]

In like fashion, Zigarelli concludes that verses such as Prov 18:13 suggest that we should "respect and consider *unsolicited* advice,"[12] As it states, "He who answers before listening–that is his folly and his shame" One common pitfall for the leader is to ignore unsolicited counsel. This is rooted in the sin of pride. Zigarelli observes, "Proverbs invites us to learn from others, to take a posture of teachability (sic), considering the potential merits of unsolicited

---

10. Wood, *A Survey of Israel's History*, 287.
11. Woolfe, *Leadership Secrets from The Bible*, 104.
12. Zigarelli, *Management by Proverbs*, 140.

advice. . . . Soliciting advice and respecting unsolicited advice are acts of pure humility, something with which legions of bosses struggle. But let's be clear about this for the record: Refusing counsel and answering before listening are manifestations of pride."[13] Murphy observes that a failure to seek advice is associated with pride.[14] As shown in Prov 13:10, "Pride only breeds quarrels, but wisdom is found in those who take advice." It is actually one's pride that stands in the way of asking for advice. Zigarelli's analysis on this point is excellent. He writes, "Many people sing the virtues of gathering advice from others, but when it comes to implementing that virtue, they fall short. It is often a pride thing; if someone else has valuable ideas–ideas that are better than mine–then adopting those ideas is a tacit admission to that person's superiority. Leaders are strong, we tell ourselves. Leaders have all the answers. Leaders tell other people what to do, rather than ask what they should do."[15] Leaders who have a problem with pride find it difficult to receive advice or correction and fail to value the opinions of others. Godly leaders who possess a humble spirit are more grounded in reality and thus are able to avoid the pitfalls of pride (cf. Prov 13:10). Estes concludes:

> In contrast to pride, which elevates a false estimation of oneself above others and God, humility views life accurately. Those who are humble see God as he is, they view other people with the value with which God created them, and they regard themselves in terms of how God has designed them. From this perspective, they are able to submit to God, appreciate others, and value themselves appropriately.[16]

Another obstacle to planning in partnership with others by a failure to listen to counsel is the time element. For the sake of saving time and expediency, the listening-to-advice stage is often circumvented. This oversight can be a real issue for the busy Christian leader. His problem may not be pride, but the time factor. As noted in Prov 21:5, "The plans of the diligent lead to profit as surely as haste leads to poverty." Whatever the reason, Proverbs generally warns against an independent approach to planning: "The way of a fool seems right to him, but a wise man listens to advice" (Prov 12:15). The old English aphorism states the same concept, "Two heads are better than one." Garry Friesen, in his classic work on seeking the will of God,

13. Ibid.
14. Murphy, *Proverbs*, 114.
15. Zigarelli, *Management by Proverbs*, 72.
16. Estes, *Handbook on the Wisdom Books and Psalms*, 245.

offers some good practical advice for those who are seeking wise counselors. He writes:

> In obtaining advice, one should seek out two kinds of counselors. Of those who possess deep *spiritual insight,* the question should be asked: "Are you aware of any biblical principles that touch upon my decision?" To those who have gone through relevant *personal experiences,* the query should be: "When you went through a similar experience, did you gain any insights that would be of value to me?"[17]

The leader should never seek out sycophants who seek to flatter him and always agree with his plan of action. Rather, they should listen to those who have the courage to disagree and suggest another course of action. Blackaby and Blackaby suggest, "The key to effective counselors is not that they agree with their leaders and always support their decisions but that they tell their leaders things that they would not know or recognize otherwise."[18] As the book of Proverbs observes, "As iron sharpens iron, so one man sharpens another" (Prov 27:17).

Proverbs also employs a war or battle motif as a metaphor for planning: "Make plans by seeking advice; if you wage war, obtain guidance" (Prov 20:18). The intent of the verse is clear: One does not engage in battle or warfare without sober reflection and consideration of wise counsel. The application is not limited to warfare. The implication is that anyone making plans on such a large scale as waging war apart from seeking advice is foolish. James E. Smith writes of this verse, "One should consult with experienced counselors on every issue, and especially before undertaking a war."[19] Garrett adds to the analysis of this verse, "To enter into so serious an undertaking as a war without carefully considering the matter is the ultimate in superficial judgments."[20] Thus, one seeks advice when making any type of plans, no matter now minor, but *especially* when making such major plans as engaging in battle or war.

There is another verse that uses this battle motif: "For lack of guidance a nation falls, but many advisers make victory sure" (Prov 11:14). The contrast here is between a nation whose ruin is assured because of a lack of wise counsel and one whose victory is assured because of many such

---

17. Friesen, *Decision Making and the Will of God: A Biblical Alternative to the Traditional View,* 196.

18. Blackaby and Blackaby. *Spiritual Leadership,* 183.

19. Smith, *The Wisdom Literature and Psalms,* 610.

20. Garrett, *Proverbs,* 177.

advisers. The language suggests a military situation. However, George Lawson gives it a broader application. He writes:

> In our private concerns it is dangerous to trust our own wisdom, and it is our interest to advise with wise and faithful friends, in every important business of life. But in the affairs of countries, public calamity must be the inevitable consequence of the sovereign's being not wise enough to know his need of asking and following the advice of wise men. If he asks the advice of wise men, and yet follows that of fools, he is no better than Rehoboam, who by such conduct rent his kingdom.[21]

It is possible that Qoheleth had this verse in mind when he penned the anecdote in Eccl 9:13–16 some years after the writing of Proverbs: "I also saw under the sun this example of wisdom that greatly impressed me: There was once a small city with only a few people in it. And a powerful king came against it and built huge siegeworks against it. Now there lived in that city a man poor but wise, and he saved the city by his wisdom."

The godly leader does not plan for the future in isolation or in a vacuum. He takes prudent steps to ensure that he makes wise decisions. First, he plans in partnership with God. Such planning always places God's will in the forefront. As commended in Prov 16:3, "Commit to the Lord whatever you do, and your plans will succeed." Then he relies upon the wise counsel of other people by planning in partnership with others. This increases the odds against making an unwise or impetuous decision in the planning process. It is true that the decision making process may be slowed somewhat, but the built-in safeguards of this approach more than offsets the disadvantages. Estes suggests, "Good decisions come from following good advice."[22] The book of Proverbs warns against making impetuous decisions: "It is not good to have zeal without knowledge, nor to be hasty and miss the way" (Prov 19:2); "The plans of the diligent lead to profit as surely as haste leads to poverty" (Prov 21:5). Again, Estes writes, "Good decisions are not impulsive; they are reached after careful consideration of the facts."[23]

---

21. Lawson, *Exposition of Proverbs*, 203.
22. Estes, *Handbook on the Wisdom Books and Psalms*, 233.
23. Ibid.

Summary

A godly leader plans in partnership with God and with others. Such planning places God in the forefront of the decision-making process. It also requires humility and a willingness to listen to the advice of other godly counselors. It is God's prescription for making wise and godly decisions.

Chapter 4

The Leader's Speech
The Proper Use of the Tongue

A GODLY LEADER ORDERS his priorities and plans by the wisdom contained in Proverbs, but he also controls his tongue. He realizes the tremendous power of the tongue for good and evil (cf. James 3:1–12), and he soberly weighs the words of Proverbs. He also heeds the warning of James from the New Testament, "If anyone considers himself religious and yet does not keep a tight rein on his tongue, he deceives himself and his religion is worthless" (Jam 1:26). Peterson's challenge is timely, "The tongue is a powerful force that can be used for good or evil. Try to master yours if you can. Some leaders don't realize the power of the words coming out of their mouth. Everything they say has an impact just by virtue of their personality and position. And because they are in charge, there is often no one who will point out their faults."[1] The book of Proverbs also brings out this theme: "A fool's talk brings a rod to his back, but the lips of the wise protect them" (Prov 14:3).

The book of Proverbs has more to say about the use of the tongue and a person's words than almost any other topic. An informal tally by this writer demonstrates the great number of verses that deal with the tongue in either a positive or a negative sense. The actual recording of proverbs begins in chapter 10. James T. Draper writes, "The first nine chapters are exhortations, admonishing the reader to prepare himself to heed the sayings that follow."[2] Beginning, then, with "The Proverbs of Solomon" from 10:1—22:17, there are 132 verses out of a total of 376 that specifically

---

1. Peterson, *The Message of Leadership*, 35.
2. Draper, *Proverbs: The Secret of Beautiful Living*, 13.

mention lips, tongue, mouth, speaking, quarreling, mocking, or some other aspect of the vehicle of speech. Thus, in the initial section of proverbs by Solomon, 35.1 percent of the verses mention the use of the tongue in some way. There is a dramatic drop in percentage in the next section, "The sayings of the wise," in 22:17—24:22. Of the seventy total verses in this brief section, only six, or 8.6 percent, specifically mention some aspect of the tongue. The next section, the further "sayings of the wise," comprise only twelve verses, of which three, or twenty-five percent, are related to the tongue. The percentages rise again dramatically in the final section of proverbs from Solomon, described as "more proverbs of Solomon, copied by the men of Hezekiah king of Judah" (Prov 25:1). From 25:1—29:27 there are 138 verses, of which forty-two, or 30.4 percent, mention some aspect of the tongue. This tabulation certainly demonstrates that the tongue is not an inconsequential subject in the book of Proverbs.

The prescriptions in the book of Proverbs, for the most part, are not given specifically to the leader, but more generally to anyone who would be wise. However, they certainly apply to the leader who would consider himself to be wise. Any leader who would ignore the Proverbs' teaching on the use of the tongue would not be wise, but rather a fool, as stated in Prov 17:27-28, "A man of knowledge uses words with restraint, and a man of understanding is even-tempered. Even a fool is thought wise if he keeps silent, and discerning if he holds his tongue" and in Prov 21:23, "He who guards his mouth and his tongue keeps himself from calamity." Goldberg writes of the solemn responsibility that leaders accept whenever they speak. Although he writes of kings in the Old Testament, certainly there is a broader application here. He writes, "Leaders of a nation must ever be careful how they use their mouths. In the Old Testament, the king was God's regent, and when he spoke, it was as if God rendered His decision for the nation Israel."[3] Although the godly leader today would be most reluctant to speak at the behest of God, he must be acutely aware that in his leadership position, he must be most careful how and what he speaks. He dare not wield his tongue in a cavalier fashion.

It is beyond the scope of this book to deal exhaustively with this subject. However, Proverbs outlines both the proper use and the improper use of the tongue. Although there are many more warnings and prohibitions of a negative nature in Proverbs against the improper use of the tongue, there is still a large amount of material commending the proper use of the

---

3. Goldberg, *Savoring the Wisdom of Proverbs*, 188.

tongue. The proper use of the tongue includes imparting knowledge and wisdom, encouragement, protection, nurture, healing, telling the truth, pleasant speech, praise, advice, confessing sin, discretion, and rebuke.

Imparting Knowledge and Wisdom

One positive use of the tongue is to impart wisdom and knowledge. Another way to refer to this concept is instruction, which is highly valued in the book of Proverbs: "Hold on to instruction, do not let it go; guard it well, for it is your life" (Prov 5:13); "The discerning heart seeks knowledge" (Prov 15:14); "Pay attention and listen to the sayings of the wise; apply your heart to what I teach, for it is pleasing when you keep them in your heart and have them ready on your lips" (Prov 22:17–18). Often in Proverbs, the two words 'wisdom' and 'knowledge' are indistinguishable; for example, "The tongue of the wise commends knowledge, but the mouth of the fool gushes folly" (Prov 15:2); "The lips of the wise spread knowledge; not so the hearts of fools" (Prov 15:7). This connection between the lips (or tongue) and the heart is found elsewhere in Proverbs, as well as in the words of Jesus (cf. Luke 6:45[4]). The point is that the tongue reveals what is going on inside the heart. Smith explains that the wise man spreads knowledge ". . . either by expressing that knowledge (1) at the right time and place; or (2) in the right manner. The wise man not only possesses knowledge, he can give it proper expression."[5] The wise man educates; the fool obfuscates.

The value of knowledge is seen in Prov 15:2 and 15:7. In the former verse, knowledge is commended by the wise; in the latter, it is disseminated. Toy translates תֵּיטִיב (from the verb *yatab*) in 15:2 as "dispenses," but its meaning is actually "makes good"; that is, it "does or treats in a good, excellent way."[6] Some translators and commentators understand the verb as actually improving the knowledge of the recipients. For example, Robert Alter translates the verse thus, "The tongue of the wise improves knowledge, but the mouth of dullards bubbles with folly."[7] The Jewish commentators, Leonard Kravitz and Kerry Olitzky, reference the medieval Jewish

---

4. Luke 6:45, "A good man brings good things out of the good stored up in his heart, and an evil man brings evil things out of the evil stored up in his heart. For the mouth speaks what the heart is full of" (NIV).

5. Smith, *The Wisdom Literature and Psalms*, 571.

6. Toy, *Proverbs*, 303. See also Murphy, *Proverbs*, 110.

7. Alter, *The Wisdom Books*, 258.

writer Levi ben Gershom (1288–1344 A.D.) as arguing that "the speech of the wise improves the knowledge of those who listen to them by correcting their ideas."[8] Whether that is a correct translation and interpretation of the verse or not, it is clear that Solomon is holding knowledge in very high regard and deprecating the words of the fool. Rabbi A. Cohen writes of the fool, "He talks nonsense and, the parallelism suggests, his language is badly phrased."[9] This antithesis between the wise man and the fool is reinforced by Prov 15:7, which states, "The lips of the wise spread knowledge." In other words, they disseminate knowledge. They impart knowledge and wisdom. They are instructors. Verse 7 continues the general sense of the antithesis of verse 2 in stating that such wise words are not the ways (hearts) of fools. "Lips of the wise" is parallel to "hearts of fools" in this verse, in that, as Cohen observes, the heart is "the seat of intelligence" in that "it directs speech."[10] The practical implications of these two verses is noted by Bruce Waltke, in his majestic commentary on the Proverbs, thus:

> The wise have tongues controlled by loving emotions and sound thought and so speak in a way that makes their internalized knowledge of the moral order attractive. Instead of brutalizing people with their knowledge of the cause-effect relationship in God's ordained moral order, the wise state it kindly, sensitively, and gently with an aim to save their audience, not to condemn and destroy it. Their content and their form of speech make them convincing (see 25:1). By contrast, the mouth of fools, who are out of control, excitedly and heatedly *gushes forth* ... an abstraction for their morally insolent speech that destroys a person and/or the community.[11]

The wise man also promotes wisdom and instruction by the winsomeness of his words, shown in Prov 16:25 ("The wise in heart are called discerning, and pleasant words promote instruction.") and 16:23 ("A wise man's heart guides his mouth, and his lips promote instruction."). Such leaders and teachers create a hunger for wisdom and learning in their followers. The old English proverb certainly fits here, "You can lead a horse to water, but you cannot make him drink." Garrett writes of this passage, "The overall thrust of this text is that wise teachers choose their words carefully and in so doing enhance the learning experience for their students. The

---

8. Kravitz and Olitzky, *Mishlei: A Modern Commentary on Proverbs*, 146.
9. Cohen, *Proverbs in The Soncino Books of the Bible*, 95.
10. Ibid., 96.
11. Waltke, *The Book of Proverbs* Chapters 1–15, 614.

wisdom of the true sage not only benefits the disciples morally, but is a joy to receive as well."[12] Alden's comments on Prov 16:21[13] add to this description of the effective, wise teacher as suggesting "... a teacher whose words are so sweet that they increase the appetite of those who listen to them. The words do not flatter or trick those that hear them; rather the motivation for using them is the noble one of making learning pleasant."[14] Unfortunately, such wise and winsome teachers are few and far between.

The rarity of such an instructor is reflected in Prov 20:15: "Gold there is, and rubies in abundance, but lips that speak knowledge are a rare jewel." This verse uses hyperbole to accent the antithetical parallelism that wisdom is more highly valued than even gold and rubies. Gold and rubies are considered very rare and are valuable commodities. If they were in such abundance, they would not be so valuable. As Garrett notes, "The rarest and finest treasure is a person who has sound judgment and can give good advice."[15] Both Toy and Cohen argue that this verse is not an example of antithetical parallelism, but rather it is one continuous sentence.[16] However, this interpretation does not fully capture the force of the contrast being made here. This verse appears to be teaching that the one who speaks knowledge is rarer than even gold or rubies. Rubies were considered the most valuable jewels in the ancient world.[17] Speaking of the man who finds wisdom, Solomon writes, "Blessed is the man who finds wisdom, the man who gains understanding, for she is more profitable than silver and yields better returns than gold. She is more precious than rubies; nothing you desire can compare with her" (Prov 3:13–15). Kidner argues that the contrast is not between wise teaching and wealth, but "between kinds of adornment. . . . To be justly admired, study to catch the ear, not the eye; and offer it things of more than scarcity-value."[18] Peterson's translation of this verse captures that nuance: "Drinking from the beautiful chalice of knowledge is better than adorning oneself with gold and rare gems."[19] However, the note

---

12. Garrett, *Proverbs*, 157.

13. Proverbs 16:21, "The wise in heart are called discerning, and gracious words promote instruction" (NIV).

14. Alden, *Proverbs*, 129.

15. Garrett, *Proverbs*, 177.

16. Toy, *Proverbs*, 388–89; Cohen, *Proverbs*, 134.

17. See NIV Study Bible note on 3:15.

18. Kidner, *Proverbs*, 138.

19. Peterson, *The Message of Leadership*, 111.

on this verse in the *NIV Study Bible* simply notes, "Wisdom is valued more highly than gold or rubies."[20] Whether the emphasis is on adornment or the comparative values of wisdom and gold/rubies, the meaning is clear that wise instruction is in relatively short supply.

The exhortation in Prov 22:17 commands his readers (hearers) to "pay attention and listen to the sayings of the wise." This phrase, דִּבְרֵי חֲכָמִים (*dibre hakamim*), is a title much like the one in Prov 10:1, "The proverbs of Solomon" (מִשְׁלֵי שְׁלֹמֹה; *misle selomoh*). The reason why these sayings are to be heeded is found beginning in the following verse, which declares that "it is pleasing when you keep them in your heart and have all of them ready on your lips" (Prov 22:18). The writer concludes his explanation in verses 20 and 21: "Have I not written thirty sayings for you, sayings of counsel and knowledge, teaching you true and reliable words, so that you can give sound answers to him who sent you." These thirty sayings are actually thirty units, which are divided into three separate sections each containing ten units (Prov 22:22—24:22). It has been noted by Old Testament scholars that the Egyptian *Wisdom of Amenemope* also contains thirty units. The correspondences between Amenemope's writing and that of this section of the book of Proverbs have been well-documented by scholars.[21]

There is an emphasis in Prov 22:17–21 on the memorization of Scripture, a discipline also found elsewhere (Ps 119:11). Alden explains the necessity of learning Scripture "by heart" both then and now thus:

> The Hebrew literally advises us to "keep them in your belly" and "fix them on your lips." In ancient times, the scarcity of books and literacy made the skill of memorizing almost a necessity. Still, despite the availability of Bibles and people who read today, memorizing Proverbs and other portions of Scripture to tuck them away in our hearts remains an excellent practice.[22]

Certainly, the Apostle Peter was in sympathy with this view when he wrote, "Always be prepared to give an answer to everyone who asks you to give the reason for the hope that you have" (1 Pet 3:15). A logical apologetic is much easier to make when one has a sound grasp of Scripture. Much is

---

20. *NIV Study Bible*, 987.

21. Oesterley, *The Teaching of Amen-Em-Ope and The Book of Proverbs*, 36–74. Also, see Chapter 5 of this book under the subsection, 'Quarreling', for a fuller discussion of this issue.

22. Alden, *Proverbs*, 165.

demanded of one who would hear the Word of God, especially the Proverbs. Kidner's impassioned comments on this text are worth quoting:

> A series of proverbs demands much of the reader, if it is not to remain for him a string of platitudes. The present call to attention is salutary not only in its immediate context but beyond it, to enable the disciple to review his response to all Scripture. Does he read with alert concentration (17)? How much is retained and ready for passing on (18)? Does he receive it in the spirit in which it was given–to deepen his trust (19), guide his decisions (20) and strengthen his grasp of truth (21)? Does he see himself as the virtual envoy (cf. *send thee,* 21) of those whose knowledge of the truth depends on him?[23]

The final verse dealing with instruction under consideration begins the second main section of "the sayings of the wise" in Prov 23:12, "Apply your heart to instruction and your ears to words of knowledge." This verse epitomizes the message of the book of Proverbs, as well as all wisdom literature, whether Jewish or not.[24] There is a common thread throughout all wisdom literature exhorting the reader/hearer to be receptive to words of wise instruction. It is worth noting that henceforth in the book of Proverbs, there are no parallels with Egyptian wisdom literature.[25] Thus, the acquisition of wisdom and listening to instruction are not unimportant matters. This is an endeavor to revolve one's life and priorities around. It is not inconsequential. Having applied one's heart to instruction and one's ears to words of knowledge, the next step is to impart that knowledge and wisdom to others. That mandate is expressed by the Apostle Paul as an essential task of the Christian leader. In writing to young Timothy, he enlarges the sphere of influence that the leader should have: "You then, my son, be strong in the grace that is in Christ Jesus. And the things you have heard me say in the presence of many witnesses entrust to reliable men who will also be qualified to teach others" (2 Tim 2:1–2). Four generations are in view in these verses: (1) Paul, (2) Timothy, (3) reliable men, (4) others. Thus, the essential task of the Christian leader is to receive instruction and then pass on that instruction in such a way that that wisdom and knowledge is passed on to others in an endless cycle.

---

23. Kidner, *Proverbs*, 149.
24. Alden, *Proverbs*, 169.
25. Ibid.

Encouragement

Another important positive use of the tongue is encouragement, as expressed in Prov 12:25, "An anxious heart weighs a man down, but a kind word cheers him up." The ancient Hebrews did not fully understand the terrible effects that stress has on the human body. Stress exacerbates diseases such as heart disease and diabetes. However, Solomon seemed to have a deep understanding of the physical and emotional effects of stress. Anxiety can be totally debilitating, leading to depression and a complete inability to function. This verse is a reminder of the power of words for good or for ill. One kind word can have a miraculous impact upon the anxious heart. Waltke observes, "Whereas anxiety knocks a person out of commission, the personal and kind, pleasant and sweet, timely and thoughtful word restores him with encouragement and hope."[26]

Another verse that deals with encouragement uses a simile to describe a timely word: Prov 25:11, "A word aptly spoken is like apples of gold in settings of silver." Cohen explains that this verse is interpreted by traditional Jewish commentators who teach that the apples of gold are not actual fruit, but rather carvings of apples overlaid with gold in a silver setting.[27] According to this verse, the timing is just as important as the content of the message spoken. In the book of Proverbs, the setting in which words are spoken are just as important as the words themselves. In wisdom literature, silence is often a virtue. Also, not every wise word is an effective antidote if spoken in the wrong setting. As Longman observes, "The wisdom formula is to speak the right word to the right person at the right time."[28] Only the fool speaks all of the time without regard for timing and circumstance. Waltke explains this concept:

> The shape of the apple and perhaps the lovely fragrance associated with it refer to the loveliness of a proper decision, and the gold, to its great value. However, like a gold ring in a swine's snout, its beauty and value can be undone without the proper setting. Handing down the carefully crafted decision that in every way is proper to the circumstances of the composition and delivery (i.e., at the right time and in the right way) enhances its aesthetic impression and its moral influence.[29]

26. Waltke, *The Book of Proverbs* Chapters 1–15, 541.
27. Cohen, *Proverbs*, 168.
28. Longman, *Proverbs*, 453.
29. Waltke, *The Book of Proverbs* Chapters 15–31, 321.

The Leader's Speech

The wise Christian leader soon learns that it is easier to motivate with encouragement and by "a word aptly spoken" than by criticism and ugly words, especially in an organization such as a church that relies largely upon a volunteer work force. Zigarelli offers several practical suggestions on how to encourage or praise others. He writes that leaders should offer praise as a reward, praise in public whenever possible, offer timely praise, and that praise does not always have to be verbal.[30] James Kouzes and Barry Posner list "Encourage the Heart" as the fifth of their Five Practices of Exemplary Leadership. They write, "Leaders *encourage the heart* of their constituents to carry on. Genuine acts of caring uplift the spirit and draw people forward."[31]

One verse, Prov 25:20, is a reminder that not all words meant to encourage indeed have that effect: "Like one who takes away a garment on a cold day, or like vinegar poured on soda, is one who sings songs to a heavy heart." The Hebrew is uncertain in this verse. Alden explains that it is "uncertain whether the singer has a sad heart or sings songs to someone who has a sad heart."[32] Whatever the actual meaning of the verse, it is clear that the emphasis is on the timeliness and appropriateness of the message. One who speaks inappropriately is the polar opposite of the person spoken of in Prov 25:11, who communicates "a word aptly spoken."[33] To the contrary, this singer lacks sensitivity to the circumstances and feelings of others, and instead of being an encouragement, rubs salt in the wounds. Waltke labels him "the insensitive and inept speaker."[34] He explains, "The proverb implicitly compares the incompatibility of one singing joyful songs to a sullen heart to the incongruities of putting off a warm garment on a frosty day and to pouring stinging vinegar on a wound. All three foolishly inflict pain with no therapeutic value."[35]

Another verse that lacks clarity in the Hebrew is Prov 27:9, which reads, "Perfume and incense bring joy to the heart, and the pleasantness of one's friend springs from his earnest counsel." Although the second line is difficult, taking the verse as an example of synonymous parallelism is the

---

30. Zigarelli, *Management by Proverbs*, 169–72.
31. Kouzes and Posner, *The Leadership Challenge*, 22.
32. Alden, *Proverbs*, 184.
33. Proverbs 25:11, "Like apples of gold inlaid with silver is a word that is aptly spoken" (NJB).
34. Waltke, *The Book of Proverbs* Chapters 15–31, 329.
35. Ibid.

most reasonable solution to the problem. There is no reason to conclude that the second line is "unintelligible," as Toy suggests,[36] or to say, as does Clifford, that the entire proverb is in doubt.[37] Understanding the proverb as synonymous parallelism would require that the second line be synonymous to the first. Peterson's translation renders the verse correctly: "Just as lotions and fragrance give sensual delight, a sweet friendship refreshes the soul."[38] Alden's translation also gets it right: "Perfume and incense bring joy to the heart like the counsel of a friend brings sweetness to the taste."[39]

The final verse under consideration in this section on Encouragement is Prov 27:11: "Be wise, my son, and bring joy to my heart; then I can answer anyone who treats me with contempt." The first line of this verse sounds like many other proverbs in that it is a father exhorting his son to be wise and thus "brings joy" (encourages) to his heart. The second line introduces a new element of explanation. Apparently, the wisdom of the son or pupil so encourages the heart of the teacher (father) that it "gives him such a lift that he can answer anyone, even someone that criticizes him."[40] It is clear that one's successes or failures can either encourage or dishearten his teacher.

Encouragement is a valuable use of the tongue. This usage is seen in several passages in the book of Proverbs. The godly leader ought to be an encourager. Encouragement builds up; its counterpart tears down. The anonymous author of the book of Hebrews in the New Testament also had much to say about encouragement. He wrote, "But encourage one another daily, as long as it is called Today, so that none of you may be hardened by sin's deceitfulness" (Heb 3:13).

Likewise he adds, "And let us consider how we may spur one another on toward love and good deeds. Let us not give up meeting together, as some are in the habit of doing, but let us encourage one another–and all the more as you see the day approaching" (Heb 10:24–25). Encouraging speech is so easy to give, but so hard to do for so many. Encouragement should be the habit of every godly leader.

---

36. Toy, *Proverbs*, 484.
37. Clifford, *Proverbs*, 238.
38. Peterson, *The Message of Leadership*, 126.
39. Alden, *Proverbs*, 191.
40. Ibid., 192.

The Leader's Speech

Protection

Proper use of the tongue also includes protection, as shown in Prov 12:6, "The words of the wicked lie in wait for blood, but the speech of the upright rescues them." The meaning of this verse is somewhat cryptic. The situation is not specified, although it could be an actual ambush or possibly even a judicial setting.[41] Murphy renders this "ambush" or lying "in wait for blood" (NIV) more graphically and literally as "ambush for blood."[42] Alter's translation reflects this understanding: "The words of the wicked are a bloody ambush, but the mouth of the upright will save them."[43] In like manner, Kravitz and Olitzky, using the classical Jewish commentaries of Rabbi Solomon Yitzchak ben Isaac (Rashi; 1040–1105 A.D.), Abraham ibn Ezra (1089–1164 A.D.), and Levi ben Gershom (Gersonides; 1288–1344 A.D.) to develop their translation of the text, translate: "But the words of the wicked lay in wait for blood, but the mouth of the upright will save them."[44] However, Solomon Yitzchak ben Isaac, as cited in Kravitz and Olitzky, understood the first line of the verse as relating to false testimony in a court of law.[45] Longman concedes the possibility of a legal setting for this proverb but writes that "it does not seem to be specifically tied to the court."[46] He emphasizes rather the consequences of the words of the wicked. He continues:

> The proverb is an observation on the consequences that flow from the speech of the "wicked" and from those "with integrity," two words used to indicate the realms of fools and the wise. As we might expect, the words of the wicked lead to a negative end, even a violent death. It is a little unclear, perhaps unintentionally, whether the ambush comes on those who listen to the advice of the wicked, whose guidance is fraudulent . . . or on the wicked themselves. Certainly, the teaching of Proverbs affirms both results.[47]

However, the emphasis here is not so much on the fate of those who are ambushed, but on the rescue provided by the "speech of the upright."

---

41. Murphy, *The Wisdom Books*, 89.
42. Ibid.
43. Alter, *Proverbs*, 245.
44. Kravitz and Olitzky, *Mishlei*, 119.
45. Ibid.
46. Longman, *Proverbs*, 272.
47. Ibid.

Smith summarizes the focus of this verse and the protection that the mouth of the upright provides: "If the righteous have the opportunity, they warn the unwary and protect them from the wicked. They plead the cause of the oppressed and use their eloquence in their behalf."[48]

It is likely, as some commentators argue, that verse 6 should be linked with the preceding verse, which would place the emphasis on the fact that the schemes of the wicked may have deadly consequences. In fact, Garrett links Prov 12:5–7 together as a thematic unity, as suggested by the Hebrew structure.[49] He writes, "These three proverbs follow a logical progression: the righteous make plans that are just, but the wicked scheme with deceitful counsel (v. 5); the wicked attempt to ambush the righteous with their lies, but the righteous are delivered by their integrity (v. 6); the wicked are totally destroyed, but the righteous stand secure."[50] Whatever traps the wicked may devise, it is the words of the righteous and the wise that enable them to escape them. Thus, their ministry is one of rescue and protection. The godly leader uses his tongue as an instrument for good as he protects the weak and unwary.

Nurture

Another proper use of the tongue by the godly leader is nurture or nourishment as shown in Prov 10:21, "The lips of the righteous nourish many, but fools die for lack of judgment." Commentators are divided on the precise meaning of this verse. Some take it as a reference to prayer, while others interpret it as the teaching of the righteous.[51] Whatever the exact meaning of "the lips of the righteous," it is clear that a contrast is being drawn. It is that the words of the righteous lead to life, whereas the words of the foolish lead to death. Alter's translation seems to miss the point of the proverb entirely: "The righteous man's lips guide the many, but dolts die for lack of sense."[52] Peterson's take on this verse is much closer to the real meaning: "The talk of

---

48. Smith, *The Wisdom Literature and Psalms*, 549.

49. Garrett, *Proverbs*, 130. Proverbs 12:5–7 reads, "The plans of the righteous are just, but the advice of the wicked is deceitful. 6 The words of the wicked lie in wait for blood, but the speech of the upright rescues them. 7 The wicked are overthrown and are no more, but the house of the righteous stands firm" (NIV).

50. Ibid.

51. Smith, *The Wisdom Literature and Psalms*, 538.

52. Alter, *The Wisdom Books*, 238.

The Leader's Speech

a good person is rich fare for many, but chatterboxes die of an empty heart."[53] Longman writes, "The picture the proverb draws is of the righteous person guiding listeners to refreshing pastures. They do this not just for themselves, or even for one other person, but for many. The righteous, thus, build community."[54] Toy correctly observes that the antithetic parallelism contrasts "... the nutritive power of wise thought and speech, and the incapacity of moral folly to gain life–earthly life, taken in the widest sense, with physical and moral content."[55] The verb translated "nourish" in the New International Version is רעה (ra'a), which actually means to "pasture, tend, graze" in the sense of a shepherd or herdsman feeding his sheep.[56] Thus, the idea of feeding or nourishment is certainly prominent in this verse.

Although Prov 10:21 is apparently the only verse that clearly speaks of the ministry of nourishing or nurture, the concept is found throughout Scripture. Perhaps the best-known chapter in the Bible is Psalm 23. Certainly, the idea of nurture, nourishment, and restoration almost leap off the page. "He makes me lie down in green pastures, he leads me beside quiet waters" (Ps 23:2). That is where the sheep are able to derive nourishment in a safe haven. Sheep are not the most intelligent of animals, and they must be led and protected. Kravitz and Olitzky refer to the commentary of Levi ben Gershom on how the lines of this verse well described the ignorant masses of the Medieval Period. Often they are compared to sheep. They write, "Gersonides, reflecting the medieval philosophical tradition that distinguished between the philosophically learned elite and the philosophically unlearned masses, understands the first clause to say that not only do the lips of the righteous (which he equates with those who are philosophically astute) provide life for them, those same lips guide the masses and provide for them as a shepherd provides for the sheep."[57] They conclude with ben Gershom's correlation, "Fools cannot help the masses. Moreover, since they lack correct ideas, they cannot help themselves. For Gersonides, incorrect ideas in this life negate the possibility of providence in this life and eternal life in the next. For him, folly leads to error, and error leads to death."[58]

---

53. Peterson, *The Message of Leadership*, 90.
54. Longman, *Proverbs*, 239.
55. Toy, *Proverbs*, 212.
56. *BDB* § 9172.
57. Kravitz and Olitzky, *Mishlei*, 102.
58. Ibid.

Leadership Secrets from the Proverbs

The concept of nourishment is found again five verses later, in Ps 23:5, "You prepare a table before me in the presence of my enemies. You anoint my head with oil; my cup overflows." The imagery suggests a banquet table at which a vassal king would sit as an honored guest. The metaphor of feeding and nourishment is a prominent feature of Psalm 23.

Both W. Gunther Plaut and Waltke suggest that nourishment or the lack of it is the blame of the fool who lacks the good sense to take or feed on what is provided.[59] As Prov 10:21 states clearly, "The lips of the righteous nourish many." However, the fool in the antithesis apparently starves to death in the pasture or at the banquet table because he is too stupid to feed on what has been abundantly provided. Plaut writes, "The wise nourish others with their wisdom, the foolish have not enough for themselves. . . . the foolish die for lack of good advice, i.e., they will not listen."[60] Waltke is even more pointed in his comments. He writes that ". . . though the fool is surrounded by the life-preserving words of the righteous that nourish many, he starves to death because he lacks the good sense to feed on them. He can neither receive life nor give it."[61] He is much like the proverbial poor soul who is on a raft in the middle of the ocean who cries out, "Water, water, everywhere, and not a drop to drink!" However, in this instance, the body of water is a freshwater lake, yet "the fool" lacks the common sense to dip his cup. What a tragedy that this describes so many people today!

The godly leader is called to nurture and nourish. The pastor feeds his flock through the preaching and teaching ministry of the church. But whether he is engaged in parish ministry or not, the Christian leader is called to nurture his followers. He does this by building and storing a repository in himself, and that is accomplished by feeding on the Word of God. The godly leader must be a man/woman who feeds daily upon the Word of God and is nourished. Only then can he nurture or nourish others. He must heed the words of the psalmist:

> How can a young man keep his way pure?
> By living according to your word.
> I seek you with all my heart;
> do not let me stray from your commands.
> I have hidden your word in my heart
> that I might not sin against you.

---

59. Plaut, *Proverbs*, 132; Waltke, *The Book of Proverbs* Chapters 1–15, 472.
60. Plaut, *Proverbs*, 132.
61. Waltke, *The Book of Proverbs* Chapters 1–15, 472.

> Praise be to you, O Lord;
> teach me your decrees.
> With my lips I recount
> all the laws that come from your mouth.
> I rejoice in following your statutes
> as one rejoices in great riches.
> I meditate on your precepts
> and consider your ways.
> I delight in your decrees;
> I will not neglect your word (Ps 1:9–16).

The leader who adheres to the words of the psalmist is able then, having himself been fed, to nurture and nourish others. "The lips of the righteous nourish many." They nurture.

Healing

Closely akin to nurture is healing. There are four verses in the book of Proverbs that specifically mention healing within the context of the tongue or speech: "Reckless words pierce like a sword, but the tongue of the wise brings healing" (Prov 12:18); "The tongue that brings healing is a tree of life, but a deceitful tongue crushes the spirit" (Prov 15:4); "A cheerful look brings joy to the heart, and good news gives health to the bones" (Prov 15:30); "Pleasant words are a honeycomb, sweet to the soul and healing to the bones" (Prov 16:24). The overall thrust of these four verses is that the wise choose their words carefully. Words have the potential to wound or to heal. The wise Christian leader always chooses words that soothe and heal. That is not to say that he flatters or practices insincerity. Alden concludes that "what we say should always be tempered with kindness rather than cruelty."[62] Charles Turner outlines the twofold benefit that pleasant words can provided to the wounded. He writes:

> Pleasant words are like the honeycomb in two senses. They are sweet to the soul, which is certainly helpful to the inner man. We human beings really need strength in the inner man. The Bible encourages this. Sweet words are also health to the bones the physical. This speaks of the same thing as the merry heart that makes us to be well in the body. A kind word from a kind friend can bring healing to the heart as well as healing to the bones and body.[63]

62. Alden, *Proverbs*, 118.
63. Turner, *Studies in Proverbs*, 58.

Words can indeed act as a balm to the wounded soul.

The wise leader also realizes that constructive criticism can be an opportunity for healing. Criticism does not always have to be destructive. In Prov 12:18, the reckless words of the fools are contrasted sharply with the words of the wise which promote healing.[64] A wise leader or manager learns to choose his words carefully realizing the tremendous power that they wield. They can wound like a sword, as the simile suggests, or they can do the opposite and heal. Zigarelli's analysis of how to deal with such management situations is timely. He writes:

> Our choice of words has the power to escalate or to ameliorate. That is, how we communicate our concern and dissatisfaction can largely determine the trajectory of the conversation: more confrontational or more cordial. If at any point we recklessly abandon a Christ-like attitude, allowing our frustration free reign to "pierce like a sword," the discussion can quickly degenerate into something counterproductive.... If, on the other hand, we're shrewder in our choice of words and in our tone ... we unleash the power to ameliorate, even to "bring healing." This is wisdom's path, the path of diplomacy.... When delivering negative feedback, vigilantly guard against reckless words spoken out of emotion, and instead speak with "the tongue of the wise."[65]

Both Waltke and Garrett argue that Prov 12:18 is part of a four verse arrangement (verses 16–19) linked by an alternating parallelism conjoined by the common verse, 12:19, to a four verse chiasmus (verses 19–22).[66] Garrett arranges the pattern thus:

    A: Thoughtless reactions (v.16)

        B: Honesty and lying (v.17)

    A': Reckless words (v. 18)

        B': Honesty and lying (v. 19)

            C: Plotting evil and promoting peace (v. 20)

            C': Trouble to the wicked, not the righteous (v. 21)

        B'': Honesty and lying (v. 22)[67]

---

64. Proverbs 12:18, "The words of the reckless pierce like swords, but the tongue of the wise brings healing" (NIV).

65. Zigarelli, *Management by Proverbs*, 163.

66. Waltke, *The Book of Proverbs* Chapters 1–15, 532; Garrett, *Proverbs*, 132.

67. Garrett, *Proverbs*, 132.

The Leader's Speech

In these verses, as in much of the book of Proverbs, the way of the fool and the way of the wise are brought into sharp contrast. In verse 18, the contrast is between the way that words are used. Cohen writes of this contrast thus, "Whereas the fool's thoughtless chatter inflicts pain and harm, the words of a wise man produce the opposite effect: they sooth anguish and undo injury."[68] The dangers of reckless speech and loquaciousness will be dealt with further in Chapter 5.

In Prov 15:4, the contrast using antithetical parallelism is between the truthful tongue that brings healing and the deceitful tongue that crushes the spirit. Peterson's translation brings out this contrast: "Kind words heal and help; cutting words wound and maim."[69] In like manner, Toy titles his discussion of this verse, "Gentle Words," and translates the first line, 'A soothing tongue is a tree of life.'[70] A gentle tongue soothes wounded feelings. A companion verse to this is Prov 15:1, which reads in part, "A gentle answer turns away wrath." Waltke understands the metaphor, "a tree of life," to hearken back to the Garden of Eden, as he writes that the imagery "... whets the appetite to restore Paradise in a broken world through healing speech that gives eternal life to those who 'eat' it."[71] Biting or hurtful speech is a direct result of the Fall. The speech of the godly leader should always be seasoned with grace and kindness rather than a spirit of meanness or cruelty. The intent should always be to heal, rather than to wound or crush the spirit.

An interesting Hebrew idiom is found in Prov 15:30, which speaks of giving "health to the bones."[72] Alter translates it as putting "sap in the bones."[73] Fox says that "it fattens the bones."[74] Whereas obesity in ancient times was considered a sign of prosperity and good health, today the opposite is implied. Alden's explanation of this Hebrew idiom is enlightening:

> The man who is truly happy is affected clear down to his bones.... The Hebrew idiom says his bones become greasy with fat. The idiom makes sense when we remember the arid conditions of

---

68. Cohen, *Proverbs*, 77.
69. Peterson, *The Message of Leadership*, 100.
70. Toy, *Proverbs*, 303.
71. Waltke, *The Book of Proverbs,* Chapters 1–15, 615.
72. Proverbs 15:30, "Light in a messenger's eyes brings joy to the heart, and good news gives health to the bones" (NIV).
73. Alter, *The Wisdom Books*, 261.
74. Fox, *Proverbs* 10–31, 603.

Solomon's country. Drought was a curse while moisture was a blessing. Fat or greasy bones were connected in his mind with wealth and happiness, while sickness and poverty accompanied dry bones.[75]

Fat in the bones literally means to be "full of marrow."[76] Waltke understands "bones" to be "a synecdoche for the entire person, both physical and psychical."[77] Thus, being made "fat" in the bones means "gives health to the bones," as the NIV correctly translates and as Waltke interprets, "connotes abundance, full satisfaction, and health."[78] A good word has positive psychological benefits which in turn have a corresponding benefit to the body. A godly leader should be in the habit of bringing positive reports instead of always being the harbinger of bad news. He does not color the truth or practice deception, but his perspective is always one of optimism, not negativity. Such a person is a joy to be around. He lifts the spirits, which, in turn, brings healing.

The same Hebrew idiom is found in the final verse under consideration in this section, Prov 16:24.[79] It also speaks of "healing to the bones," but it adds the words, "sweet to the soul." This verse will be dealt with in more detail in the later in this chapter in the section titled "Pleasant Speech."

The spoken word has the power to impact both physical and mental health. It can have a positive effect or a negative effect. The godly leader should always be careful that his words are seasoned with salt and that they have a positive impact on his hearers. Such words will always promote healing. It is true that the godly leader sometimes must exercise correction or reproof, but he always does so suffused with the love of Christ and with the ultimate goal of promoting healing.

Telling the Truth

The message of the book of Proverbs is unequivocal on the subject of honesty. Honesty is a virtue to be exalted. This topic will be explored in more detail from the converse side, lying, in the next chapter, "The Improper Use of the Tongue." *The Talmud* states, "Truth stands, falsehood does not

75. Alden, *Proverbs*, 123.
76. Cohen, *Proverbs*, 102; Toy, *Proverbs*, 317.
77. Waltke, *The Book of Proverbs* Chapters 15–31, 7.
78. Ibid.
79. Proverbs 16:24, "Gracious words are a honeycomb, sweet to the soul and healing to the bones" (NIV).

The Leader's Speech

stand;" and a Rabbinic proverb says, "Truth is the seal of God."[80] Proverbs 12:17–22 provides "a positive portrayal of the character that responds truthfully even under duress."[81]

> A truthful witness gives honest testimony,
> but a false witness tells lies. (v. 17)
> Reckless words pierce like a sword,
> but the tongue of the wise brings healing. (v. 18)
> Truthful lips endure forever,
> but a lying tongue lasts only a moment. (v. 19)
> There is deceit in the hearts of those who plot evil,
> but joy for those who promote peace. (v. 20)
> No harm befalls the righteous,
> but the wicked have their fill of trouble. (v. 21)
> The Lord detests lying lips,
> but he delights in men who are truthful. (v. 22)

The impact from the two witnesses in verse 17 appears to be intentional testimony given in the courtroom, whereas the reckless words in verse 18 appear to inflict unintentional damage. Waltke notes, "Although motivated differently, the character informing them is the same, as the effects, and it must be compensated for."[82] Most commentators identify the setting in verses 17–19 as a courtroom. Clifford argues that in all six instances of the verb פּוּחַ (*puah*) in Proverbs in which it has "lies" as its direct object, the meaning is "to testify in court."[83] Thus, the truth must be established through courtroom testimony. As it is often declared, "the truth, the whole truth, and nothing but the truth" is paramount in a court proceeding. Murphy explains the importance of this kind of testimony. He writes, "Wisdom's concern is with the inner nature of the individual, the honesty and sincerity that must be displayed in critical cases. The verb 'tells' is literally 'breathes'; truth is to be something as natural as breathing. It is not surprising then that he 'proves trustworthy,' literally 'proclaims justice.'"[84]

The implied courtroom setting lends the words of Prov 12:17 more gravitas. Often testimony in a courtroom can literally mean life or death. It is not unheard of in the judicial annals for a person to be condemned

---

80. As cited in Cohen, *Proverbs*, 77.
81. Waltke, *The Book of Proverbs*, Chapters 1–15, 535.
82. Ibid.
83. Clifford, *Proverbs*, 132.
84. Murphy, *Proverbs*, 91.

to death upon fraudulent testimony. Although the truth of verse 17 is not limited to the courtroom, Longman observes that "the consequences of lying in a legal setting make the contrast even more dramatic."[85]

At first glance, verse 18 ("The words of the reckless pierce like swords, but the tongue of the wise brings healing.") does not seem to deal with either truthfulness or falsehood. There is a contrast drawn here between reckless speech and thoughtful speech. Reckless speech wounds like a sword, whereas thoughtful, hence truthful, speech brings healing. Waltke opines, "The proverb promotes thoughtful speech by explicitly comparing the spiritual damage done by the thoughtless 'tongue' to the physical damage done by the lethal sword and contrasting it with one that heals."[86] Delitzsch states it this way, "But on the other hand, the tongue of the wise, which is in itself pure gentleness and a comfort to others, since, far from wounding, rather, by means of comforting, supporting, directing exhortation, exercises a soothing and calming influence."[87] Thus, truthful words always have a positive effect, but reckless words tend to wound.

Verse 19 ("Truthful lips endure forever, but a lying tongue lasts only a moment.") reverts to the contrast between truthful speech and false testimony. Two metonymies appear here: "Truthful lips" are substituted for "truthful speech," and "a lying tongue" is substituted for "lie." There is a decided contrast between "the enduring truth and the lie of the moment."[88] Thus, the Hebrew antithetic parallelism sets in contrast the truth that endures and falsehood that does not endure. Clifford, however, identifies a double contrast in this verse. He writes, "The saying seems to have a double meaning: (1) lies are quickly found out, whereas truthful statements endure; (2) truth-tellers, being favored by God, live long, whereas liars will not live or prosper."[89]

Garrett sees a linked parallelism and chiasmus in Prov 12:16–22 in which the dominant theme is "honesty and lying."[90] He treats these seven

---

85. Longman, *Proverbs*, 276.
86. Waltke, *The Book of Proverbs, Chapters 1–15*, 536.
87. Delitzsch, *Proverbs*, 261.
88. Murphy, *Proverbs*, 91.
89. Clifford, *Proverbs*, 132.
90. Proverbs 12:16–22, "Fools show their annoyance at once, but the prudent overlook an insult. 17 An honest witness tells the truth, but a false witness tells lies. 18 The words of the reckless pierce like swords, but the tongue of the wise brings healing. 19 Truthful lips endure forever, but a lying tongue lasts only a moment. 20 Deceit is in the hearts of those who plot evil, but those who promote peace have joy. 21 No harm

verses as a unit in which verses 16–18 are arranged in parallel "conjoined by a common verse to a four-verse chiasmus" in verses 19–22.[91] Garrett's structure of these verses is as follows:

> A: Thoughtless reactions (v. 16)
> > B: Honesty and lying (v. 17)
>
> A': Reckless words (v. 18)
> > B': Honesty and lying (v. 19)
> > > C: Plotting evil and promoting peace (v. 20)
> > >
> > > C': Trouble to the wicked, not the righteous (v. 21)
> >
> > B'': Honesty and lying (v. 22)[92]

Seen in this context, verse 20 makes perfect sense, whereas at first glance one might wonder how it fits in with honest speech. This fraud or "deceit in the hearts of those who promote evil" demonstrates their utter disregard for the truth. As Longman observes, "Those who plan evil do not care for the truth; they are happy to deceive others or even themselves. On the other hand, joy comes to people who advise peace. The difference between planning evil and advising peace seems to be that the former leads to social disintegration but the latter to social cohesion."[93]

Verse 21 appears on the surface to be a general blanket statement contrasting the fates of the righteous and the wicked. No harm befalls the righteous, whereas the wicked experience many troubles. Longman writes of this verse:

> This statement taken alone is quite bold. It says simply that a righteous person will avoid the pitfalls of life, but the wicked person will not escape trouble. However, anyone with a modicum of life experience realizes that this cannot be taken as an ironclad promise, nor can it be used as a kind of barometer of righteousness of other people in the way that the three friends of Job so used it. In other words, this verse begs discussion of the issue of retribution.[94]

---

overtakes the righteous, but the wicked have their fill of trouble. 22 The LORD detests lying lips, but he delights in people who are trustworthy" (NIV).

91. Garrett, *Proverbs*, 132.
92. Ibid.
93. Longman, *Proverbs*, 277.
94. Ibid.

However, the Proverbs do not provide the reader with legal guarantees that if "A" happens, then "B" will automatically occur. Stuart's reminder is timely that "people often misunderstand wisdom terms and categories as well as wisdom styles and literary modes."[95] Leland Ryken, who has written extensively on the literary modes of the Bible, explains the limitations of the proverb form:

> Proverbs are true in the same way a story or poem is true: they are true to human experience and to reality. Proverbs express truths and experiences that are continually being confirmed in our own lives or the lives of people around us. Proverbs are timeless and never go out of date. The one unanswerable proof that proverbs can be trusted to tell the truth is a long, hard look at what is going on around us in the world.[96]

Waltke suggests that the chiastic linkage of verse 21 with verse 20 is the key to understanding the contrast between the fates of the righteous and the wicked.[97] Thus, the center of the chiasm, "C": Plotting evil and promoting peace (v. 20) and "C'": Trouble to the wicked, not the righteous (v. 21), is not to be taken as a legal promise guarantee in every situation in life. Rather, the principles presented in the Proverbs are to be understood as generally true maxims by which to live a godly life. If all other things are equal, the statement will most likely prove to be true. Longman explains, "It is more likely that life will be easy for the righteous man than it is for the wicked. The intention behind stating this principle so boldly is to encourage righteous rather than wicked behavior."[98] William McKane sees a different application to this verse in "that those who act to the detriment of the community are their own worst enemies, while those who make plans for the common good enjoy a personal satisfaction and fulfilment (sic)."[99]

Verse 22 returns to the main theme of the linked parallelism and chiasm, that of honesty and lying. This same general thought is found over and over again in the book of Proverbs outside of this section (Prov 10:31, 32; 11:20; 13:5; 16:13; 20:23).[100] Actually, the first line of the verse reads, "Lying lips are

---

95. Stuart, *How To Read the Bible For All Its Worth*, 188.
96. Ryken, *How to Read the Bible as Literature*, 125.
97. Waltke, *The Book of Proverbs, Chapters 1–15*, 538.
98. Longman, *Proverbs*, 277–78.
99. McKane, *Proverbs: A New Approach*, 447.
100. Toy, *Proverbs*, 255.

an abhorrence to have."[101] McKane sees the contrast in verse 22 as between "those who behave with integrity, or whose action has a quality of truth" with "liars who are 'an abomination to Yahweh.'"[102] Waltke characterizes the latter as those who "so repulse his [God's] nature that he casts them aside."[103]

Although these verses will not be developed, Prov 14:5 and 14:25 also address the need for truthfulness: "A truthful witness does not deceive, but a false witness pours out lies" (14:5); "A truthful witness saves lives, but a false witness is deceitful" (14:25). It is obvious that the Proverbs place a great emphasis upon and extol the virtue of honesty. As Estes suggests, "Truthfulness, then, should affect every area of life. As a result, truthfulness has consequences across the full range of experience. In the realm of individual life, truthfulness keeps one from trouble."[104] Although this should not be the primary motivation to speak the truth for the believer or the godly Christian leader, it adds another gentle prod for him to do the right thing.

Pleasant Speech

Two verses in the book of Proverbs teach about the value of pleasant speech, 16:24, "Pleasant words are a honeycomb, sweet to the soul and healing to the bones," and 22:11, "He who loves a pure heart and whose speech is gracious will have the king for his friend." The former verse was mentioned earlier under the section, "Healing." Pleasant words bring healing to the bones. They promote good health. Here the metaphor compares them to a honeycomb, which is "sweet to the soul." If the Psalms titles can be believed, David compared the Law of God both to gold and to the honeycomb. He wrote, "They are more precious than gold, than much pure gold; they are sweeter than honey, than honey from the comb" (Ps 19:10). Precisely what constitutes pleasant words is never expressly defined in this verse. Pleasant speech is not simply—as Toy opines—"charm of expression and manner."[105] In like manner, Cohen writes with regard to pleasant words that "wisdom adorns words with graciousness."[106] However, it is obvious that this verse, Prov 16:24, suggests that pleasant speech goes far beyond simply one's de-

---

101. Delitzsch, *Proverbs*, 264.
102. McKane, *Proverbs: A New Approach*, 448.
103. Waltke, *The Book of Proverbs*, Chapters 1–15, 539.
104. Estes, *Handbook on the Wisdom Books and Psalms*, 260.
105. Toy, *Proverbs*, 330.
106. Cohen, *Proverbs*, 108.

meanor while speaking; however, other verses in the Proverbs render some assistance in this regard. They are words that are spoken at the right time ("a timely word"; Prov 15:23). They are words "aptly spoken" (Prov 25:11). They are gracious words (Prov 22:11). Waltke argues that the thrust of the pleasant words of this verse "stands in contrast to 'evil thoughts' in Prov 15:26, suggesting that the expression denotes a moral as well as an aesthetic quality."[107] Certainly pleasant words can overlap with other categories such as encouragement, instruction, protection, healing, and honest words. Bridges conveys this thought. He writes, "Description may give a fancied notion of it. However, the taste affords the only true apprehension. Such is the mysterious delight and refreshment conveyed to us in *pleasant words*. When they are words of counsel, sympathy, or encouragement, they are medicinal also."[108]

Speech that is gracious is also the subject of Prov 22:11. Speech that is gracious is linked with the person who loves a pure heart. The synthetic parallelism used by the writer here adds the thought that such a person "will have the king for a friend." Garret sees a contrast between the mocker in verse 10 and the one "whose minds and words are peaceable."[109] It is clear that this person is not a sycophant because his heart is pure. A flatterer would have ulterior motives. Plaut observes that "A man should cultivate two things: character (pureness of heart) and good manners (grace in his lips).[110] Cohen comments on these two virtues. He writes, "The verse mentions two essential qualifications which must be possessed by a man who wishes to make his way up the social ladder to the top, viz. the king's friendship. Some attempt to reach it by intrigue and insincere flattery, a method which succeeds only for a time because eventually the king obtains a true estimate of them."[111]

There is a logical progression in Prov 22:11. The person whose heart is pure will speak pleasant or gracious words. What a man says is a reflection of what is in his heart. Jesus recognized and taught this progression. He said to the Pharisees who had accused him of driving out demons only by the power of Beelzebub, "Make a tree good and its fruit will be good, or make a tree bad and its fruit will be bad, for a tree is recognized by its fruit. You

---

107. Waltke, *The Book of Proverbs*, Chapters 15–31, 30.
108. Bridges, *Proverbs*, 244.
109. Garrett, *Proverbs*, 189.
110. Plaut, *Proverbs*, 229.
111. Cohen, *Proverbs*, 147.

The Leader's Speech

brood of vipers, how can you who are evil say anything good? For out of the overflow of the heart the mouth speaks. The good man brings good things out of the good stored up in him, and the evil man brings evil things out of the evil stored up in him" (Matt 12:33–35). Later in addressing some Pharisees and teachers of the law who had accused him of allowing his disciples to transgress the tradition of the elders by not washing their hands prior to eating, he replied, "But the things that come out of the mouth come from the heart, and these make a man unclean" (Matt 15:18).

The result of this progression is seen in the second line of this verse, that he "will have the king for his friend." Thus, a "pure heart" + "gracious speech" = royal influence. The proverbial saying comes true in the end: "The cream always rises to the top." Such is true of some of the most unlikely individuals in the annals of Scripture (e.g., Joseph from prison to Pharaoh's court; David from shepherd to king). As Longman concludes, "It is always good to have friends in high places."[112] This is true of the person whose pleasant speech manifests itself from a pure heart.

Praise

The Puritan John Watson eloquently wrote of the duty of praise thus: "Praising God is one of the highest and purest acts of religion. In prayer we act like men; in praise we act like angels."[113] The theme of the book of Psalms is praise to God, as represented Ps 147:1, "Praise the Lord. How good it is to sing praises to our God, how pleasant and fitting to praise him."

However, praise has a lower use and different connotation when it is used to commend man. The criteria for such praise to man is found in Prov 12:8, "A man is praised according to his wisdom, but men with warped minds are despised." Solomon uses antithetical parallelism here to set in contrast a man of wisdom and men with warped minds. The wise man is praised; the men with warped minds are despised. Toy writes of this contrast, "The contrast intended is not of learning and ignorance, or of philosophical depth and shallowness, but of ability and inability to think justly in common matters of life."[114] The word translated here "warped" (or "perverse" in the AV and RSV) is עָוָה (*'awa*), which means "bend, twist,"

---

112. Longman, *Proverbs*, 407.
113. Thomas, *The Golden Treasury of Puritan Quotations*, 209.
114. Toy, *Proverbs*, 245.

thus "one perverted of mind."[115] Toy softens the sense of willfulness that "perverse" suggests and writes that "the sense of the latter is better expressed by our *wrongheaded* . . . incapable of just, discriminating thought, lacking in judgment."[116] The flip side of this is the "wisdom" in the first line of the verse. The word for wisdom found in this verse, שׂכל (*sekel*), is found in its noun form six times and as a verb eight times.[117] It literally means "prudence, insight," and it carries the nuance here of possessing common sense or good judgment.[118] Garrett explains, "The term here implies integrity and capacity to deal with problems in life."[119] There is always a sharp distinction made between intelligence and common sense. Common sense, of course, is simply applied intelligence, but it must always have a God-ward component. Kravitz and Olitzky differentiate thus, that "mere intelligence that is lacking moral direction is dangerous for the individual and for society."[120] Such a person will demonstrate his wisdom through his behavior and, thus, will merit praise.

In the book of Proverbs, wisdom is often mentioned in association with the fear of the Lord, as in 1:7, "The fear of the Lord is the beginning of knowledge, but fools despise wisdom and discipline." This association is so prominent that most scholars believe that it expresses the theme of the book. The Epilogue of the book is The Wife of Noble Character. This woman's character is so singular that "her children arise and call her blessed; her husband also, and he praises her" (Prov 31:28). The final two verses of the Proverbs mention the word "praise" twice in connection with this woman: "Charm is deceptive, and beauty is fleeting; but a woman who fears the Lord is to be praised. Give her the reward she has earned, and let her works bring her praise at the city gate" (Prov 31:30–31). Here is a picture of the truly liberated and fulfilled woman. She is worthy of praise because she exemplifies the concepts of wisdom outlined in the rest of the book of Proverbs. So should the godly leader be. He should not only be worthy of praise, but also be willing to give praise when it is due.

---

115. *BDB* § 6859.

116. Toy, *Proverbs*, 245.

117. Strong, *Strong's Exhaustive Concordance*, 1175–76.

118. *BDB* § 9445.

119. Garrett, *Proverbs*, 130.

120. Kravitz and Olitzky, *Mishlei*, 119.

The Leader's Speech

Advice

The benefits of seeking and heeding wise counsel are dealt with in detail in Chapter 3. In those verses marshaled as support in that chapter, the emphasis is upon seeking counsel and heeding wise counsel. Proverbs 27:9 is one verse that speaks about the advice offered by a friend and how it brings joy to the heart: "Perfume and incense bring joy to the heart, and the pleasantness of one's friend springs from his earnest counsel." Cohen observes, "His earnest counsel" is literally "from advice of the soul."[121] It is advice given with a sincere desire to be of assistance. Admittedly, the Hebrew construction of 9b is difficult; however, the parallelism that the writer employs appears to be synonymous. McKane concludes that the verse is "a type of simile," which then makes interpretation easier.[122] Peterson captures the essence of the simile in his translation of this verse, although he ignores the advice or counsel aspect: "Just as lotions and fragrance give sensual delight, a sweet friendship refreshes the soul."[123] The comparison appears to be between the physical refreshment that perfume and incense bring and the spiritual refreshment that the words of advice of a friend provide. Waltke agrees thus, "The gladdening oil and incense are similes for the agreeable and delightful counsel of a friend that originates in his very being. Both the outward fragrances and the whole-some counsel produce a sense of well-being."[124] Offering wise counsel when asked is one of the responsibilities of friendship as is the receiving of the same one of the benefits. Good advice is always in season and a valuable and proper use of the tongue.

Confession of Sin

The confession of sin is an important component of the believer's walk with the Lord, as noted in Prov 14:9, "Fools mock at making amends for sin, but goodwill is found among the upright." The godly leader should set the example in this regard. Although only one verse in the book of Proverbs expressly mentions this use of the tongue, it is an extremely important element of the ongoing process of sanctification. Often in the Old Testament, as here, the withholding of confession is linked with material prosperity,

---

121. Cohen, *Proverbs*, 180.
122. McKane, *Proverbs: A New Approach*, 613.
123. Peterson, *The Message of Leadership*, 126.
124. Waltke, *The Book of Proverbs*, Chapters 15–31, 378.

as implied in Prov 28:13, "He who conceals his sins does not prosper, but whoever confesses and renounces them finds mercy." David's lament about his experience with withholding sin is perhaps the classic Old Testament expression of Prov 28:13, as recorded in Ps 32:1–4,

> Blessed is he
> whose transgressions are forgiven,
> whose sins are covered.
> Blessed is the man
> whose sin the Lord does not count against him
> and in whose spirit is no deceit.
> When I kept silent,
> my bones wasted away
> through my groaning all day long.
> For day and night
> your hand was heavy upon me;
> my strength was sapped
> as in the heat of summer (Ps 32:1–4).

It is also possible that the Apostle John was inspired by Prov 28:13 when he wrote, "If we confess our sins, he is faithful and just and will forgive us our sins and purify us from all unrighteousness" (1 John 1:9). Certainly, the two verses are very similar.

Although Prov 28:13 appears to be on the surface explicitly theological, Garrett posits a nontheological understanding of the verse on the basis that verse 13 is part of a section (Prov 28:12—29:2) which "relates to how good versus evil relates to the social fabric of society."[125] He explains further, "Thus those who confess their crimes and are remorseful are more likely to get the mercy of the court than those who try to the end to conceal their guilt, and the hardened criminal will be more severely treated than someone who shows fear of the power of the state."[126] Alter's translation takes an entirely secular slant and appears to favor this interpretation: "Who covers his crimes will not prosper, but who admits and leaves off will be granted mercy."[127] To this writer, however, a secular rather than theological interpretation of Prov 28:13 is incorrect. Although the general context does indeed relate to the social fabric of society, the immediate context does not. The very next verse speaks explicitly of fearing the Lord and not hardening

---

125. Garrett, *Proverbs*, 225.
126. Ibid.
127. Alter, *The Wisdom Books*, 317.

one's heart, which argues strongly for a theological interpretation. Both the RSV and the ESV translations appear to favor this slant: "He who conceals his transgressions will not prosper, but he who confesses and forsakes them will obtain mercy" (RSV). Almost totally identical is the ESV, "Whoever conceals his transgressions will not prosper, but he who confesses and forsakes them will obtain mercy" (ESV). Murphy's position is that the confession mentioned in this verse is public. He writes, "This verse stands out as being the only one in Proverbs to indicate the need of public confession, and also the divine offer of mercy that this entails."[128] However, there is nothing in the text that indicates that this confession needs to be public. Clifford, on the other hand, argues that the confession is made solely to God.[129] It has been argued by some writers that the book of Proverbs "has no real notion of God, that its concept of God is rather primitive."[130] However, Garrett argues thus, "Actually, God is no afterthought or incidental truth in Proverbs. He is at the very heart of the book."[131] Here in Prov 28:13 is found part of the foundation of the Gospel message, that of confession of sins and repentance. The person who does so is the recipient of God's mercy. Certainly the godly leader should do this on a regular basis.

Discretion

This category is titled "Discretion" for want of a better title. In his book of admonitions for youth, Solomon wrote, "My son, pay attention to my wisdom, listen well to my words of insight, so that you may maintain discretion and your lips may preserve knowledge" (Prov 5:1–2). Again, wisdom is linked with discretion.: "I, wisdom dwell together with prudence; I possess knowledge and discretion" (Prov 8:12); "Wisdom is found on the lips of the discerning" (Prov 10:13). Discretion can be defined as "a being careful about what one does and says; prudence."[132] Several verses in the book of Proverbs speak of this use of the tongue. Some of them overlap into other categories, but all speak of the use of discretion in some form. One passage, Prov 11:12–13, concludes a section on the proper use of the tongue: "A man

---

128. Murphy, *Proverbs*, 216.
129. Clifford, *Proverbs*, 245.
130. Garrett, *Proverbs*, 153.
131. Ibid.
132. *Webster's New World Dictionary of the American Language*, 418.

who lacks judgment derides his neighbor, but a man of understanding holds his tongue. A gossip betrays a confidence, but a trustworthy man keeps a secret." Garrett concludes that Prov 11:9–13 constitutes a chiasmus with an afterword (verse 13). He writes, "Verses 10–11 are an obvious pair in parallel, whereas vv. 9, 12 are bound by the theme of the slanderous gossip of the wicked against the restrained silence of the righteous."[133] Verse 12 contrasts, using antithetical parallelism, the man who openly demonstrates his contempt for his neighbor by deriding him with the man of understanding who holds his tongue. This man who derides his neighborhood is the same godless man who in verse 9 with his tongue "destroys his neighbor." The "man of understanding" of verse 12b possesses the judgment that the one of 12a lacks. He shows discretion in his speech. This verse contrasts an improper use of the tongue with a proper use, holding his tongue. It is not condemning thinking contemptuous thoughts about one's neighbor, but rather expressing those thoughts outwardly in a way that brings him down. Kravitz and Olitzky write, "A sensible person does not express contempt for one's neighbor, no matter how much one might think it. A wise person keeps silent, particularly if there is nothing appropriate to say."[134] This comment brings to mind an old saying, "If you can't say anything nice about a person, don't say anything at all." Another term for that kind of behavior is discretion.

Verse 13, according to Garrett, comprises the Afterword of this section on the tongue.[135] In this verse the gossip of 13a is contrasted, again by use of antithetical parallelism, with the "trustworthy man" of 13b who is able to keep a secret. He writes of the gossip, "The wicked are not only malevolent with their words, but they are also indiscreet and cannot be trusted. The wise not only refrain from lies and slander, but they also know how to keep a matter private."[136] An oft-quoted aphorism that is usually attributed to Benjamin Franklin is, "Three can keep a secret if two of them are dead."

"A prudent man" is the subject of Prov 12:16, "A fool shows his annoyance at once, but a prudent man overlooks an insult" and 12:23, "A prudent man keeps his knowledge to himself, but the heart of fools blurts out folly." The former verse is the more straightforward of the two. It contrasts using antithetical parallelism a fool who responds to the slightest provocation with a prudent man who exercises discretion. The fool is what is referred to

133. Garrett, *Proverbs*, 125.
134. Kravitz and Olitzky, *Mishlei*, 111.
135. Garrett, *Proverbs*, 125.
136. Ibid.

The Leader's Speech

today as "thin-skinned." Christ's words in the Sermon on the Mount are an application of this verse when he noted, "You have heard that it was said, 'Eye for eye, and tooth for tooth.' But I tell you, Do not resist an evil person. If someone strikes you on the right cheek, turn to him the other also" (Matt 5:38–39). Toy comments that this proverb "condemns thoughtless, passionate resentment, and enjoins calmness and deliberateness in the face of an insult."[137] He argues further that it does not teach pacifism, cowardice, or weakness.[138] What it does teach is the use of discretion and prudence in the face of insult. It condemns impulsive displays of annoyance or retribution. It teaches that silence is a better alternative. Longman's commentary on this verse reveals another possible reason for such discretion. He writes, "There is benefit for those who do not let their rivals know how upset they are. If one's intent is to hurt another person, then the victim's immediate display of negative emotion will be received and celebrated as a victory. Prudence is the ability to regulate one's emotional display for one's own advantage."[139] Murphy appears to echo this thought in writing that the proverb ". . . envisages some sparring with others. . . . Anger will only lead one to play into the hands of an opponent."[140]

A companion to Prov 12:16 is 12:23, which praises the "prudent man" who "keeps his knowledge to himself." He is contrasted using antithetical parallelism with the fool who "blurts out folly." Both proverbs enjoin the virtue of silence instead of rash response. The wise or prudent man is commended in the latter for using few words and knowing when to speak. Rabbi Solomon Yitzchak ben Isaac pointed out that a prudent person is cautious about revealing what he knows.[141] The fool shows no discretion, which only makes his stupidity apparent. Often a conversation is dominated by someone who knows the least. That person "blurts out folly." A parallel passage to this is found in the writings of Yeshua ben Eleazar ben Sira: "The mind of fools is in their mouth, but the mouth of the wise is in their mind" (Sirach 21:26). Peterson's translation of Prov 12:23 captures this understanding: "Prudent people don't flaunt their knowledge; talkative

---

137. Toy, *Proverbs*, 252.
138. Ibid.
139. Longman, *Proverbs*, 276.
140. Murphy, *Proverbs*, 91.
141. Kravitz and Olitzky, *Mishlei*, 123.

Fools broadcast their silliness."[142] Humility is at issue here as well. Flaunting one's knowledge is boasting, which is rooted in pride. Pride is uniformly condemned in Scripture.

A person who practices discretion has a tight control over his tongue. He "guards his lips," as Prov 13:3 says, "He who guards his lips guards his life, but he who speaks rashly will come to ruin." In this verse, the cautious speaker is contrasted using antithetical parallelism with the one who speaks recklessly or rashly. Yeshua ben Eleazer ben Sira wrote, "So make balances and scales for your words. So make a door and bolt for your mouth" (Sirach 28:25). Kidner suggests a range of possibilities for both the rashness and the resultant ruin thus, "This rashness could show itself in promises, assertions, disclosures; the ruin could be financial, social, physical, spiritual."[143] It is unlikely, as Clifford attests, that verse 3b includes a "touch of sardonic humor."[144] This verse touches on issues of life and death. There is nothing even remotely humorous about behavior that can result in death or ruin. As Waltke attests, "The stakes are high; good and bad speech is a matter of life and death."[145] The power to control one's tongue is one of the clearest evidences of wisdom. It would indeed appear strange that a book devoted to the pursuit of wisdom would have so much to say about the control of the tongue if it were not an evidence of that quality.

Discretion can also be seen in the manner in which a person replies, as stated in Prov 15:1, "A gentle answer turns away wrath, but a harsh word stirs up anger." In his *Homily on Our Lord 22.3*, Ephraem the Syrian said in regard to this verse as cited in the *Ancient Christian Commentary on Scripture*, "Our Lord gave most of his assistance with persuasion rather than with admonition. Gentle showers soften the earth and thoroughly penetrate it, but a beating rain hardens and compresses the surface of the earth so that it will not be absorbed."[146] An illustration of this type of answer can be seen Gideon's answer to the Ephraimites in order to placate their wrath against him:

> Now the Ephraimites asked Gideon, "Why have you treated us like this? Why didn't you call us when you went to fight Midian?" And they criticized him sharply. But he answered them, "What have I

---

142. Peterson, *The Message of Leadership*, 95.
143. Kidner, *Proverbs*, 101.
144. Clifford, *Proverbs*, 136.
145. Waltke, *The Book of Proverbs, Chapters 1–15*, 553.
146. Wright, *Old Testament IX: Proverbs*, 103.

accomplished compared to you? Aren't the gleanings of Ephraim's grapes better than the full grape harvest of Abiezer? God gave Oreb and Zeeb, the Midianite leaders, into your hands. What was I able to do compared to you?" At this, their resentment against him subsided" (Judges 8:1–3)

It has been said that "Discretion is the better part of valor." Rather than further inflame an already incendiary situation, Gideon chose to practice discretion. He gave the Ephraimites a "gentle answer" which turned away their wrath. Jephthah faced a nearly identical situation later in Israel's history, but his harsh answer produced a vastly different result:

> The men of Ephraim called out their forces, crossed over to Zaphon and said to Jephthah, "Why did you go to fight the Ammonites without calling us to go with you? We're going to burn down your house over your head." Jephthah answered, "I and my people were engaged in a great struggle with the Ammonites, and although I called, you didn't save me out of their hands. When I saw that you wouldn't help, I took my life in my hands and crossed over to fight the Ammonites, and the Lord gave me the victory over them. Now why have you come up today to fight me? Jephthah then called together the men of Gilead and fought against Ephraim. The Gileadites struck them down because the Ephraimites had said, "You Gileadites are renegades from Ephraim and Manasseh." The Gileadites captured the fords of the Jordan leading to Ephraim, and whenever a survivor of Ephraim said, "Let me cross over," the men of Gilead asked him, "Are you an Ephraimite?" If he replied, "No," they said, "All right, say 'Shibboleth.'" If he said, "Sibboleth," because he could not pronounce the word correctly, they seized him and killed him at the fords of the Jordan. Forty-two thousand Ephraimites were killed at that time" (Judges 12:1–6).

Garrett comments on Prov 15:1 thus, "The ability to avert needless quarreling and to live in harmony with others is a virtue of wisdom. Many conflicts arise not because the issues separating the parties are so great but because of the temperaments people bring to a confrontation."[147] The respective responses of Gideon and Jephthah are a commentary on this verse. The former gave a gentle answer; the latter a harsh word. Gideon turned away wrath, whereas, Jephthah's response initiated a bloodbath. Both approaches have been used throughout history with similar results.

---

147. Garrett, *Proverbs*, 150.

A companion verse to Prov 15:1 is found later in the same chapter: "A hot-tempered man stirs up dissension, but a patient man calms a quarrel" (Prov 15:18). This verse is dealt with in greater detail in Chapter 5 under the section titled 'Quarreling'; however, suffice to say that the "patient man" mentioned here is one who uses discretion. The result is that he does not stir up dissension and he is able to calm a quarrel.

A highly valued skill in wisdom literature is the ability to give an "apt reply," as stated in Prov 15:23, "A man finds joy in giving an apt reply–and how good is a timely word." Garrett suggests that the verse's placement here is because of verse 22, which stresses the need of counsel in making plans.[148] The type of parallelism used here is likely synthetic of the completion type. The first line speaks of the joy a speaker has in giving "an apt reply." However, as the second line states, the timing of the reply is just as important as the substance of the words. Waltke comments on this verse: "It is not a hasty word . . . , but a ready, thoughtful word from the mouth, assuming that the speaker has stored up knowledge to give the fitting word on just the right occasion."[149] The timing of such a word is crucial. It is possible to give a good reply but at the wrong time. It is also possible to give an unsatisfactory reply, but to give it at the right time. What this verse endorses is the practice of saying the right word at the right time. As Alden says, it is "the right word and the right time for that word."[150] It is important to have both. Kravitz and Olitzky give this passage a leadership context thus: "What is important is how we use the gift of speech–to help or to cause hurt. Moreover, learning how and when to speak is extremely important for those who seek roles in government."[151] The annals of history are full of leaders who "put their foot in their mouths." In today's media age, those types of leaders do not usually last very long in leadership positions.

The final passage under consideration, Prov 26:4–5, could just as easily be classified under "Rebuke," as it reads, "Do not answer a fool according to his folly, or you will be like him yourself. Answer a fool according to his folly, or he will be wise in his own eyes." These verses constitute a paradox, which was the major reason that the book of Proverbs was considered to be one of the Old Testament Antilegomena in the canonicity discussion. Plaut summarizes the Rabbinic concern in this regard. He writes, "These

---

148. Ibid., 154.
149. Waltke, *The Book of Proverbs*, Chapters 1–15, 634.
150. Alden, *Proverbs*, 121.
151. Kravitz and Olitzky, *Mishlei*, 151–52.

two proverbs stand in contradiction to one another, and all pious attempts to reconcile the differences are futile. The Rabbis of the past took a very serious view of this, and the Talmud reports that because of this contradiction, there was objection to the inclusion of proverbs in the Bible. For, so they argued, how could the Book be inspired if it contained this manifest contradiction?"[152] Plaut, along with other Jewish commentators in the Rabbinic tradition have mistakenly concluded that verses 4 and 5 contradict one another. Verse 4 basically is saying that one must not stoop to the level of a fool in answering him. In other words, it is sometimes better not to answer a fool at all. Verse 5, on the other hand, says that sometimes foolishness must be denounced and the fool rebuked. Alden suggests, "Perhaps the real lesson here is no matter what you do, you won't win in your dealings with a fool."[153] The Rabbis eventually were able to reconcile the apparent contradiction by ". . . applying verse 4 to secular matters (silence is advisable), and verse 5 to religious controversy (speak up for a principle)"[154] Thus, the book of Proverbs was included in the Hebrew Bible along with the other books of the Antilegomena: Esther, Ecclesiastes, Song of Songs, and Ezekiel. The perpetual Jewish frustration with fools can be seen in some of the old secular proverbs: "A fool can ask more questions in an hour than ten wise men can answer in a year"; or "When a wise man talks to a fool, two fools are conversing."[155] Again, this is an area of speech where timing is important. There is a time for silence in the presence of a fool and there is a time to answer him. Ryken correctly observes, "Paradox always imposes on the reader the obligation to *resolve* the apparent contradiction."[156] Discretion gives one the wisdom to know what is the proper course of action.

Rebuke

The final type of the proper use of the tongue under consideration in this chapter is rebuke. There are at least four verses in the book of Proverbs which speak clearly of this type of speech. Two speak of the effect of a rebuke to a man of discernment: "A rebuke impresses a man of discernment more than a hundred lashes a fool" (Prov 17:10); and, "Flog a mocker, and

152. Plaut, *Proverbs*, 266.
153. Alden, *Proverbs*, 186.
154. Plaut, *Proverbs*, 266.
155. Alden, *Proverbs*, 186.
156. Ryken, *How To Read The Bible As Literature*, 101.

the simple will learn prudence; rebuke a discerning man, and he will gain knowledge" (Prov 19:25). These two verses have much in common. Both speak of the flogging of either a fool or a mocker. The hundred lashes of Prov 17:10 is doubtless hyperbole with the attention on the extreme measures that must be taken to get a fool's attention. Both also speak of rebuking either a "man of discernment" or a "discerning man" and its effect upon him. In the former verse, the "man of discernment" is impressed by the rebuke, whereas in the latter, he gains knowledge. Bridges comments on Prov 17:10 thus, "If this be true of man's *reproof*, much more of God's. A word was enough for David. A look *entered more into* Peter's heart, *than an hundred stripes into* Pharaoh."[157] Alden writes, "People who are wise are also sensitive; their consciences are tender and their wills are pliant. Fools, on the other hand, are stiff-necked and unresponsive."[158]

A simile is employed in Prov 25:12: "Like an earring of gold or an ornament of fine gold is a wise man's rebuke to a listening ear." Both Garrett and Waltke pair this verse with the preceding one.[159] Garrett writes, "The metaphor of jewelry dominates both proverbs, and both concern the importance of good counsel."[160] Here the wise man's rebuke falls upon a " listening ear." The rebuke is like an adornment of gold or a golden earring. Wisdom and its effects are often portrayed in the book of Proverbs as an adornment: "They will be a garland to grace your head and a chain to adorn your neck" (Prov 1:9); "They will be life for you, an ornament to grace your neck" (Prov 3:22); "She will set a garland of grace on your head and present you with a crown of splendor" (Prov 4:9). Kravitz and Olitzky comment on the Rabbinic writings on Prov 25:12, "The delicate relation between the one who offers reproof and the one who receives it received the attention of the Rabbis. Rabbi Tarfon wondered if there was anyone in his generation who knew how to offer reproof and Rabbi Eliezer ben Azariah wondered if there was anyone in his generation who knew how to receive it."[161]

The final verse extolling the virtues of a timely rebuke is Prov 28:23: "He who rebukes a man will in the end gain more favor than he who has a flattering tongue." This verse is an example of synthetic parallelism (comparison type) in which a comparison is made by way of contrast between

---

157. Bridges, *Proverbs*, 262–62.
158. Alden, *Proverbs*, 134.
159. Garrett, *Proverbs*, 206; Waltke, *The Book of Proverbs, Chapters 15–31*, 321.
160. Garrett, *Proverbs*, 206.
161. Kravitz and Olitzky, *Mishlei*, 248.

the one who rebukes and the flatterer. Clifford sees a paradox in the verse. He writes, "The paradox is that frank and truthful speech wins more favor than flattery. People learn best through honest dialogue that includes the possibility of reproof and correction. Reproof leads to wisdom that wins favor."[162] This verse teaches that the reward for a frank assessment does not come immediately, but only later after much reflection on the truth of the rebuke. The rebuke may cause an initial estrangement, but in the end the person will appreciate the speaker's frankness. An example of this type of rebuke in Prov 28:23a can be seen in Paul's opposition to Peter after he had led some Jews astray in withdrawing from Gentile believers.

> When Peter came to Antioch, I opposed him to his face, because he was clearly in the wrong. Before certain men came from James, he used to eat with the Gentiles. But when they arrived, he began to draw back and separate himself from the Gentiles because he was afraid of those who belonged to the circumcision group. The other Jews joined him in his hypocrisy, so that by their hypocrisy even Barnabas was led astray. When I saw that they were not acting in line with the truth of the gospel, I said to Peter in front of them all, "You are a Jew, yet you live like a Gentile and not like a Jew. How is it, then, that you force Gentiles to follow Jewish customs?" (Gal 2:11–14).

Peter's initial response is not recorded either in Galatians or the Acts of the Apostles. However, Paul's position is later vindicated in Acts 15 with James' pronouncement at the Jerusalem Council (Acts 15:19–21). An example of the one who has a flattering tongue seen in Prov 28:23b is Balaam (Numbers 22–24), the hypocritical prophet who sought to lead Israel astray. Steven Barabas writes of this woeful prophet, "No Bible character is more severely excoriated."[163] Thus, one who speaks without regard for wealth or personal benefit, such as the Apostle Paul, wins out in the end, whereas the insincere flatterer, as exemplified by Balaam, in the end gains nothing of value. As Toy asserts, the teaching of this verse is that "men's good sense will prefer honest reproof to flattery."[164] The ear may prefer flattery, but the honest mind realizes that a sincere rebuke is of much greater value in the end.

---

162. Clifford, *Proverbs*, 247.
163. Barabas, "Balaam," in *NIDB*, 121.
164. Toy, *Proverbs*, 104.

Summary

The tongue has well been described as a double-edged sword. It has the capacity to do great good and to inflict great harm. The nineteenth century commentator William Arnot opines about the duty incumbent upon the man or woman who dares to speak. He writes,

> It is not safe for a man or woman to open the lips and permit the heart to pour itself forth by that channel without selection or restraint. If the spring within were pure, the stream could not be too constant or too strong; but the heart is full of corruption; and from a corrupt fountain sweet waters cannot flow. It is the part of a wise man to set a watch upon his own lips.[165]

This chapter has outlined the first of two courses of action that the tongue can take: The Proper Use of the Tongue. The Proper Use of the Tongue includes Imparting Wisdom and Knowledge, Encouragement, Protection, Nurture, Healing, Telling the Truth, Pleasant Speech, Praise, Advice, Confessing Sin, Discretion, and Rebuke. This is not a comprehensive or exhaustive listing of categories that could be classified under The Proper Use of the Tongue, but it does cover the major ones in at least a representative or overview fashion. It is easy to see that the book of Proverbs has much to say on the subject and clearly extols the proper use of the tongue in its many manifestations.

---

165. Arnot, *Studies in Proverbs*, 182.

Chapter 5

The Leader's Speech

The Improper Use of the Tongue

THE IMPROPER USE OF the tongue includes a multiplicity of sins such as lying, gossip, foolish talk, slander, quarreling, speaking rashly, boasting, flattery, mockery, and perverse talk. The book of Proverbs speaks in a general sense about the dangers of the improper use of the tongue. Proverbs 4:24 commands, "Put away perversity from your mouth; keep corrupt talk from your lips. Proverbs 18:6 observes, "A fool's lips bring him strife, and his mouth invites a beating, and 18:7 notes, "A fool's mouth is his undoing, and his lips are a snare to his soul." This section will outline briefly the scriptural teaching from Proverbs on these ten improper uses of the tongue. As the apocryphal writer, Yeshua Ben Sira, summarized so well the importance of this teaching in the second century B.C.E., "Happy is the one who does not sin with the tongue" (*Sirach* 25:9).

Lying

One topic upon which the book of Proverbs deals most emphatically is the need for truthfulness. A disturbing trend of modern culture that has also permeated the church, para-church organizations, and Christian-owned businesses, is that of dishonesty. This inclination includes lying, fraud, cheating, and evasion. The prevailing attitude seems to be that if one is not caught, then these forms of dishonesty are acceptable. Sir Walter Scott long ago wrote of the practical problems that a liar faces in his L'Envoy, "Oh, what a tangled web we weave, when first we practice to deceive."[1] An old Chinese proverb states, "A liar is not believed even if he tells the truth." Proverbs unequivocally declares that all forms of dishonesty are unacceptable, and are, in fact, sin. By contrast, Proverbs elaborates the virtue of truthfulness and emphasizes its importance. Proverbs 8:7 proclaims, "My mouth speaks what is true, for my lips detest wickedness." In the first listing in Proverbs of practices that are hateful to God, lying is featured prominently:

> There are six things the Lord hates,
> seven that are detestable to him:
> haughty eyes,
> a lying tongue,
> hands that shed innocent blood,
> a heart that devises wicked schemes,
> feet that are quick to rush into evil,
> a false witness who pours out lies
> and a man who stirs up dissension among brothers. (6:16–19)

This succinct listing of things that God hates using the X + 1 formula is not meant to be an exhaustive listing of detestable practices, but rather a "way of stating something indefinite."[2] This structure is not unique to the book of Proverbs. It is also used by the prophet Amos (chapters 1 and 2). Smith defines the sin of lying as ". . . the willful perversion of the truth with the intent to harm another. The sin is committed mainly with the mouth, but also when by any other means a false impression is deliberately conveyed."[3]

Proverbs also sets forth the dichotomy between truthfulness and lying using antithetic parallelism: "The Lord detests lying lips, but he delights in men who are truthful" (Prov 12:22). Longman translates this verse even more strongly, "False lips are an abomination to YHWH; his favor is on those who do what is true."[4] It is clear that God hates lying. It should not be the practice of any Christian, much less the Christian leader. The modern maxim states it very well, "Honesty is the best policy." Someone has amended this to read, "Honesty is the *only* policy." Certainly, this policy should characterize the godly leader. It is clear that God places a premium on honesty and hates dishonesty.

1. Bartlett, *Familiar Quotations*, 431.
2. Smith, *The Wisdom Literature and Psalms*, 509.
3. Ibid., 509–10.
4. Longman, *Proverbs*, 278.

The Leader's Speech

Zigarelli explains why dishonesty in speech is so reprehensible to God. He writes:

> Honesty is an elemental virtue. It's a tenet that transcends almost every system of ethics, whether religious or philosophical. What distinguishes the Judeo-Christian construction of this belief, though, is its insight into God's vehemence about honesty.... We must be honest because when we're not, *the Lord detests it*. Our dishonesty is an *abomination* to Him.... We must elevate our behavior, as we view our actions through the eyes of God. Dishonesty and deception are wholly unacceptable to God. They separate us from Him.[5]

The book of Proverbs quite possibly devotes more emphasis to the sin of lying than any other sin. Numerous verses deal with the subject of lying lips or a deceitful tongue. Several of those were dealt with in some detail in the section "Telling the Truth" in Chapter 4, "The Proper Use of the Tongue." A representative sampling of other verses that deal with this subject include the following: "He who conceals his hatred has lying lips, and whoever spreads slander is a fool" (Prov 10:18); "A man of perverse heart does not prosper; he whose tongue is deceitful falls into trouble" (Prov 17:20); "A false witness will not go unpunished, and he who pours out lies will not go free" (Prov 19:5); "A malicious man disguises himself with his lips, but in his heart he harbors deceit" (Prov 26:24); and, "Though his speech is charming, do not believe him, for seven abominations fill his heart" (Prov 26:25).

The first line of Prov 10:18 deals specifically with the sin of lying, whereas the second line deals with slander, which is a substratum of deceitful speech. However, Roy Zuck links the two words as both, in this case, are sired from the same seed, hatred. He writes, "The second line in verse 18 begins with 'and' rather than 'but' to show that the two thoughts of hatred and slander are not opposites. Such lying and slander, born out of hatred, characterize a fool."[6] More will be said about this verse later under the subheading of "Slander," but suffice to say that the clear intent of the person mentioned here is to "hurt, belittle, or demean the other person."[7] As Longman opines, "Through such actions, relationships are destroyed."[8]

---

5. Zigarelli, *Management by Proverbs*, 104–5.
6. Zuck, *Learning From the Sages*, 269.
7. Ibid.
8. Longman, *Proverbs*, 238.

Another verse which condemns lying is Prov 17:20, "One whose heart is corrupt does not prosper; one whose tongue is perverse falls into trouble." This verse emphasizes the consequences of lying to the one who perpetrates verbal fraud, not to the victim, as might be expected. It is one of many Old Testament admonitions that are boldly reinforced by the Apostle Paul who wrote: "Do not be deceived: God cannot be mocked. A man reaps what he sows. The one who sows to please his sinful nature, from that nature will reap destruction" (Gal 6:7–8a). Alden writes, "Over and over the sages state this lesson, perhaps hoping that if it is repeated often enough, we'll obey it."[9]

Proverbs 17:20 is an example of synthetic parallelism in which the second line builds upon or completes the first. The heart and the tongue are paralleled in verse 20. The central concept seems to be that a deceitful tongue springs from a perverse heart. Longman observes that the use of these two words in such parallel fashion is not uncommon and "recognizes that people's speech reflects their core personality."[10] This concept is developed more fully in the Gospels by Jesus. For example, he says in a confrontation with the Pharisees, "You brood of vipers, how can you who are evil say anything good? For out of the overflow of the heart the mouth speaks. The good man brings good things out of the good stored up in him, and the evil man brings evil things out of the evil stored up in him. But I tell you that men will have to give account on the day of judgment for every careless word they have spoken" (Matt 12:34–36). Jesus knew as did Solomon about 1000 years earlier that a person's speech is simply an outward manifestation of what is in his heart or mind. Words do not just slip out unless they are spoken hastily, and even then they accurately reflect what the speaker actually believes and the values that he holds in his heart. Perhaps he did not want to display to the world that he is "a man of perverse heart," but his words are an accurate reflection of who he is. People can be fooled only for a time, because eventually "he whose tongue is deceitful falls into trouble." The Puritan Thomas Brooks wisely said, "We know metals by their tinkling, and men by their talking."[11] So words do reveal what a person really is. Lying reveals a great deal about a person. It demonstrates what is really in his heart. Kouzes and Posner have extensively researched the question, "What values, personal traits, or characteristics do you look for and admire in a leader?"[12] Over the

---

9. Alden, *Proverbs*, 136.
10. Longman, *Proverbs*, 349.
11. Thomas, *The Golden Treasury of Puritan Quotations*, 296.
12. Kouzes and Posner, *Christian Reflections on the Leadership Challenge*, 28.

course of more than a quarter century, they have survey thousands of business and government executives from six continents (Africa, North America, South America, Asia, Europe, and Australia) asking them that very question. Twenty characteristics regularly make the list, but only four have consistently received over sixty percent of the votes as recorded in the 1987, 1995, 2002, and 2007 editions of *The Leadership Challenge*.[13] These traits are Honest, Forward-looking, Inspiring, and Competent.[14] Honesty has dominated the survey, with eight-three percent of the respondents selecting it in the 1987 edition, eight-eight percent in the 1995 edition, eighty-eight percent in the 2002 edition, and a zenith of eighty-nine percent in the latest edition, 2007.[15] Thus, executives consider honesty in their leaders as more important than competence, intelligence, fairness, dependability, loyalty, and a host of other worthy characteristics. Blackaby and Blackaby conclude how important it is to be honest, which is the polar opposite of lying. They write, "Spiritual leaders, of all people, ought to be known for their honesty."[16] Honesty and lying are two sides of the same coin. One is commended by God and is to be practiced by the godly leader; the other is roundly condemned and is to be eschewed at all costs.

Gossip

Gossip is another sin of the tongue that is widely condemned throughout Scripture, but no place more so than in the book of Proverbs. Zigarelli defines gossip as "discrediting talk about someone who is not present."[17] Elsewhere he describes further what it is, its origins, and its ultimate fruit. He writes, "Gossip is a venomous misuse of the tongue, induced by its scriptural companions arrogance, jealousy, insolence, and the like, culminating in strife."[18] Six verses in Proverbs mention the term "gossip" in the NIV

---

13. The complete list is Honest, Forward-looking, Inspiring, Competent, Intelligent, Fair-minded, Straightforward, Broad-minded, Supportive, Dependable, Cooperative, Courageous, Determined, Caring, Imaginative, Mature, Ambitious, Loyal, Self-controlled, and Independent. For complete percentages of Characteristics of Admired Leaders, see Appendix 3. For Cross-Cultural Comparisons of the Characteristics of Admired leaders, see Appendix 4.
14. Ibid., 30.
15. Ibid.
16. Blackaby and Blackaby, *Spiritual Leadership*, 104.
17. Zigarelli, *Management by Proverbs*, 185.
18. Ibid., 187.

translation (Prov 11:13; 16:28; 18:8; 20:19; 26:20, 22). Four verses translate the verb רָגַן (ragan), which literally means to murmur, whisper, backbite, or slander, as gossip.[19] Another form of the verb can be rendered as whisperer or talebearer.[20] The verb is found in Prov 16:28: "A perverse man stirs up dissension, and a gossip separates close friends." The Hebrew word translated "stirs" here is שָׁלַח (shalah), which has been variously translated "soweth" (AV) and "spreads" (RSV). It is the same verb found in Judges 15:5 where Samson "released" the flaming foxes in the standing grain of the Philistines. It literally means to "send forth" or "drive" as in cattle to pastures.[21] In Prov 16:28, the emphasis is on the tremendous damage that the words of a gossip can cause. Alden writes of this verse: "This despicable sin not only separates the gossip from his friends, but also drives a wedge between people who are close friends. . . . God despises the insidious work of the gossip."[22]

Proverbs 18:8 is another verse using נִרְגָּן (nirgan) that describes the appeal of a gossip's words as well as the deep damage they can accomplish: "The words of a gossip are like choice morsels; they go down to a man's inmost parts." People are attracted to the words of a gossip as a hungry man is attracted to delicious food. Murphy writes of this attraction, "Experience bears out the attraction that gossip exerts over human beings; it enters deeply into a person; the second line suggests this penetration and . . . the hearer's relishing."[23] Thus, gossip does not make a superficial impression; rather, it is eaten like a meal and thoroughly digested. Longman's concluding comments on this verse are helpful. He writes, "Even though so harmful, people often find the words of gossips irresistible, and this proverb likens gossip to fine food that is hard not to eat, but once eaten, it penetrates deeply into a person."[24] Two other verses from Proverbs using נִרְגָּן (nirgan) are 26:20, "Without wood a fire goes out; without gossip a quarrel dies down." and 26:22, which copies 18:8, "The words of a gossip are like choice morsels; they go down to a man's inmost parts."

Proverbs 11:13, "A gossip betrays a confidence, but a trustworthy man keeps a secret." and 20:19, "A gossip betrays a confidence; so avoid a man who talks too much." also copy one another in the first line using the noun,

19. *BDB* § 8908.
20. Ibid.
21. *BDB* § 9972.
22. Alden, *Proverbs*, 130.
23. Murphy, *Proverbs*, 135.
24. Longman, *Proverbs*, 356.

The Leader's Speech

רָכִיל (*rakil*), which means "talebearer" or "informer."[25] The former verse employs antithetic parallelism to contrast the gossip with the trustworthy man, whereas the latter verse uses synthetic parallelism (completion type) to advise against consorting with people who are too talkative.

There has been a movement in recent years to curtail gossip in the workplace among the rank and file. Because gossip can be so debilitating to the corporate culture, some of the literature has urged businesses to regulate it. However, some policies, when put in place, are extremely difficult to enforce and can lean heavily in the direction of political correctness. Zigarelli concludes that "... the trick, then, is to craft a no-gossip policy that honors God without unduly suffocating employee interaction. It must meet organizational interests of extinguishing rumor and encouraging respect, while simultaneously treating adults as adults."[26] He suggests a twofold criteria for companies considering such policies: "(1) narrowly tailoring the policy to deal only with gossip and (2) focusing the policy more on education about the problem than on punishment."[27]

Although the issue that Zigarelli raises is more of a management issue than a leadership one, it is certainly a benefit to the organization if gossip is regarded by leaders and followers alike as not an inconsequential sin, but rather as a cancer that spreads poison wherever it appears. It is not—as preachers sometimes like to label gossip—as one of the "sins in good standing."[28] The Apostle Paul includes this sin in a listing of sins practiced by those of a "depraved mind" who do "what ought not to be done." He describes them as follows: "They have become filled with every kind of wickedness, evil, greed and depravity. They are full of envy, murder, strife, deceit, and malice. They are gossips, slanderers, God-haters, insolent, arrogant and boastful; they invent ways of doing evil; they disobey their parents; they are senseless, faithless, heartless, ruthless" (Rom 1:29–30). Gossip is not a minor issue among leaders or in the workplace.

Zigarelli suggests that workplace efforts to deal with this problem should be educational rather than punitive. Certainly the godly leader must model appropriate behavior by not engaging in gossip himself. Zigarelli's analysis on this remedy is compelling. He writes:

---

25. BDB § 9102.
26. Zigarelli, *Management by Proverbs*, 188.
27. Ibid.
28. This designation is usually attributed originally to G. Campbell Morgan, but has also been used by such modern preachers/writers as Warren Wiersbe.

Of course, the no-gossip policy cannot be *exclusively* educational since a law without teeth is no law at all. There must be some established consequence for violation of the policy. Let common sense be your guide here; penalties must fit the crime, and, most importantly, you should remain mindful of the principles of due process.... However, remembering the warning in Proverbs 20:19 "to avoid a [gossip]," you should be sure that the policy underscores that severe and repeated violations of the no-gossip policy are cause for dismissal. As the policy matures, though, self-enforcement may prevail in lieu of the more severe tactics. That is, by raising consciousness about this issue, by focusing on education about the effects of workplace gossip, and by offering regular reminders that management is indeed serious about this issue, you can gently shape a workplace culture so a stigma is associated with gossiping.... Herein lies the long-term ideal for any no-gossip policy. If narrowly tailored and educationally oriented, after years of its operation it may become institutionalized as part of the corporate culture.[29]

Foolish Talk

There are numerous passages in the book of Proverbs that warn against the dangers of foolish talk. The first passage is actually two verses separated by an aphorism, which does not appear to fit into the context of either verse: "The wise in heart accept commands, but a chattering fool comes to ruin" (Prov 10:8), and, "He who winks maliciously causes grief, and a chattering fool comes to ruin" (Prov 10:10). The repetition of the second line in both verses appears to accentuate the major emphasis of this section. Ted Hildenbrandt rightly observes that in the book of Proverbs "needless talking is often associated with folly."[30] Garrett takes verse 6–11 as a unit, an inclusio within which is the parallel structure of verses 7–10 arranged in an A B A B pattern.[31] He writes, "Deceitfulness is the mark of the wicked, but the godly are known by the evidence of God's favor upon them and the salutary effects of their words (vv. 6, 11). Thus, the righteous secure their place in the world, whereas a life of deception holds only the promise of detection and disgrace (vv.7, 9)."[32] On the other

---

29. Zigarelli, *Management by Proverbs*, 189.
30. Zuck, *Learning From the Sages*, 269.
31. Garrett, *Proverbs*, 118.
32. Ibid.

hand, Alden speculates that the repetition of the words, "a chattering fool comes to ruin," is possibly a case of "dittography caused by homoeoteleution," as a result of "a scribal error caused by the close similarities of the last words in the first half of each verse."[33] Longman reinforces this view and prefers the LXX rendering, which he translates, "but those who reprimand with boldness bring peace."[34] Regardless of whether the LXX reading of the second line of verse 10 better fits the context or not, the intent of verse 8 seems clear. The fool is characterized by endless prattling. Whereas the wise in heart recognizes his limitations and humbly accepts commands, the fool lacks this capacity, and he chatters endlessly with speech that is devoid of true wisdom. One is reminded of the old adage, "Better to be quiet and be thought a fool than to open one's mouth and remove all doubt." Arnot describes such an individual:

> All his folly comes out. Every one sees through him. The fool, being empty, busies himself giving out, instead of taking in, and he becomes still more empty. From him that hath not shall be taken. He is known, by the noise he makes, to be a tinkling cymbal. People would not have known that his head was so hollow if he had not been constantly ringing on it. If ever he becomes wise, he will begin to receive commandments; and when he receives them, he will grow wiser thereby. To receive a lesson and put it in practice implies a measure of humility; whereas to lay down the law to others is grateful incense to a man's pride and self-importance.[35]

The fool seems to be compelled to share the fruits of his ignorance with others. There appears to be a correlation in play here: The less one knows about a subject, the louder and more vociferous he is in advertising his lack of knowledge. One is reminded in another verse where there is a link of the personified "Folly" with the adulteress: "The woman Folly is loud; she is undisciplined and without knowledge" (Prov 9:13). She prattles on loudly and undisciplined in her ignorance. This "chattering" brings the fool "to ruin."

The prudent man and the fool are contrasted in Prov 12:23, "A prudent man keeps his knowledge to himself, but the heart of fools blurts out folly." A similar verse is found in Prov 15:2, "The tongue of the wise commends knowledge, but the mouth of the fool gushes folly." In the former the fool "blurts out" folly; in the latter he "gushes."

---

33. Alden, *Proverbs*, 85.
34. Longman, *Proverbs*, 233.
35. Arnot, *Studies in Proverbs*, 172.

It would be possible to classify Prov 18:6–7 under another category, as it states, "A fool's lips bring him strife, and his mouth invites a beating. A fool's mouth is his undoing, and his lips are a snare to his soul" (18:6–7). Garrett, for example links the obvious chiasmus in these verses (lips, mouth, mouth, lips) to verse 5, which "refers to heeding evil talk at the gate" and to verse 8, which "describes the pleasure that malicious slander can give."[36] Thus, the classification could easily be either gossip or slander. On the other hand, Waltke seems to favor a quarreling classification for these verses. He writes, "The fool's misuse of speech foments controversy and conflict, hurting himself and perhaps others. . . . In starting his quarrel he intends to damage others, but in so doing it boomerangs against him."[37] McKane explains, "The effect of his speech is always to alienate himself from public sympathy and to attract feelings of hostility. . . . The fool's words have a socially destructive intent, and he thereby draws on himself the disapproval and retaliation of the community and condemns himself to isolation, ineffectiveness, loss of vitality and ultimately death."[38]

However, it seems best to this writer to give these verses a more general classification, Foolish Talk. It is the "fool's lips" and the "fool's mouth" which lead to "strife" and "invites a beating" and which are "his undoing" and "a snare to his soul." He is a fool, and it should surprise no one that the fruit of his lips is foolish talk. Rabbi Solomon Yitzchak ben Isaac understood the "beating" in verse 6 to be the "suffering brought on by folly."[39] He is a fool and his words spew out without forethought or consideration. Alden explains, "His words are so stupid, so careless, and so provocative that others become angry enough to come after him with fists."[40] Thus, it is not necessary to understand these verses as having the malicious intent that Garrett suggests nor the combative spirit as does Waltke. He is a fool and his lips bring forth foolish talk. But his words lead to unpleasant consequences and are his undoing and a snare to his soul.

Another passage in Proverbs which condemns foolish talk is 26:18–19, "Like a maniac shooting flaming arrows of death is one who deceives their neighbor and says, 'I was only joking!'" (NIV). This verse belongs to a section that is a departure from previous structures employed in the book of

---

36. Garrett, *Proverbs*, 164.
37. Waltke, *The Book of Proverbs,* Chapters 15–31, 73.
38. McKane, *Proverbs*, 515.
39. Kravitz and Olitzky, *Mishlei,* 181.
40. Alden, *Proverbs,* 139.

The Leader's Speech

Proverbs. Raymond Van Leeuwen writes, "Prov 26:17–28 is unusual in that it employs regular sub-units of three proverbs or 'triplets.' These sub-units have strong *internal* cohesion thematically, a cohesion which also manifests itself on the poetic level principally by means of word repetition and the devices of parallelism."[41] This phenomenon is considered to be something of a rarity in biblical Hebrew poetry. However, this structural cohesion must be kept in mind in attempting to interpret verses 18–19 in that they are thematically linked to verses 20–28 which have as their major emphasis "malicious talk."[42] Thus, malice aforethought appears to be in the mind of the writer. It is not simply a harmless prankster whose practical joke goes awry, but rather a devious schemer who intends grave harm. Alden apparently does not see the malicious intent in these verses. He writes, "Even if this man *was* just playing a trick, it was hardly funny. Good humor does not laugh at another man's discomfort. The prankster here shows insensitivity as well as poor moral judgment."[43] This analysis hardly gets at the heart of the matter. The verb translated "deceive," רָמָה (*rimmah*),[44] shows that the actions described in verse 18 are not just a serendipitous prank gone wrong. The perpetrator intended harm. Waltke's analysis is much better in that he gets to the heart of the matter. He writes:

> The verb "deceive," however, shows that the jester intends to harm his neighbor. He is a fool for whom villainy is like the pleasure of laughter (10:23); he is not merely a prankster or practical joker. He condemns himself by his self-quotation to explain his behavior, for his question betrays his meanness and cynicism (cf. 6:10; 24:12). The cruel buffoon cannot discern the difference between a joke and cruelty. The comparison of the treacherous clown with an armed and berserk warrior is double. Both cannot distinguish right from wrong and both inflict horrible tragedy on the community. However, the madman is out of his mind and cannot plot evil, whereas the mischief maker is cunning, showing that he is intellectually capable of carrying out a crime. His problem is not intellectual but spiritual; he lacks kind affections. The madman is not culpable for his crime; the mischief maker is.[45]

---

41. Van Leeuwen, *Context and Meaning in Proverbs, 25–27*, 116.
42. Kidner, *Proverbs*, 164.
43. Alden, *Proverbs*, 188.
44. BDB § 9112.
45. Waltke, *The Book of Proverbs, Chapters 15–31*, 359.

The malicious intent of the fool's action is what separates it from a mere practical joke. He intends to inflict harm, and he covers up his crime by saying that it was all a joke.

This discussion leads to the obvious question: Is all joking or use of humor forbidden by Scripture? The subject of the role of humor in the Christian life, especially in the proclamation of God's Word, has been much discussed and analyzed in recent decades. For example, a Jewish writer, Hershey H. Friedman, discusses the subject of humor in the Old Testament in an article which was published in *Humor: International Journal of Humor Research*. He lists the many types of humor which are found in the Hebrew Bible, many of which are understandable only by an understanding of the Hebrew language. His list includes "puns, wordplays, riddles, jokes, satires, lampoons, sarcasm, irony, wit, black humor, comedy, slapstick, farce, burlesque, caricature, parody, and travesty."[46] The Old Testament writers also use "humorous names, humorous imagery and exaggeration, and humorous situations."[47] According to Friedman, "Humorous stories and exaggerations make the moral lessons of the Hebrew Bible more memorable, and the irony behind punishments that are 'measure for measure' hints at a world in which justice does truly prevail."[48] It is true that humor in the Old Testament is usually subtle and underplayed, but it is there nonetheless.

John D. Drakeford, in his book *Humor in Preaching*, notes the playful spirit of God with three examples from the Old Testament, "God making a sea creature to play with (Psalm 104:26), God playing with a crocodile (Job 41:5), and wisdom personified and playing for God's delight (Proverbs 8:30)."[49] God's sense of humor and playful spirit can also be seen in the Old Testament's employment of paradox, incongruity, absurdity, epigrams, subtleties, clever turns of phrases, and pungency of speech.

Two verses from the Psalms are often marshaled as proof that God is a God of humor, Ps 24:4, "The One enthroned in heaven laughs; the Lord scoffs at them," and Ps 37:13, "But the Lord laughs at the wicked, for he knows their day is coming." However, the laughter described in these verses is not one of humor or merriment, but one of mockery and scorn. They should not be considered as proofs that God has a sense of humor.

---

46. Friedman, "Humor in the Hebrew Bible," 258.
47. Ibid.
48. Ibid.
49. Drakeford, *Humor in Preaching*, 22.

The Leader's Speech

On the other hand, while it is probably true that there is no place in the New Testament where Jesus appears to be laughing, it would be wrong to say that he did not utilize humor in his ministry. Much has been written about Jesus' use of humor in his ministry and teaching. Jesus used puns (Matt 23:24), word play (Matt 16:8), irony, gentle teasing (John 1:47), sarcasm (Luke 5:27–39), and even a joke in Luke 12 about the rich fool who had no place to store his possessions.

Thus, the "foolish talk" that the writer of the book of Proverbs condemns was probably not just an instance of somebody employing a sense of humor. Were that true, Jesus himself would stand condemned. Rather, the writer is describing something else. Certainly, what is in view in the book of Proverbs is a fool arrogantly chattering and revealing the fruits of his ignorance. His words are often malicious with the intent to cause harm. The Apostle Paul lists this sin within a catalogue of sins associated with immorality, impurity, and greed. He writes, "But among you there must not be even a hint of sexual immorality, or of any kind of impurity, or of greed, because these are improper for God's holy people. Nor should there be obscenity, foolish talk, or coarse joking, which are out of place, but rather thanksgiving" (Eph 5:3–4). Therefore, those who enjoy the use of humor are probably not being condemned in these two verses. After all, "A cheerful heart is good medicine, but a crushed spirit dries up the bones" (Prov 17:22); however, it would probably be wise for the godly leader keep his sense of humor in check and not allow his tongue free reign.

Slander

Another example of improper use of the tongue is slander. Slander is essentially false witness, which is condemned by the Decalogue: "You shall not give false testimony against your neighbor" (Exod 20:16). It is making a claim against another person that is known by the speaker to be false. It is defined as "a malicious utterance designed to hurt or defame the person about whom it is uttered."[50] James Draper defines it thus, "Slander is gossip. It has no basis in fact. It is the repetition of something that is not true or even something that is half true, giving a false impression."[51] Slander is a serious sin in that it steals the reputation of a person and can be terribly destructive. Perhaps the best example of a slanderer from the annals of world

50. Unnamed, "Slander," *NIDB*, 949.
51. Draper, *Proverbs: The Secret of Beautiful Living*, 122.

literature is William Shakespeare's character, Iago, from the tragedy *Othello*. Iago's poisonous words ultimately lead to three tragic deaths: himself, Othello, and Desdemona. His words serve as a condemnation of himself:

> Good name in man and woman, dear my lord,
> Who steals my purse, steals trash; 'tis something, nothing;
> 'Twas mine, 'tis his, and has been slave to thousands:
> But he that filches from me my good name
> Robs me of that which not enriches him
> And makes me poor indeed.[52]

Proverbs has much to say on this topic: "A truthful witness does not deceive, but a false witness pours out lies" (Prov 14:5); "A truthful witness saves lives, but a false witness is deceitful" (Prov 14:25).

Slander is a general term for false witness, but when it is used in a courtroom setting, it is known by the specialized term "perjury," which is addressed by Prov 25:18, "Like a club or a sword or a sharp arrow is the man who gives false testimony against his neighbor." Here the writer utilizes a simile to liken the harm accomplished by false testimony to that of a club, sword, or sharp arrow. Longman is probably correct in concluding, "It is likely that the primary setting of the teaching is in the courtroom."[53] Smith writes, "False testimony can shatter, slash, and pierce as surely as these weapons of war."[54] It is not common, but by no means unheard of, for an innocent person to be convicted and executed on the basis of false testimony. Naboth is a case study of false testimony leading to capital punishment (1 Kgs 21).

False words can be as destructive as weapons of war. Ben Sira's observations on the destructive nature of slander, while not canonical, are still compelling. He writes:

> Slander has shaken many,
> and scattered them from nation to nation;
> it has destroyed strong cities,
> and overturned the house of the great.
> Slander has driven virtuous women from their homes,
> and deprived them of the fruit of their toil.
> Those who pay heed to slander will not find rest,
> nor will they settle down in peace.

---

52. Shakespeare, *Othello*, 58 (Act 3, Scene 3, lines 154–60).
53. Longman, *Proverbs*, 455.
54. Smith, *The Wisdom Literature and Psalms*, 646.

The blow of a whip raises a welt,
but the blow of a tongue crushes the bones.
Many have fallen by the edge of the sword,
but not as many as have fallen because of the tongue" (Sirach 28:14–18).

There is a well-known statement from the *Talmud*, "The slanderous tongue kills three: the slandered, the slanderer, and him who listens to the slander." Christian organizations are not immune to the destruction wrought by slander. The godly leader should have no part in them. Nor should he be a liar or a gossip. Such conduct is unbecoming in a Christian leader and should be avoided at all costs.

The only other instance in which the word for slander is found in the book of Proverbs is 10:18, where the second half of the verse reads, "and whoever spreads slander is a fool." Alden entertains the possibility that slander does not necessarily have to be untrue and he introduces the possibility of rancor. He writes, "Gossip or slander might be defined as saying something about your neighbor he wouldn't say about himself. What you say might be true, but saying it might be unnecessary as well as cruel."[55] However, Waltke sees the entire verse as an enjambment with the slanderer of the second line of the verse being identical with the liar of the first line ("He who conceals his hatred has lying lips.") with a compound predicate. He explains, "The construction leaves no doubt that hatred inspires slander informed by innuendoes, half-truths, and facts distorted and exaggerated beyond recognition (cf. 6:17, 19). In other words, this fool spreads slander, concealing his hatred with lying lips."[56] This verse abandons the characteristic antithetic parallelism of this book and is likely a rare example of synthetic parallelism in the book of Proverbs in that the second stitch advances the line of thought of the first. Toy sheds some light on the thought process of the writer of this verse. He writes, "There might thence seem to result the antithesis of secrecy and publicity: a secret hater is a liar, an open slanderer is a fool. But this antithesis does not really exist in the verse–the suggestion rather is that concealed hatred expresses itself in slander (the two are related as cause and effect), which is itself an underhand, secret procedure."[57] In any case, the intent is the same as is the resultant damage that it causes. As Delitzsch rightly observes, "Such slandering can generally

---

55. Alden, *Proverbs*, 88.
56. Waltke, *The Book of Proverbs*, Chapters 1–15, 469.
57. Toy, *Proverbs*, 210.

bring no advantage; it injures the reputation of him to whom ... the secret report, the slander, refers; it sows discord, has incalculable consequences, and finally brings guilt on the tale-bearer himself."[58] In other words, it sullies and defiles not only the slandered, but the slanderer as well. The perpetrator of this vicious sin does as much damage, if not more, to himself as to the inflicted.

The psalmist David asked a question about who would be the inhabitants of God's sanctuary. He inquired of the Lord and then answered his own question:

> Lord, who may dwell in your sanctuary?
> Who may live on your holy hill?
> He whose walk is blameless
> and who does what is righteous,
> who speaks the truth from his heart
> and has no slander on his tongue,
> who does his neighbor no wrong
> and casts no slur on his fellowman,
> who despises a vile man
> but honors those who fear the Lord,
> who keeps his oath
> even when it hurts" (Psalm 15:1–4).

Therefore, it behooves the godly leader to speak the truth from his heart and to have no slander on his tongue. He must never do his neighbor harm or cast a slur on his fellowman. This is a necessity for the godly leader.

Quarreling

The person who is quarrelsome is a frequent feature in the book of Proverbs. The strife and dissension stirred by such a person is a common theme in the book. There are several verses which use the Hebrew word, רִיב (*rib*), often translated "quarrel" or "quarrelsome," which literally means "strife, dispute."[59] A representative sample of these verses are as follows: "A hot-tempered man stirs up dissension, but a patient man calms a quarrel" (Prov 15:18); "It is to a man's honor to avoid strife, but every fool is quick to quarrel" (Prov 20:3); "Like one who seizes a dog by the ears is a passer-by who meddles in a quarrel not his own" (Prov 26:17); "Without wood a fire

---

58. Delitzsch, *Proverbs*, 221.
59. *BDB* § 9061.

goes out; without gossip a quarrel dies down. As charcoal to embers and as wood to fire, so is a quarrelsome man for kindling strife" (Prov 26:20–21); "An angry man stirs up dissension, and a hot-tempered one commits many sins" (Prov 29:22); and, "For as churning the milk produces butter, and as twisting the nose produces blood, so stirring anger produces strife" (Prov 30:33). Not all of the aforementioned verses translate רִיב (*rib*) as either "quarrel" or "quarrelsome," but the idea is certainly present there.

Quarreling is a sin of the tongue that often has its root in anger, a bad temper, or a contentious spirit. "A hot-tempered man" is the cause of the quarrel in Prov 15:18. He is contrasted with the "patient man," as shown by the antithetic parallelism. The man with the hot temper "stirs up dissension," whereas the latter "calms a quarrel." Some scholars see a parallel between this verse and the Egyptian wisdom teachings of Amenemope, which frequently contrast the "hot-tempered man" who provokes dissension with the "silent one" "who is quiet and composed."[60] This verse is often linked with Prov 22:24–25, which is comparable to the teachings of Amenemope.[61] Those verses read, "Do not make friends with a hot-tempered man, do not associate with one easily angered, or you may learn his ways and get yourself ensnared." The similarities of Prov 22:24 with Amenemope IX. xi. 13–14 are striking: "Consort not with a passionate man, and press not thyself upon him with talk."[62] W. O. Oesterley comments on the link between the two: "The repetition in Proverbs is somewhat jejune; there is more point in Amen-em-ope's couplet. Still, the relationship between the two is clear; one only wonders why the second line in the former finds no place in the latter."[63] There are many similarities between Prov 22:17—24:34 and the work of Amenemope, leading to scholarly speculation as to who borrowed from whom. Was Solomon dependent upon Amenemope as many liberal scholars argue or vice versa? Even a conservative scholar such as Garrett simply assumes that Proverbs is modeled after the writings of Amenemope rather than vice versa.[64] When the late Egyptian hieratic manuscript, *The Wisdom of Amenemope,* was discovered by E. A. Wallis Budge in 1888, he initially dated the manuscript as Eighteenth Dynasty, which naturally led scholars

---

60. Fox, *Proverbs,* 10–31, 598.
61. Ibid.
62. Oesterley, *The Teaching of Amen-Em-Ope and The Book of Proverbs,* 66.
63. Ibid.
64. Garrett, *Proverbs,* 193.

to assume that the dependence had to be on Solomon's part.[65] However, subsequent dating has revised the date for Amenemope to around 1000 B.C., leading to the possibility that Solomon's work was entirely original in this instance. Archer explains, "A close examination of the linguistic data indicates quite conclusively that borrowing must have been the other way around in this particular case."[66] He then goes on to present four strands of argument which support his case.[67] Thus, it is not necessary to assume that similarities between the two works automatically means that Solomon was the borrower and not the other way around.

Garrett links Prov 15:18 with 15:1, which reads, "A gentle answer turns away wrath, but a harsh word stirs up anger," and he concludes that it is not so much the issues which lead to a quarrel, but rather the personalities involved. He writes, "The ability to avert needless quarreling and to live in harmony is a virtue of wisdom. Many conflicts arise not because the issues separating the parties are so great but because of the temperaments people bring to a confrontation."[68] Proverbs 15:1 deals with two types of personality: the hot-tempered man and the patient man. The former pours gasoline on the fire, whereas the latter pours water in an attempt to extinguish it. Alden describes these two widely divergent personalities, as he writes, "The man who stirs up dissension is hot tempered, easily irritated, and itching to pick a fight. The peacemaker, on the other hand, is patient, longsuffering, and calm; a man who eases tension rather than adds to it."[69] Peterson's translation of this verse aptly captures the nature of these two hypothetical people: "Hot tempers start fights; a calm, cool spirit keeps the peace."[70] It is clear from this verse that quarrels depend far more upon the personalities of the people involved rather than the actual issues under consideration.[71] Draper believes that the derivation of all quarrels can be explained by one principle. He writes, "Here is the basic principle: quarrels do not depend on issues, but on people. The particular issues do not matter. The real problem is in the heart. . . . Issues are never the real causes of strife."[72]

65. Ibid.
66. Archer, *SOTI*, 442.
67. Ibid., for a complete discussion.
68. Garrett, *Proverbs*, 150.
69. Alden, *Proverbs*, 120.
70. Peterson, *The Message of Leadership*, 101.
71. Kidner, *Proverbs*, 115.
72. Draper, *Proverbs*, 141.

The Leader's Speech

A characteristic of the fool is that he is "quick to quarrel," according to Prov 20:3. This verse teaches the value of exercising self-control. Both Waltke and Garrett link this verse with the preceding verse ("A king's wrath is like the roar of a lion; he who angers him forfeits his life," 20:2) as well as with Prov 19:11–12 ("It is not fitting for a fool to live in luxury–how much worse for a slave to rule over princes! A man's wisdom gives him patience; it is to his glory to overlook an offense.").[73] Garrett understands these verses to be structural markers, which taken together are in a chiastic structure: "patience, the king's wrath, the king's wrath, patience."[74] Thus, the emphasis of these verses is placed in a royal context. Garrett writes, "The point of the whole is that the patient person knows how to avoid quarrels and quarrelsome people and stays out of trouble with the government as well."[75]

It is easy to misinterpret Prov 20:3; however, it is clear that there are two things that this verse is not teaching. First, not every fool is eager to get involved in a dispute. The "every fool" is an example of hyperbole for poetic emphasis. Second, this verse should not be understood to teach a universal principle that always in all cases strife must be avoided. Plaut explains, "It certainly should not apply where a principle or where the welfare of others are involved; it encourages no ivory tower morality. But fighting over trivia or over superficial ego-satisfactions (often called points of honor) does not befit a real man. He settles, gives in, or forgets it all."[76] As Kravitz and Olitzky observe, "This is another way of saying 'Pick your battles.' Everybody needs to know what battles are worth fighting."[77]

It is not difficult to begin or continue an argument. Proverbs 20:3 teaches that any fool can do that. It takes honor and self-control to avoid an argument. The truly wise man is able to do this as well as resolve issues and turn enemies into friends. This avoidance of strife adds to a man's honor and demonstrates his mettle.

A busybody is the person who is described in Prov 26:17 ("Like one who seizes a dog by the ears is a passer-by who meddles in a quarrel not his own."). This person is not necessarily contentious. He simply cannot resist the impulse to get involved in the business of other people. Cohen observes that the information given about the meddler that he is a passer-by

---

73. Waltke, *The Book of Proverbs*, Chapters 15–31, 129; Garrett, *Proverbs*, 173.
74. Garrett, *Proverbs*, 173.
75. Ibid.
76. Plaut, *Proverbs*, 209.
77. Kravitz and Olitzky, *Mishlei*, 196.

"emphasizes the fact that he was not really concerned in the quarrel. He just chanced to be passing at the time."[78] Although this verse speaks out against meddling in the affairs of others as much as it does against quarreling, it exposes the utter stupidity and lack of caution demonstrated by anybody who would foolishly get involved in another's argument.

It should be noted that dogs in Palestine during the days of Solomon were not domesticated as pets, but were wild animals that ran wild in the streets.[79] Such animals were never approached to be petted or even touched, much less grabbed by the ears. Such behavior was dangerous, as there was a grave risk of being bitten or worse. The person who needlessly intrudes into someone else's quarrel risks the wrath of both participants in the quarrel. Garrett notes, "Busybodies cannot resist the temptation to inject themselves into private disputes, and they have no excuse for being surprised at the violent outbursts that are sure to follow."[80] This verse is different from the other verses dealing with quarrels in that the person described is not the initiator of the quarrel. However, by virtue of the fact that he involves himself, he becomes guilty by association.

Another passage that also does not portray the person who is involved in a quarrel as the stereotypical "hot head" is Prov 26:20–21.[81] Rather, the emphasis in these verses is on the gossip "as the fuel that maintains quarrels."[82] Employing emblematic parallelism, the imagery here is that of a fire that is fueled by wood. Without wood or some other suitable fuel, a fire will eventually burn itself out. The person described here is apparently not actively involved in the quarrel. He works his wickedness behind the scenes sowing discord instead of allowing the quarrel to die a natural death. Van Leeuwen notes that the word translated as "gossip" or "whisperer" here, רָגָן (ragan), "connotes the attempt, by verbal calumny, to wrongfully attack the rights, reputation, or authority of another to secure one's own will."[83] Waltke points out, "His tools of trade are innuendoes, half-truths, and facts distorted and exaggerated beyond recognition. . . . As a storm whips up the

---

78. Cohen, *Proverbs*, 176.

79. Kravitz and Olitzky, *Mishlei*, 258.

80. Garrett, *Proverbs*, 214.

81. Proverbs 26:20–21, "Without wood a fire goes out; without gossip a quarrel dies down. As charcoal to embers and as wood to fire, so is a quarrelsome man for kindling strife."

82. Garrett, *Proverbs*, 214.

83. Van Leeuwen, *Context and Meaning in Proverbs, 25–27*, 111.

sea, this slandering rebel whips up strife so strong that it divides even the closest friends."[84]

In Prov 29:22,[85] יְגָרֶה (*yagareh*) is translated "dissension" in the New International Version. Although the word "quarrel" is not used, the idea underlies the meaning of the verse. Alter translates the first line of this verse, "An angry man stirs up strife."[86] Peterson translates the verse as follows: "Angry people stir up a lot of discord; the intemperate stir up trouble."[87] Bridges captures the essence of this verse in his description. He writes, "The general tendency of anger is however here most truly described. Its active energy *stirreth up strife*. It quarrels even upon trifles, or matters, which a forbearing consideration might have satisfactorily explained."[88] The first line of this verse reads the same as Prov 15:18 except that it substitutes the word "angry" for "hot-tempered." In Prov 15:18, the antithetical parallelism contrasts the hot-tempered man with the patient man who is able to calm a quarrel. In this verse (Prov 29:22), the angry man is equated by synonymous parallelism with a hot-tempered man who "commits many sins." In any event, the angry man/hot-tempered man is indeed a quarrelsome individual. Kidner says that this is not a temporary state as in a normally calm person who loses his temper. Rather, it is his "general disposition," a seemingly permanent state of mind.[89] In other words, it seems as if there are people who go through life with a perpetual chip on their shoulders. Peterson's translation of Prov 3:30 describes this type of individual: "Don't walk around with a chip on your shoulder, always spoiling for a fight."[90] Every word spoken is a personal affront to them. They are always in a foul mood. This verse is a clear warning to keep a tight rein on one's emotions.

The final verse in the book of Proverbs that uses רִיב (rib) is Prov 30:33, which the NIV translates "strife."[91] The verb, מִיץ (mits) occurs three times in this verse. The NIV translates it differently each time it occurs. In the

---

84. Waltke, *The Book of Proverbs,* Chapters 15–31, 360.

85. Proverbs 29:22, "An angry man stirs up dissension, and a hot-tempered one commits many sins" (NIV).

86. Alter, *The Wisdom Books,* 321.

87. Peterson, *Proverbs,* 132.

88. Bridges, *Proverbs,* 581.

89. Kidner, *Proverbs,* 177.

90. Peterson, *Proverbs,* 79.

91. Proverbs 30:33, "For as churning cream produces butter, and as twisting the nose produces blood, so stirring up anger produces strife" (NIV).

first line it is translated as "churning," in the second as "twisting," and in the third as "stirring." Longman renders the wordplay in verse 33 as follows: "For pressing milk yields curds, and pressing the nose yields blood, and pressing anger yields accusations."[92] Although the tripartite structure of this verse is clear even in English, the analogy and wordplay are not so obvious and "cannot be duplicated in translation."[93] Alden explains the playful spirit that Agur, the author of this chapter, exhibits in this verse. He writes, "It's a down-home sort of analogy with an additional play on words because in Hebrew 'nose' and 'anger' are the same word and 'blood' can also mean 'bloodshed/murder.'"[94] Just as pressing or churning milk produces butter and pressing or twisting the nose causes a nosebleed, so pressing an argument produces strife or a quarrel. Sometimes it is difficult to exercise restraint in such instances, but pressing an argument is not the course that a godly leader should pursue. Garrett suggests that such behavior can even lead to violence. He explains, "Hidden in the second simile, however, is the warning that those who make trouble are liable to get punched in the nose! Also the 'strife' that follows troublemaking may not just be discord but also lawsuits."[95] Thus, the same Hebrew word מִיץ (*mits*) describes the same basic action, which in three different contexts produces three different results. Pressing butter produces something good; pressing the nose or an argument produces something bad. Kravitz and Olitzky write, "The author makes the point that the same kind of action can have beneficial or deleterious effects. Pressure can be good or bad. The last clause contains a truth: there are people who are angry without reason. They are simply looking for an outlet for their anger. Such people 'squeeze' their anger, holding it within themselves until they find an excuse to release it. They are 'just looking for a fight.'"[96]

Three other verses in the book of Proverbs use the words quarrel or quarrels: Prov 13:10, "Pride only breeds quarrels, but wisdom is found in those who take advice"; Prov 17:14, "Starting a quarrel is like breaching a dam; so drop the matter before a dispute breaks out"; and Prov 17:19, "He who loves a quarrel loves sin; he who builds a high gate invites destruction." The antithetic parallelism of Prov 13:10 contrasts the proud or arrogant

---

92. Longman, *Proverbs*, 533.
93. Plaut, *Proverbs*, 308.
94. Alden, *Proverbs*, 212.
95. Garrett, *Proverbs*, 243.
96. Kravitz and Olitzky, *Mishlei*, 303.

The Leader's Speech

person with the one who takes advice. Pride is seen here as the source of all quarrels. Longman properly translates זָדוֹן (*zadon*) as "insolence."[97] He explains precisely what this sin is: "Insolence is a pride that will not listen to other people, especially of behavior or thought. On the other side are those who are open to correction and new ideas. The latter is the way of wisdom, and the implication is that the way of wisdom avoids 'quarrels.'"[98] A closed mind is a symptom of pride. The proud person already thinks that he knows everything and he is unbending in his opinions. He is contrasted here with the wise person who is open to advice. This arrogant spirit leads to quarrels.

Starting a quarrel is likened to a leak in a dam in Prov 17:14. According to Toy, the text and translation of this verse is doubtful.[99] The ancient Jewish commentator, Rashi, explains the meaning of this verse as that "as one drills a hole in a water pipe, it lets out more water and the flow itself enlarges the hole."[100] Kravitz and Olitzky explain the meaning of the simile. They write, "Similarly, a contention starts with very little and ends with very much. Since quarrels develop a life of their own beyond their initial reasons, the wise person will either avoid them or turn away as quickly as possible from them."[101] A quarrel, then, is like a breach in a dam. Once it begins, it is hard to stop and it tends to enlarge. Kidner writes, "Opening such a sluice lets loose more than one can predict, control or retrieve."[102] It is better to plug the leak before it becomes a flood or to put out a small fire before it becomes a conflagration. It is better to drop a matter of contention before it becomes a quarrel. Whatever the precise meaning of the aphorism may be, the general meaning is certainly clear: Avoid strife and quarrels before they get out of hand.

Garrett considers Prov 17:14 as a companion piece to 17:19,[103] a verse that uses synthetic parallelism, completion type, in which the second line completes or further explains the first; however, the explanation is by no means clear to the reader. Longman considers this proverb to be

---

97. Longman. *Proverbs*, 286. Compare this meaning with BDB § 2598, which gives zadon the meaning of "insolence, presumptuousness."

98. Ibid.

99. Toy, *Proverbs*, 344.

100. Kravitz and Olitzky, *Mishlei*, 173.

101. Ibid.

102. Kidner, *Proverbs*, 125.

103. Garrett, *Proverbs*, 161. Proverbs 17:19, "Whoever loves a quarrel loves sin; whoever builds a high gate invites destruction" (NIV).

"one of the most difficult in the book."[104] Clearly the first line is criticizing the person who loves a quarrel, but which is the subject and which is the predicate is unclear. Murphy describes this verse's grammatical construction as "the juxtaposition of four participles" and simply claims that "the verse is difficult."[105] Is the subject the lover of quarreling or the lover of sin? The NIV properly renders the former as the subject according to Waltke's understanding,[106] although Longman renders 17:19a: "Those who love an offense love a quarrel."[107] Alden does not address the difficulty, but simplifies the matter by writing that "sin and trouble go hand in hand. You can't have one without the other."[108]

The real difficulty appears to be the meaning of the second line of the verse. What does it mean by "builds a high gate invites destruction"? This part of the verse, to this writer, is the *crux interpretum*. According to Murphy, the meaning of this is a total mystery of which nobody knows the answer.[109] He also believes that the parallelism used is synonymous, not synthetic.[110] In trying to make sense of this line, the ancient Jewish commentators, Solomon Yitzchak ben Isaac and Abraham ibn Ezra, reference Micah 7:5 ("watch the opening of your mouth"; c.f., the NIV rendering is "be careful of your words") and thus understand it to refer to proud speech.[111] Toy disagrees with this approach and calls it "an improbable metaphor."[112] His understanding of this phrase is that it refers ". . . to the pride and ostentation shown by building the house-door high," but he admits that "no such custom is known to have existed in antiquity."[113] Alden suggests that "high gate" is an idiom that has no English counterpart, but reads literally "He who makes high his door. . . ."[114] He attempts to explain the intention of the author as he writes, "This image may literally refer to people who show off their wealth by building huge homes with grand entrances, or

---

104. Longman, *Proverbs*, 348.
105. Murphy, *Proverbs*, 131.
106. Waltke, *The Book of Proverbs, Chapters 15–31*, 58.
107. Longman, *Proverbs*, 348.
108. Alden, *Proverbs*, 136.
109. Murphy, *Proverbs*, 131.
110. Ibid.
111. Kravitz and Olitzky, *Mishlei*, 174.
112. Toy, *Proverbs*, 348.
113. Ibid.
114. Alden, *Proverbs*, 136.

may figuratively refer to the mouth of a braggart which pours out all kinds of proud words."[115] An interesting variation on this theme is seen in Clifford's translation of verse 19b, "who makes his doorway high is asking for a collapse."[116] Alter's translation of the line is very similar: "who builds a high doorway seeks a downfall."[117] Peterson's translation of the line, on the other hand, is nonsensical: "build a wall, invite a burglar."[118] A high wall is normally a deterrent, not an invitation to crime. Such an understanding of the verse totally ignores the context as well as common sense. Garrett's interpretation of 17:19b is worth mentioning in that it is totally original and seems plausible. He writes, "Those who love to quarrel and bring suits, however, build a 'high gate'; that is, they become isolated. Such persons are alone in the world and bring disaster upon themselves."[119] This idea that the person who loves to quarrel brings upon himself a kind of social isolation because of his propensity to sin is highly original and may not be too far off the mark. Despite the myriad of interpretational possibilities, one thing is clear: The person who loves a quarrel loves sin and invites destruction.

There are five verses in the book of Proverbs that speak pejoratively of a quarrelsome person, four of a quarrelsome wife and one of a quarrelsome man: "A foolish son is his father's ruin, and a quarrelsome wife is like a constant dripping" (Prov 19:13); "Better to live on a corner of the roof than share a house with a quarrelsome wife" (Prov 21:9); "Better to live in a desert than with a quarrelsome and ill-tempered wife" (Prov 21:19); "As charcoal to embers and as wood to fire, so is a quarrelsome man for kindling strife" (Prov 26:21); and, "A quarrelsome wife is like a constant dripping on a rainy day" (Prov 27:15). The verse addressing the quarrelsome man (Prov 26:21) was dealt with earlier in this book and will not be reconsidered here.

Delitzsch relates an Arab proverb about conditions which make living in a house intolerable: "the trickling through of rain . . . the contention of the wife . . . and bugs."[120] The connection in Prov 19:13 of the "foolish son" and the "quarrelsome wife" is unclear. What is clear is that the poor father/husband is to be pitied.[121] In the modern world—at least in developed

---

115. Ibid.
116. Clifford, *Proverbs*, 163.
117. Alter, *The Wisdom Books*, 268.
118. Peterson, *The Message of Leadership*, 106.
119. Garrett, *Proverbs*, 161.
120. Delitzsch, *Proverbs*, 27.
121. Murphy, *Proverbs*, 144.

countries—a dripping faucet or a dripping from a hole in the roof is usually a minor inconvenience that can be easily remedied. The Hebrew word דֶּלֶף (*delep*) is also found in Prov 27:15, which also compares "a quarrelsome wife" with "constant dripping," but it specifies that it comes on a rainy day, implying that it refers to a leaking roof.[122] The same word is found in Eccl 10:18, which explicitly mentions a leaking house.[123] Garrett warns against assuming that the quarrelsome woman and the constant dripping are minor irritations. He writes:

> First of all, the modern reader should beware of making an anachronistic transfer of imagery. This is not the "leaky faucet" that is irritating and may deprive one of sleep but is only a minor household problem and is easily repaired. . . . A leaking roof is an irritation, but it is more than that. It can cause severe damage to a house, be expensive to repair, and can render a building unfit to live in. Second, a "quarrelsome wife" is more than a nagging wife. The Hebrew word implies antisocial behavior that stirs up discord and even prompts lawsuits. Such a woman no doubt does nag her husband . . . , but she is equally apt to create quarrels with those outside the home (neighbors, people in the market, etc.).[124]

Taking these factors into consideration, the unclear connection between the "foolish son" in 19:13a and the "quarrelsome wife" in 19:13b becomes clearer. Like a family member with a drug or gambling problem today who brings down the family and impoverishes it, so a "foolish son" and a "quarrelsome wife" can be the ruin of the father, husband, and even the entire family. One or both can reduce the family to poverty.

A different perspective on the "quarrelsome wife" is found in Prov 21:9 ("Better to live on a corner of the roof than share a house with a quarrelsome wife."), which uses synthetic parallelism (comparison type) to make the drastic comparison that any living conditions are preferable to living sharing a house with a quarrelsome wife. This same thought is echoed later in the same chapter in verse 19, with a change in locale, "a desert" instead of "a corner of the roof."[125] The verse also adds the adjective, "ill-tempered," to

---

122. Proverbs 27:15, "A quarrelsome wife is like the dripping of a leaky roof in a rainstorm" (NIV).

123. Ecclesiastes 10:18, "Through laziness, the rafters sag; because of idle hands, the house leaks" (NIV).

124. Garrett, *Proverbs*, 170.

125. Proverbs 21:19, "Better to live in a desert than with a quarrelsome and nagging wife" (NIV).

"quarrelsome," making this woman especially troublesome. Garrett's judgment is that verses 9 and 19 constitute an inclusio, but that "the proverbs between the inclusio do not themselves examine domestic harmony but concern a variety of topics."[126] That statement is a surprising interpretation to this writer. It seems more plausible to understand the arrangement as more of a random pattern than to postulate an inclusio in which the intervening verses sandwiched between have no relationship to one another nor to the first and last verses.

These verses seem to be teaching the simple truth that it is difficult to live with a quarrelsome spouse. Plaut recounts an old Jewish proverb, which says that "three things ... shorten a man's life: a sour stomach, living on the third floor, and a contentious wife."[127] Yeshua ben Eleazer ben Sira also has some pointed comments about bad wives. He writes, "I would rather live with a lion and a dragon than live with an evil woman" (Sirach 25:16). Daniel J. Harrington remarks about Ben Sira's negativity towards women in his introduction to the book in NOAA, "Sirach's very negative remarks about a woman are striking even in the context of a patriarchal culture."[128] He explains further:

> Ben Sira was a man of his place and time, that is, Palestine in the early second century BCE. His opinions on many social issues, especially on women and slaves, may strike modern readers as benighted, even outrageous. Ben Sira and his contemporaries perceived themselves as embedded in various groups (family, clan, village, city, etc.). They judged their own importance by what others thought of them, in what anthropologists call an honor-shame society. His social world was hierarchical, with everyone having a relatively fixed place and little opportunity for upward social mobility. People then considered wives to be naturally subordinate to their husbands, and children and slaves under the ultimate control of the male head of the household.[129]

Murphy wonders at the gender bias in this (verse 9) and others like it and concludes that the application of such is of a universal nature. He muses, "One wonders why the sexual roles are never reversed; such sayings

---

126. Garrett, *Proverbs*, 180–81.
127. Plaut, *Proverbs*, 218.
128. Harrington, "Introduction to Sirach," in *NOAA*, 133.
129. Ibid., 99.

are just as applicable to an autocratic and 'quarrelsome' male."[130] Longman comes to the same conclusion and explains his reasoning thus: "In its primary setting, this proverb, consistent with the whole book, is directly addressed to a male audience. Women who read it today must simply substitute 'man/husband' into the proverb; it can apply with equal force in that direction."[131] Longman further explains the interpretation of this proverb by arguing that the values presented here (and by logical extension in verse 19) are in a "... better-than-form, which gives relative, not absolute values. While marriage and companionship are positive things in Proverbs, it is better to be alone than with a person who makes life unbearable."[132]

In verse 9, the place of refuge for the beleaguered husband is "a corner of the roof"; in verse 19 it is "a desert." Neither description is hyperbole. In Palestine the roofs were flat to which people retreated for repose in hot weather (c.f. Matt 24:17; Luke 5:19; Acts 10:9).[133] Similarly, desert places were commonplace in Palestine. Alden takes a different approach in interpreting the intent of this verse as well as the gender bias debate. He writes that "... the verse does not recommend divorce, though, as much as prudence in dealing with a bad situation. Just as it is wise to steer clear of an angry king ... so verse 9 advises staying a safe distance away from a quarrelsome mate until some of the anger passes."[134] With respect to the gender issue, he departs from the views of Murphy and Longman, "Note the verse doesn't say the angry wife should go to the roof. The house is her territory; his is the city gate or the field. If he invades her turf and thus provokes her anger, he invites his own banishment to the roof."[135] Regardless of one's understanding of these verses, one thing is clear: It is better to avoid a quarrelsome person, whether it is a wife, husband, or other.

The final verse dealing with a quarrelsome wife is Prov 27:15.[136] This verse, like Prov 19:13, compares, by using a simile, a quarrelsome woman to a constant dripping. Solomon adds the words "on a rainy day," implying that it is the roof that is leaking. Then he adds a further description of

130. Murphy, *Proverbs*, 159.
131. Longman, *Proverbs*, 392.
132. Ibid.
133. Alden, *Proverbs*, 155.
134. Ibid.
135. Ibid.
136. Proverbs 27:15, "A quarrelsome wife is like the dripping of a leaky roof in a rainstorm" (NIV).

her contentiousness in the next verse: "Restraining her is like restraining the wind or grasping oil with the hand" (Prov 27:16). Cohen renders the constant dripping as "a downpour which drives out the dwellers from a house."[137] In like fashion, the quarrelsome wife drives her family members away. Jewish commentators Kravitz and Olitzky understand the verse in terms of the growing spirit of egalitarianism of Palestine of that time period (c.f., "The Wife of Noble Character" in Prov 31:11-23). They explain:

> City life gave new freedom to women. Some men accepted such women and lauded those who operated in the city. Others were threatened by that freedom and upset by those who exercised it. This verse reflects the view of those who opposed such freedom. The end of the Book of Proverbs and its praise of the woman of valor ultimately show support for women who seized the limited freedoms that society offered.[138]

However, this interpretation does not appear to be supported by the verse. If anything, this woman is the counterpart to the wife of noble character of Proverbs 31 or the "prudent wife" of Prov 19:14. Garrett believes that verses 15–16 are part of a section, Prov 27:11–27, which constitute a "series of paternal teachings."[139] Verse 11 begins with a fatherly exhortation, "Be wise, my son, and bring joy to my heart." Then follows what appears to be a series of random teachings that a father might logically teach his son before he goes out into the world. An exhortation to exclude a contentious woman as possible wife material would thus be natural in such a section.

A simile is used in verse Prov 27:16 to describe how difficult it is to restrain such a woman ("restraining her is like restraining the wind or grasping oil with the hand."). Although most commentators believe that this verse is difficult to interpret, its application is clear. Longman claims that the first line is enigmatic and the second line "downright obscure."[140] For example, Murphy translates the second line, "the oil of his right hand calls" or "to declare one's right hand to be oil."[141] Clifford translates, "The woman's perfume (oil) on her fingers gives her presence away," which he explains is "another illustration that concealing her is futile."[142] Alter's

---

137. Cohen, *Proverbs*, 182.
138. Kravitz and Olitzky, *Mishlei*, 268.
139. Garrett, *Proverbs*, 219.
140. Longman, *Proverbs*, 480.
141. Murphy, *Proverbs*, 208.
142. Clifford, *Proverbs*, 239.

translation is equally puzzling, "Who conceals her conceals the wind, and her name is called 'right hand.'"[143] It is obvious that the meaning of verse 16 cannot be understood apart from the context of the preceding verse that talks about how a quarrelsome wife is like the incessant dripping that one cannot escape from on a rainy day. If it is raining outside, where can one go to escape the constant dripping from the rain? The implied answer is that there is no place to escape. Thus, verse 16 must deal with something akin to trying to escape from the rain when it is raining outside and leaking inside. It is an impossibility. According to this writer's opinion, the translators of the NIV got this verse right even if their translation philosophy of dynamic equivalence tended to stretch the Hebrew language into something more readable and understandable. Therefore, trying to get this contentious woman to stop quarreling is like trying to restrain the wind or hold oil in one's hand. The point of the verse is that both scenarios are equally impossible. The wind cannot be controlled, and oil will simply run through the fingers. Getting back to the point of verse 15, Waltke aptly summarizes the sad fate of the man with a contentious wife:

> The man takes shelter under the roof of his home expecting to find protection from the storm. Instead, he finds that his leaky roof provides him no shelter from the torrential downpour. Likewise, he married with the expectation of finding good, but the wife from whom he expected protection from the rudeness of the world attacks him at home. Both render his home intolerable.[144]

He married seeking to find heaven on earth and a sanctuary from the world outside; instead, his marriage turned into a hell on earth. As so often happens in real life, he finds that he is unable to restrain his wife, and his daily existence becomes a perpetual misery.

The consistent witness of the book of Proverbs on the subject of quarrels is clear and unequivocal. Quarrels, quarrelsome people, and strife in general are to be avoided by anyone who would seek to be wise. This is especially true of the godly leader. He should be characterized by his peaceful and quiet spirit.

---

143. Alter, *The Wisdom Books*, 313.
144. Waltke, *The Book of Proverbs, Chapters 15–31*, 383.

Speaking Rashly

There is tremendous power in the spoken word. It has the power to uplift and encourage. It also has the capacity to pierce and wound. In writing about the Persuasion of words, Draper argues, "Words are compelling. They have a great impact for good or ill. They can crush a person's feelings. A thoughtless word can devastate one's life. There are people who can say a word and they might as well pierce you through with a sword."[145] Reckless words are usually thrown about without forethought and once spoken cannot be taken back.

Solomon had much to say in the book of Proverbs about speaking rashly. Following are verses representative of this teaching about reckless words: "Reckless words pierce like a sword, but the tongue of the wise brings healing" (Prov 12:18); "He who guards his lips guards his life, but he who speaks rashly will come to ruin" (Prov 13:3); "A hot-tempered man stirs up dissension, but a patient man calms a quarrel" (Prov 15:18); "A man of knowledge uses words with restraint, and a man of understanding is even-tempered" (Prov 17:27); and, "Even a fool is thought wise if he keeps silent, and discerning if he holds his tongue" (Prov 17:28).

It is clear from Prov 12:18 that words can wound or heal, depending on how they are employed. The reckless words that "pierce like a sword" come from the verb בָּטָה (bata), which carries the meaning "speak rashly, thoughtlessly."[146] In his translation, Murphy renders the first line of the verse, "There is one who talks on and on, like sword thrusts."[147] Delitzsch likens it to a word that is "imitative of the sound, like the Greek βαπταρίζειν, to stammer, and βαπτολογειν, to babble."[148] This comparison of reckless words to a sword thrust indicates the seriousness of this sin in the mind of Solomon. Murphy intones, "This drastic comparison indicates how seriously loquaciousness is condemned."[149]

Reckless words are a subcategory of thoughtless reactions, which is the thrust of Prov 12:16, "A fool shows his annoyance at once, but a prudent man overlooks an insult." As mentioned previously, Garrett believes that Prov 12:16–22 form a linked parallelism and chiasmus in which verses 16–19 create a four verse parallelism joined to a four-verse chiasmus of

---

145. Draper, *Proverbs*, 119–20.
146. *TWOT* 1: 101.
147. Murphy, *Proverbs*, 87.
148. Delitzsch, *Proverbs*, 261.
149. Murphy, *Proverbs*, 91.

verses 19–22, of which verse 19 constitutes the link between the two.[150] Thus, verse 16 begins the parallelism with the general theme of Thoughtless Reactions (A). Verse 18 completes the A section of the parallelism with a refinement of the general theme, Reckless Words (A'). In the A, B, A', B' parallel structure, verse 18 provides the reader with a concrete example of the general truth contained in verse 16. Reckless words are a form of thoughtless reactions. Michael V. Fox observes, "Verse 16 teaches that the smart man swallows his pride and conceals an insult he has suffered. This is conducive to peace and thereby shows him to be 'shrewd' . . . because avoidance of conflicts is also the counsel of self-interest."[151]

Another verse that clearly condemns speaking rashly is Prov 13:3, "He who guards his lips guards his life, but he who speaks rashly will come to ruin." This verse employs antithetic parallelism to contrast two opposing ways to use the tongue. The first line presents the person who is circumspect in his speech. Such restraint with his lips in actuality "guards his life." The image suggested in this line is that of someone who is guarding a gate.[152] Fox notes, "A fool opens his mouth wide, allowing disaster to go forth and also, less obviously, to enter."[153] Yeshua Ben Sira weighs in on this thought of guarding a gate or a door when he writes, "As you fence in your property with thorns, so make a door and a bolt for your mouth. As you lock up your silver and gold, so make balances and scales for your words." (Sir 28:24–25).

The antithesis in the second line of Prov 13:3 describes one who is the opposite of circumspect. He "speaks rashly" and this indiscretion leads to the sad consequence, that he "will come to ruin." The verb translated "speak rashly," פָּשַׂק (pasaq), is found elsewhere only in Ezek 16:25 and means to "part, open wide."[154] The Ezekiel passage compares unfaithful Israel to a promiscuous woman who indiscriminately spreads her legs to any man who passes by. It reads, "At the head of every street, you built your lofty shrines and degraded your beauty, offering your body with increasing promiscuity to anyone who passed by." In Prov 13:3 פָּשַׂק (pasaq) refers to one who indiscriminately spreads his "lips wide apart so that the words flow out unrestrained in torrents."[155] Murphy observes, "The contrast in

---

150. Garrett, *Proverbs*, 132; see 'Telling the Truth 'under "The Proper Use of the Tongue in Chapter 4: The Leader's Speech."

151. Fox, *Proverbs 1–9*, 555.

152. Ibid., 562.

153. Ibid.

154. *BDB* § 6589.

155. Waltke, *The Book of Proverbs, Chapters 1–15*, 554.

The Leader's Speech

this verse is between the silent type who chooses words well, and the fool whose open mouth is full of mere chatter that turns out to be ruinous to himself."[156] Solomon sheds some light on this concept in the book of Ecclesiastes. While writing in his old age, according to Talmudic tradition, Solomon observes, "Words from a wise man's mouth are gracious, but a fool is consumed by his own lips. At the beginning his words are folly; at the end they are wicked madness–and the fool multiplies words" (Eccl 10:12–13).

A verse that does not directly mention reckless speech, but is certainly related to the topic is Prov 15:18, where the person described in this verse is one "who stirs up dissension is hot tempered, easily irritated, and itching to pick a fight."[157] His tool to stir up the emotions is usually his injudicious use of the tongue. He is hot tempered and not in control, and his words often are spoken rashly and without aforethought. Therefore, he "stirs up dissension" usually with his words, and he pours flames upon an already volatile situation. The antithesis to the first line presents the patient man who is able to calm a quarrel.

The final section under consideration under this topic is Prov 17:27–28. These verses clearly advocate the wisdom of using restraint in speech and holding one's tongue. However, Garrett sees these verses as comprising a parallel structure "embedded in an inclusio."[158] He writes of Prov 17:27–28 and the four verses immediately following, "A parallel structure (17:28—18:3) is embedded in an inclusion (17:27; 18:4)."[159] He structures the entire section as follows:

> A: The wise person's restrained use of words (Prov 17:27)
>> B: A silent fool appears wise (17:28)
>>> C: A schismatic person is irrational (18:1)
>> B': A fool cannot remain silent (18:2)
>>> C': A base person is shameful (18:3)
> A': The wise person's words are profound (18:4)[160]

Garrett believes that the reason that the book of Proverbs places so much emphasis upon people using appropriate words "... is because it views

---

156. Murphy, *Proverbs*, 96.
157. Alden, *Proverbs*, 120.
158. Garrett, *Proverbs*, 163.
159. Ibid.
160. Ibid.

words as the index to the soul. By paying attention to what a person says (and indeed to how much he or she says), one can determine whether a person is wise or a fool."[161] He continues his analysis of this section, "Profundity, not verbosity, is the mark of wisdom (17:27; 18:4). The metaphor of water in 18:4 describes the opinions of the sage as deep (i.e., rich with meaning) and refreshing, like a flowing wadi in the desert. Even an imbecile can appear intelligent if he can avoid putting his foot in his mouth, but this is all but impossible for a fool (17:28; 18:2)."[162]

Verses 27 and 28, therefore, extol the virtue of silence. Verse 27 urges restraint in speech, whereas the following verse goes further in recommending total silence. Waltke argues that these verses are in actuality a prescription for how to respond to provocation, not just general advice in all of life's situations.[163] The author uses synthetic parallelism in these verses. In both cases the second line completes the first. It is interesting to note that in Proverbs 16–22, the predominant type of parallelism is not antithetic, which is so common elsewhere in the book, but synthetic.[164] Synthetic parallelism is extremely rare elsewhere in the book, but not in these chapters. Thus, the second line of verse 27 ("a man of understanding is even-tempered") builds upon the first line, which urges verbal restraint by "a man of knowledge." In like fashion, the second line of verse 28 ("discerning if he holds his tongue") builds upon the thought of the first that "even a fool is thought wise if he keeps silent." In verse 28, the fool who keeps silent is equated with the man of knowledge of verse 27. As Waltke observes, "The proverb mentions the fool, not to rehabilitate him but to argue from the lesser to the greater. Based on the premise that the fool does not have the wisdom imputed to him, he can be thought discerning in the absence of condemning speech."[165] At this point, some of the commentators have a bit of fun with this verse. Kidner, in writing about the advice of verse 28, says that "the fool who takes it is no longer a complete fool."[166] Murphy refers to an old Latin proverb that suggests that even a fool "had [he] kept silent ... would have been taken to be a philosopher."[167] In any event, it

---

161. Ibid.
162. Ibid., 163–64.
163. Waltke, *The Book of Proverbs,* Chapters 15–31, 64.
164. LaSor, Hubbard, and Bush, *Old Testament Survey,* 552.
165. Waltke, *The Book of Proverbs,* Chapters 15–31, 65.
166. Kidner, *Proverbs,* 127.
167. Murphy, *Proverbs,* 132.

is silence and restraint in the use of words that is commended here and demonstrates that one is "a man of understanding" and "thought wise" and discerning." Bridges pithy insight aptly summarizes these two verses, "He is a fool, not who hath unwise thoughts, but who utters them."[168]

Often reckless words are just blurted out, and sometimes they are the unfortunate residue of criticism delivered without much caution. Zigarelli offers some excellent insight into how to offer negative feedback, noting that it is clear that it is not so much *what* is being said as *how* it is being communicated.[169] As the book of Proverbs attests, "A servant cannot be corrected by mere words; though he understands, he will not respond" (Prov 29:19). Zigarelli aptly summarizes the findings of current management theory by offering ten prescriptions for delivering negative feedback. Although he is writing specifically about job performance reviews, his advice is excellent and has a more general application. He advises managers (leaders), "Do it privately.... Do it personally.... Get right to the point.... Present the negative feedback in the context of positive performance.... Speak in terms of 'I,' not 'you.'"... Be specific.... Stick to the facts.... Don't twist the knife.... Jointly craft a solution.... Offer feedback continuously."[170]

The book of Proverbs explicitly condemns the sin of speaking rashly. Once spoken, words cannot be taken back. Such careless and unguarded words have a tremendous capacity to wound. The danger is not that they do not accurately reflect the attitude of the speaker, but that in fact they do. What would not be spoken, upon reflection, is often blurted out causing untold harm and devastation. Hudson Armerding observes, "Our careless or idle words are uninhibited words, words that accurately reveal our inner condition."[171] Sometimes those words reflecting our true inner feelings are better left unspoken.

Boasting

The sin of boasting is mentioned at least three times in the book of Proverbs, in 20:14 ("'It's no good, it's no good!' says the buyer; then off he goes and boasts about his purchase"); 27:1–2 ("Do not boast about tomorrow, for you do not know what a day may bring forth. Let another praise you,

---

168. Bridges, *Proverbs*, 279.
169. Zigarelli, *Management by Proverbs*, 163.
170. Ibid., 156–64.
171. Armerding, *The Heart of Godly Leadership*, 90.

and not your own mouth; someone else, and not your own lips"); and 30:32 ("If you have played the fool and exalted yourself, or if you have planned evil, clap your hand over your mouth"). It is sometimes difficult to determine exactly what is boasting and what is simply a harmless recitation of facts regarding one's accomplishments. The Apostle Paul boasted unashamedly of his ministry to the Corinthians (2 Cor 10:1–18; 11:16–33; 12:1–10); however, the sin of boasting is generally rooted in the sin of pride, which is always roundly condemned in Scripture.

One verse that condemns both boasting and dishonesty is Prov 20:14, which suggests that one's words do not always correlate with reality.[172] One's words should not always be taken at face value. It describes a scene in the marketplace in which haggling takes place over the purchase of some goods. The buyer denigrates the product and then afterwards boasts about what a great deal he negotiated. Murphy argues that the verse is not so much a proverb as it is a description of a hypothetical scene that takes place in the marketplace.[173] Alden describes the exchange that is described in this verse as well as its implications:

> The humorous little exchange in a market place recorded in verse 14 sounds so familiar; we can all relate to the words of a buyer. In Hebrew the verse says a buyer says, "It's bad, it's bad," yet the very thing he demeans becomes the subject of boasting later to his friends. Stores which advertise "seconds" or "irregulars" at "half price" or "greatly reduced prices" know exactly what they're doing. Buyers may brag about the bargains they got, but as a rule sellers are sharper than buyers. Consider the words of an old Rabbinic proverb: "When a fool goes to market, the merchants rejoice."[174]

In the Ancient Near East, as in some places even today, negotiation and bargaining is the order of the day in the marketplace. The buyer would try to talk down the price by denigrating the merchandise. After he had succeeded in lowering the price, he would boast to his friends about his shrewd bargaining skills and his good fortune in acquiring such a deal. In many instances, he paid what the seller beforehand had already deemed to be the selling price. Even after paying the lower price, the seller ended up with the advantage in the transaction. Thus, this proverb seems to be not

---

172. Proverbs 20:14, "'It's no good, it's no good!' says the buyer; then off he goes and boasts about his purchase" (NIV).

173. Murphy, *Proverbs*, 151.

174. Alten, *Proverbs*, 150.

The Leader's Speech

only warning against boasting and dishonesty, it is likely, that it serves as "a warning against the deception of appearance," as Longman suggests.[175] Appearances do not always depict reality as Longman further argues, "Typically . . . , the warning is directed at the shrewd seller, but here it is the shrewd buyer."[176] Thus, this verse reverses the message of the old Latin proverb, *Caveat emptor,* "Let the buyer beware." It also warns the buyer about boasting about his shrewdness in bargaining.

The next two verses, Prov 27:1–2, deal with the sin of boasting, and "both begin with the same verbal root."[177] They both begin with a derivative of the verb הָלַל (*halal*), אַל־תִּתְהַלֵּל ("do not boast") and יְהַלֶּלְךָ ("let him praise you").[178] Both verses deal with the contrast between the manifestations of both arrogance and humility. Boasting is the logical outpouring of an arrogant heart; whereas humility's outgrowth is a reluctance to sing one's praises. Eugene Peterson's translation of this verse especially captures the twofold arrogance and ignorance of the one who boasts: "Don't brashly announce what you're going to do tomorrow; you don't know the first thing about tomorrow."[179]

One fact of human existence is that man has no knowledge of, nor power over, the future. This uncertainty about the future is the foundation of Prov 27:1. Fox reasons, "Do not boast (to yourself or others) of future achievements or virtues, or be confident of prosperity, for the future is opaque and beyond human control."[180] The future is entirely in the hands of God. Thus, boasting about tomorrow is to place oneself in the place of God, which is supreme arrogance. In the New Testament, James develops this idea (as does Jesus in Matt 6:34), "Now listen, you who say, 'Today or tomorrow we will go to this or that city, spend a year there, carry on business and make money.' Why, you do not even know what will happen tomorrow. What is your life? You are a mist that appears for a little while and then vanishes. Instead, you ought to say, 'If it is the Lord's will, we will live and do this or that.' As it is, you boast and brag. All such boasting is

---

175. Longman, *Proverbs*, 381.

176. Ibid.

177. Garrett, *Proverbs*, 216. Proverbs 27:1, "Do not boast about tomorrow, for you do not know what a day may bring. 2 Let someone else praise you, and not your own mouth; an outsider, and not your own lips" (NIV).

178. Ibid. See also *BDB* § 2408.

179. Peterson, *The Message of Leadership*, 126.

180. Fox, *Proverbs 1–9*, 802.

evil" (Jas 4:13–16). Thomas suggests a very logical reason for why mankind is ignorant of the future, as he writes, "This ignorance of tomorrow is *necessary to the prosecution of our duties on earth*. Could we draw aside the veil of the future, and look at the things which are coming to us, our energies would be so paralysed [sic] as to incapacitate us for the ordinary avocations of life: mercy has woven the veil of concealment. This ignorance of tomorrow *is our incentive to preparation for the future.*"[181]

What this proverb does is to forbid boasting about the future. What it does not do is to forbid making plans for the future. There is an uncertain tension inherent in this verse with those who claim that it teaches that no plans should be made for the future. Unfortunately, this is the teaching in some Christian circles today. Alden comments on this conundrum. He writes, "Don't take life for granted, warns the verse in an almost ominous tone, certainly don't brag about things that may never happen. This verse is *not* an indictment against long-range planning (e.g. 24:6); however, it is a warning against a cock-sure attitude toward controlling all the events in our lives."[182]

The next verse (Prov 27:2) is a companion verse to the previous one. Delitzsch, as well as Van Leeuwen and Waltke, understand Prov 27:1–10 to be comprised of a series of couplets thematically linked.[183] They warn against the folly of praising oneself. Murphy intones, "No one is a judge in his own case. Such judgment is bound to be biased, whereas the judgment of a stranger does not labor under that difficulty."[184] Praise of oneself is not praise at all; it is boasting and all boasting is from pride. By its very definition, praise must come from others. Waltke's analysis of this verse is instructive. He writes:

> The combined effect censures self-praise and commends a friend's praise in a most emphatic way. Since the proverbs aim for piety on the vertical axis and social success on the horizontal axis, it can be inferred that self-praise is unfitting because it destroys one's relationships with God and with people. The lord detests the proud, and society dislikes and discounts the boaster. Instead of exalting

---

181. Thomas, *Proverbs*, 675–76.

182. Alden, *Proverbs*, 190.

183. Delitzsch, *Proverbs*, 198–204. Also, Van Leeuwen, *Context and Meaning in Proverbs 25–27*, 125; and Waltke, *The Book of Proverbs*, Chapters 15–31, 372.

184. Murphy, *Proverbs*, 206.

the boaster, self-praise diminishes one's status and suggests that one is proud, feels undervalued, and is socially insecure.[185]

There are also practical reasons why a man should not promote himself. He may elevate himself to a position beyond his competence level, which could lead to an inevitable fall. McKane comments, "Self-praise does not have the significance of praise given by others and does not establish reputation.... Men will not take him seriously, for a community has processes for putting a man to the test, and trying him thoroughly before it accords him acclaim and preference and entrusts him with power."[186] Jesus told a parable that relates to this verse:

> When he noticed how the guests picked the places of honor at the table, he told them this parable: "When someone invites you to a wedding feast, do not take the place of honor, for a person more distinguished than you may have been invited. If so, the host who invited both of you will come and say to you, 'Give this man your seat.' Then, humiliated, you will have to take the least important place. But when you are invited, take the lowest place, so that when your host comes, he will say to you, 'Friend, move up to a better place.' Then you will be honored in the presence of all your fellow guests. For everyone who exalts himself will be humbled, and he who humbles himself will be exalted" (Luke 14:7–11).

Thus, the paradox of the last being first and the first being last is expressed in figurative fashion by the Savior. Praise should always come from others. If it is not forthcoming from others, it should not be self-manufactured.

The final verse related to boasting is Prov 30:32, "If you play the fool and exalt yourself, or if you plan evil, clap your hand over your mouth!" This verse comes from a section of the book of Proverbs titled, "The sayings of Agur son of Jakeh-an oracle." Kidner identifies the undercurrent of this chapter, taught either directly or by contrast, as humility.[187] Here the person who exalts himself is said to "have played the fool." He is commanded to clap his hand over his mouth. Although exalting oneself (boasting) is mentioned in this verse, commentators differ on exactly what this verse means. Waltke understands it as "a warning not to upset the divine order."[188] According to him,

---

185. Waltke, *The Book of Proverbs*, Chapters 15–31, 373.
186. McKane, *Proverbs*, 608.
187. Kidner, *Proverbs*, 182.
188. Waltke, *The Book of Proverbs*, Chapters 15–31, 500.

self-promotion is definitely in view here, which involves boasting, with the result that the person becomes an outcast. The reference to having "played the fool," according to Waltke, "points to one's resolve to commit an inappropriate and unruly act that will demean others and disrupt the social order."[189] Fox opines, "If you have behaved like a scoundrel or have sneaky intentions, shut your mouth and say no more, before you get a bloody nose! Arrogance leads to strife."[190] Alden, on the other hand, believes that the predominate emphasis of verse 32 (and 33) is teaching against anger.[191] Although there is a clear diversity of opinion on the meaning of this cryptic verse, two things are clear. First, pride and the resultant boasting are condemned. Second, the behavior should be stopped immediately as the offender is admonished to "clap your hand over your mouth."

It is clear from Scripture, and especially from the book of Proverbs, that the root of boasting is pride. Both sins are expressly condemned as behavior unfitting for the believer. As such, boasting is forbidden territory for the godly leader.

Flattery

Flattery is another example of the improper use of the tongue that at first glance appears to be rather innocuous. After all, flattery lacks the deceptive feature of lying, the malicious nature of gossip, slander, and mockery, the pride associated with boasting, the belligerence of quarreling, the impetuousness associated with speaking rashly, and the triviality and ugliness of foolish or perverse talk. Upon the surface, it would appear that flattery is quite harmless and utterly devoid of evil intent; however, Draper warns about this sin, "We need to be careful of those who would flatter us. We must also be careful of those who would condemn us. We are undoubtedly not nearly so good as our admirers think, nor as bad as our critics suggest. Our self-esteem can be blown out of proportion."[192] There are at least three passages in the book of Proverbs that speak of the sin of flattery. It is true that in chapters 5–7 the strange woman uses flattery as a lure to get the man into her bed, but those passages will not be considered here in that they deal more with sexual sin than sins of the tongue. The following passages

189. Ibid.
190. Fox, *Proverbs*, 881.
191. Alden, *Proverbs*, 212.
192. Draper, *Proverbs*, 121.

The Leader's Speech

deal directly with such sins, Prov 26:28 ("A lying tongue hates those it hurts, and a flattering mouth works ruin"); 28:23 ("He who rebukes a man will in the end gain more favor than he who has a flattering tongue"); and 29:5-6 ("Whoever flatters his neighbor is spreading a net for his feet. An evil man is snared by his own sin, but a righteous one can sing and be glad").

In Prov 26:28, "a flattering mouth" is linked with "a lying tongue." This verse further develops a concept introduced in verse 26 ("His malice may be concealed by deception, but his wickedness will be exposed in the assembly"), "that lying is an act of hatred."[193] It reveals that flattery is in reality the product of a lying tongue, that it hurts the person on the other end of the lie, and that it "works ruin." Thus, lying and its counterpart, flattery, are actually acts of hatred. Kidner writes, "The heart of the matter (20-28) is exposed in 28, with the fact that deceit, whether it hurts or soothes, is practical hatred, since truth is vital, and pride fatal, to right decisions."[194] Fox is even more straightforward. He concludes, "The unctuous hypocrite feigns friendship, but . . . actually hates his victims . . . and contrives their downfall."[195]

There is some question about who is the recipient of the harm of a lying tongue. For example, Cohen represents the traditional Jewish school of thought in that he believes that the liar/flatterer is the one who does harm to a victim. He writes, "The intention of a person who resorts to smooth speech, which screens his real thoughts, is to bring about somebody's downfall."[196] Toy entertains both possibilities, but he seems to favor the traditional understanding as being more natural to the flow of words in favoring the ruin brought upon others. He writes, "The couplet may refer to the ruin brought by the false tongue either on others or its possessor; the latter interpretation is suggested by the sense of the preceding couplet; the former is the more natural suggestion of the words."[197] Waltke, on the other hand, favors the other possibility. While admitting that at first glance ". . . it seems to refer to the ruin of the hated, but on reflection it refers to the hater. That interpretation best fits the context of the parallel B versets of the final triplet, best explains the difference between not fatally crushed and fatally ruined, and best fits the optimistic, not pessimistic, theology of the book."[198]

193. Garrett, *Proverbs*, 215.
194. Kidner, *Proverbs*, 164.
195. Fox, *Proverbs 1-9*, 801.
196. Cohen, *Proverbs*, 178.
197. Toy, *Proverbs*, 481.
198. Waltke, *The Book of Proverbs, Chapters 15-31*, 366.

It is certainly true that there is much truth to the words of verse 27 ("Whoever digs a pit will fall into it; if someone rolls a stone, it will roll back on them") as the Apostle Paul would attest, "Do not be deceived: God cannot be mocked. A man reaps what he sows" (Gal 6:7). However, there are times when a man falls into his own carefully dug trap ("pit"), and the stone that he rolls (גָּלַל; *galal*) intending to do harm to others in the second line of verse 27, does indeed roll back upon him. Rashi (Rabbi Solomon Yitzchak ben Isaac), the French Bible scholar and biblical and talmudic commentator who lived from 1040–1105, applied verse 27 to Abimelech in the book of Judges (chapter 9), whose attempts to establish himself as king involved the murder of his seventy half-brothers. He writes, "Ultimately, his crime 'rolled' (גָּלַל; *galal*) back onto himself and he in turn was killed thus proving the adage, 'Evil ultimately destroys itself.'"[199] However, the natural flow of the verse and the context seem to favor Cohen's view that the words of the perpetrator bring harm upon the victim.

This insight might lead to a logical question: Why is flattery such a dangerous endeavor? After all, a compliment, however, insincere, is still a compliment in the eyes of the recipient. In earlier centuries, it was common to be a sycophant in the king's court because to do otherwise might incur royal displeasure and even death. Longman believes that flattery is a specific subcategory under the broad category of lying as he writes about the sin of flattery, "Without conviction, it exaggerates the positive points of another person. Flattery may be used to set a person up to be taken advantage of. Flattery may also cause those who are flattered to think too highly of themselves and so act in a way that is detrimental."[200] Flattery is an especially cruel form of lying in that it makes a mockery of the person being flattered without his knowledge. It particularly attacks those who are gullible, have low self-esteem, and are vulnerable to the sin of pride. Lawson explains why flattery is such an egregious sin: "Flatterers are the worst kind of liars, and the most likely to be believed, because self-love favours their deceits. Flatterers are commonly men that intend to betray with a kiss; but, although they should only design to gain our favour by their fair speeches, yet they are very pernicious, because they are the friends of our pride, which is the

---

199. Kravitz and Olitzky, *Mishlei*, 261.
200. Longman, *Proverbs*, 472.

worst of our bosom enemies."[201] The Puritan Philip Henry warned, "Be as much troubled by unjust praise, as by unjust slanders."[202]

A second verse that deals with flattery is Prov 28:23 ("Whoever rebukes a person will in the end gain favor rather than one who has a flattering tongue."). This verse deals with a theme that is often dealt with in the book of Proverbs, the value of sincere rebuke. Such reprimand is contrasted with a flattering tongue by using synthetic parallelism (comparison type), not antithetical parallelism as Waltke[203] and Toy[204] suggest, as a means of gaining favor or position and wealth. The flattering sycophant does so with the hope of personal benefit in mind, whereas "he who rebukes a man" does so without regard for personal gain. This theme that constructive criticism is better than insincere praise was introduced earlier in the book of Proverbs (13:1; 17:10). The danger to the recipient is that praise, no matter how superficial and misleading, is always more palatable than criticism. Some commentators such as Garrett understand this verse to be speaking about the accumulation of wealth or power ("gain more favor"),[205] whereas others see it as having a more general sense. Of this latter view, McKane writes:

> Plain speaking may subject a friendship to great strain and appear to be a false step. Silence, it may be argued, would have been a better response (27:5), or even words of reassurance designed to please and flatter (cf. 27:14). But whoever takes the risk of speaking the truth in love is the kind of person who is worth having as a friend and ultimately this will be recognized. His words which seemed to wound will be seen to have had salutary effects, and he will rise in the regard of the one who has benefited from his integrity and courage. Complete honesty is the cement of friendship.[206]

Either view has credence, but the emphasis here seems to be on gaining more favor, which would seem to favor the former interpretation. Peterson's translation of Prov 28:23 would also seem to favor this position: "In the end, serious reprimand is appreciated far more than bootlicking flattery."[207] The "bootlicker" is usually in a position to gain something most

201. Lawson, *Proverbs*, 737.
202. Cited in Thomas, *Puritan Quotations*, 110.
203. Waltke, *The Book of Proverbs*, Chapters 15–31, 425.
204. Toy, *Proverbs*, 366.
205. Garrett, *Proverbs*, 227.
206. McKane, *Proverbs*, 631.
207. Peterson, *The Message of Leadership*, 130.

commonly in the workplace or political arena. In any event, the message from this verse is clear: It is better to offer sincere constructive criticism than insincere flattery.

A final passage which deals with the subject of flattery is Prov 29:5–6.[208] The dominant poetic feature in chapter 29 is antithetic parallelism.[209] Verse 5 speaks of the flatterer as spreading "a net for his feet." There is some scholarly difference of opinion as to whether the net spread is for the intended victim ("his neighbor") or the deceiver. According to Abraham ibn Ezra, a Spanish Jewish grammarian and Bible scholar who lived from 1089–1164, "it is the steps of the one who flatters."[210] Here he connects verse 5 with the verse that follows (cf., 26:27–28) which speaks of "an evil man" who is "snared by his own sin." It is possible, then, to connect this net back to the deceiver (flatterer). Murphy suggests that the "ambiguity may be deliberate."[211] Most translations seem to favor the former approach to the verse. For example, Alter's translation reads, "A man who flatters his fellow spreads a net at his feet."[212] Longman's rendering makes both the flatterer and his neighbor plurals, which makes very clear how he understands the meaning of the verse: "People who pour out flattery on their friends are spreading out a net for their feet."[213] Likewise, Peterson's approach to this verse is clear, as he translates it, "A flattering neighbor is up to no good; he's probably planning to take advantage of you."[214] Both Garrett and Waltke connect verses 5 and 6 together with the idea of a snare or trap as the linking concept in both verses. Waltke writes, "These verses are a proverb pair because both refer to deceitful people by metaphors involving hunting instruments."[215] Verse 5 uses the metaphor of a hunter or trapper attempting to ensnare a wild animal. The flatterer spreads a net before his neighbor hoping that he will fall into it. David Thomas describes the dangers of this net. He writes, "Flattery is a dangerous net that lies near to every man's

---

208. Proverbs 29:5–6, "Those who flatter their neighbors are spreading nets for their feet. 6 Evildoers are snared by their own sin, but the righteous shout for joy and are glad" (NIV).

209. McKane, *Proverbs*, 632.

210. Kravitz and Olitzky, *Mishlei*, 285.

211. Murphy, *Proverbs*, 221.

212. Alter, *The Wisdom Books*, 319.

213. Longman, *Proverbs*, 502.

214. Peterson, *The Message of Leadership*, 130.

215. Waltke, *The Book of Proverbs, Chapters 15–31*, 433.

The Leader's Speech

foot. It is a cup whose taste is generally delicious, but whose effects are always pernicious, and often mortal. The feet of the strongest men have been entangled in this net; they have fallen into it and been ruined."[216] McKane describes him as being "disarmed and trussed up while the glow of pleasure is still within him."[217]

Whether the "evil man" of verse 6 who is "snared by his own sin" is the flatterer of verse 5 who is possibly "spreading a net for his own feet" or a different individual, he is like the man in Prov 26:27 who digs a pit and then falls back into it or the man who rolls a stone only to have it roll back on him. The emphasis in Prov 29:6 is on the "righteous one" who is able to see the trap and avoid it. Poetically speaking, the proverb writer says that he "can sing and be glad." The righteous man needs to be constantly on guard for such people. As Kenneth Aitken observes, "Although flattery need not always be guileful, typically in Proverbs the flatterer is the sycophant who fawns his way through life, worming his way into favour with other people in order to manipulate them for his own advantage and to his own ends. But while his words, be they guileful or guileless, may be good for a man's ego, they are decidedly bad for his feet."[218] He needs to be on guard against such deceivers and watch where he steps.

Mockery

The sin of mockery with respect to the use of the tongue is uniformly condemned in the book of Proverbs with at least thirteen verses in the Proverbs of Solomon and the Sayings sections that clearly speak out either against it, the mocker himself in either its singular or plural form, or the verbal derivative. The verbal form of "mock" in the English language means "to hold up to scorn or contempt; ridicule."[219] In the Bible, mockery has a wide range of meanings ranging from harmless teasing (cf. Gen 21:6) to ridicule (Neh 4:1). Proverbs uniformly associates the mocker with the fool. He is contrasted sharply with the wise or the "wise son;" for example, Prov 13:1 notes, "A wise son heeds his father's instruction, but a mocker does not listen to rebuke." The antithetical parallelism of this verse contrasts wisdom and folly. The wise son listens to his father's teaching, but the mocker, an

216. Thomas, *Proverbs*, 749.
217. McKane, *Proverbs*, 637.
218. Aitken, *Proverbs*, 136.
219. *Webster's New World Dictionary*, 945.

extreme type of fool, will not. This motif recurs in the book of Proverbs (beginning in 10:1), that of adolescent or adult children and how they respond to their parents. Each child is a walking advertisement to the community of the quality of the instruction in the home. Peterson's translation of Prov 13:1 accurately captures this antithesis: "Intelligent children listen to their parents; foolish children do their own thing."[220]

Levi ben Gershom believed that the difference in the childrearing results of the "wise son" and the "mocker" lay in the ability of the parent to impart wisdom; however, some children are beyond the influence of sound instruction and will scorn everything.[221] Clifford writes of children of that ilk: "Scoffers scorn the process and end up fools, advertising to the world their parents' inability to educate them."[222] The mocker, since he will not listen to rebuke, is incapable of improvement.

Very similar to Prov 13:1 is 15:12 in meaning if not format, as it reads, "A mocker resents correction; he will not consult the wise." Whereas Prov 13:1 uses antithetical parallelism, 15:12 is likely emblematic, in which the second line gives a figurative illustration of the first. Here "a mocker resents correction" is placed loosely along with the second line, "he will not consult the wise." "A mocker resents correction" is very similar to "a mocker does not listen to rebuke" in Prov 13:1. In like manner, "he will not consult the wise" is a direct contrast to "a wise son heeds his father's instruction" in Prov 13:1. This mocker is often translated in older translations as either "the scoffer" or "the scorner." Both verbs in Prov 15:12 refer to what he will not do: he will not heed correction and he will not consult the wise. Toy refers to this person as "a man whose character is fixed. It is not suggested that he might be helped by association with the wise."[223] Alden writes, "A most accurate barometer of spiritual maturity is one's willingness to accept criticism."[224] This person does everything possible to undermine his own spiritual progress. The very ones who might point the way are the ones he refuses to consult. He is, in the common vernacular, "his own worst enemy." Although the text does not say so, the root problem is doubtless pride. This fact will be seen more clearly later in this book when Prov 21:24 is examined.

220. Peterson, *The Message of Leadership*, 96.
221. Kravitz and Olitzky, *Mishlei*, 126.
222. Clifford, *Proverbs*, 136.
223. Toy, *Proverbs*, 308.
224. Alden, *Proverbs*, 119.

The Leader's Speech

The same thought is continued in the next chapter when 14:6 notes, "The mocker seeks wisdom and finds none, but knowledge comes easily to the discerning." Again, the core reason that he is unable to find wisdom is that he refuses to accept correction and eschews the fear of the Lord. The reason why knowledge comes so easily to the discerning is that his spiritual orientation is the polar opposite of that of the mocker. Alden argues that "mockers" or "scornful ones" ". . . are afflicted with a kind of spiritual myopia; their ego is so big in their own eyes that they fail to see what is actually in front of them. Their minds are closed to everything except what they have already determined is right. Their search for wisdom is vain because they don't look in the right places and don't recognize treasure when they stumble across it."[225] They fail to heed parental advice as the key to a life of material and spiritual satisfaction on this earth. They search for wisdom on their own terms, and they come up empty in the process.

One reason that they are so arrogant in their folly is that they do not take seriously the reality of sin. As Prov 14:9 observes, "Fools mock at making amends for sin, but goodwill is found among the upright." The Hebrew in this verse is difficult. Toy maintains that both the "text and translation are doubtful."[226] Some translators such as Alter do not provide much help in the understanding of this verse. His rendering is, "Guilt dwells in the tents of scoffers, but among the upright–favor."[227] The NIV understands "making amends for sin" as the object of 14:9a. However, both Delitzsch and Toy reverse this view and make the offering for sin the subject of the sentence. Delitzsch translates the verse, "The sacrificial offering of fools mocketh; but between upright men there is good understanding,"[228] while Toy renders the first line, "The guilt offering (or, guilt) mocks fools."[229] It is unclear whether Solomon is referring to the mockery of sin or to the sacrificial system. Either is possible. Delitzsch argues that it is the Hebrew sacrificial system that mocks the fool in that he continually has to make amends for his ongoing pattern of sin because of his folly. He writes, "Fools fall from one offence into another, which they have to atone for by the presentation of sacrificial offerings; the sacrificial offering mocketh them, . . . for it equally derides them on account of the self-inflicted loss, and on account of

---

225. Alden, *Proverbs*, 111.
226. Toy, *Proverbs*, 286.
227. Alter, *The Wisdom Books*, 254.
228. Delitzsch, *Proverbs*, 294.
229. Toy, *Proverbs*, 286.

the efforts with which they must make good the effects of their frivolity and madness."[230] Longman takes a different approach in that he understands the verse to be teaching that fools ". . . disdain guilt offerings. After all, fools will not admit fault and therefore would never agree that a guilt offering is necessary."[231] Of the two approaches, Longman's is by far the more plausible. From the clear and consistent testimony of the book of Proverbs, it is difficult to conceive of a fool who is concerned enough with his sin to offer a sacrifice. He appears to be one who is totally unconcerned with religious practice and spirituality. Alden's analysis is helpful in simplifying what is admittedly a hermeneutical difficulty. He writes, "The contrast here is between fools who carelessly engage in sin while good people find acceptance with God by responsible living."[232]

However, there is an implication here that the state of being "upright" includes two things: (1) the acknowledgement of sin, and (2) the necessity of a guilt offering.

Another facet of the personality of the mocker can be seen in Prov 17:5, "He who mocks the poor shows contempt for their Maker; whoever gloats over disaster will not go unpunished."

This verse uses synonymous parallelism to teach two very simple truths: (1) Those who mock persons suffering from misfortune show contempt for God, and (2) Those mockers invite God's punishment. Cohen takes this a step further and opines that "mocking at a man's poverty is in fact blasphemy."[233] In this fashion, Ezekiel's oracle against Edom was given because that nation gloated over Israel's misfortune.

> Therefore as surely as I live, declares the Sovereign Lord, I will treat you in accordance with the anger and jealousy you showed in your hatred of them and I will make myself known among them when I judge you. Then you will know that I the Lord have heard all the contemptible things you have said against the mountains of Israel. You said, "They have been laid waste and have been given over to us to devour." You boasted against me and spoke against me without restraint, and I heard it. This is what the Sovereign Lord says: While the whole earth rejoices, I will make you desolate. Because you rejoiced when the inheritance of the house of Israel became desolate, that is how I will treat you. You will be

---

230. Delitzsch, *Proverbs*, 295.
231. Longman, *Proverbs*, 299.
232. Alden, *Proverbs*, 111.
233. Cohen, *Proverbs*, 112.

desolate, O Mount Seir, you and all of Edom. Then they will know that I am the Lord (Ezek 35:11–15).

Such persons display contempt for the Law of God, which states that the believer is to "Love your neighbor as yourself" (Luke 15:27). Jesus explained, applied, and illustrated this truth in his Parable of the Good Samaritan (Luke 15:25–37). Admittedly, the teaching of Prov 17:5 fits in with the harsh language of the Imprecatory Psalms (see Psalms 12, 35, 58, 59, 69, 70, 83, 109, 137, 140).[234] Plaut relates that Rabbi Solomon Yitzchak ben Isaac ". . . applies the proverb to people who, in the presence of someone dead, fail to talk about him and his merits. Indeed, much of the conversation in the house of mourning is tantamount to mockery."[235] This picture of attendees at a funeral gloating over the misfortune of the deceased is indeed morbid, but perhaps it is not without merit in some instances.

After an examination of related proverbs that have the ridicule of the poor as their subject (Prov 6:6–11; 10:4–5), it is apparent that it is the behavior that led to their poverty that is the object of the ridicule, not the poverty itself. Longman writes "that it is not their poverty that is being ridiculed, but the foolish behavior that got them there."[236] It is true that some cases of poverty are the result of sloth and laziness, but there are other causes that are beyond their control. The poor as well as the rich are made in the image of God, and to mock them is to mock the One who made them. Psalm 73 is a lament in which the writer Asaph confesses his sin of envy at the prosperity of the wicked. The Prosperity Gospel has led many otherwise well-meaning, but envious, saints down a road that is neither biblical nor wise. Longman cites similar proverbs from "The Teaching of Amenemope" that condemn the mocking directed at the less fortunate:

> Do not laugh at a blind man nor scorn a dwarf
> Nor spoil the plan of a lame man.
> Do not scorn a man who is in the hand of God
> Nor be fierce of countenance towards him when he has erred
> (Amenemope 24.9 12)[237]

---

234. For a fuller treatment of the problems posed by the Imprecatory Psalms see Archer, *SOTI*, 452–53; or Fee and Stuart, *How To Read the Bible For All Its Worth*, 182–84.

235. Plaut, *Proverbs*, 187.

236. Longman, *Proverbs*, 344.

237. Ibid., 344.

Garrett writes that Prov 19:25—20:1 form an inclusio that focuses on the characteristics of mockers and the punishment they can expect,[238] as shown in 12:25 ("Flog a mocker, and the simple will learn prudence; rebuke a discerning man, and he will gain knowledge."); 19:28 ("A corrupt witness mocks at justice, and the mouth of the wicked gulps down evil."); and 19:29 ("Penalties are prepared for mockers, and beatings for the back of fools."). The afterword of this section, Prov 20:1 ("Wine is a mocker and beer a brawler; whoever is led astray by them is not wise.") is not really germane to this discussion in that it does not pertain to the "mocker" as a sin of the tongue. Garrett explains, "The point here is probably that mockers are prone to consume this mocking beverage in excess and that drinking in excess in turn degrades one's respect for authority and propriety."[239] They exhibit a profound disregard for both authority and personal integrity. That is doubtless why they receive the "penalties" mentioned in verse 29 and are flogged (verse 25) and beaten (verse 29). According to verse 25, flogging serves as an object lesson to other would-be-fools. "The simple will learn prudence" and view this public punishment as a warning. Rabbi Solomon Yitzchak ben Isaac applied this verse to Jethro who converted to Judaism after seeing Pharaoh's punishment.[240]

Many commentators link the "corrupt witness" who "mocks at justice" of verse 28 with the "penalties" that are "prepared for mockers" of verse 29. For example, Waltke argues that the link between these two verses "sets forth the God-ordained punishments established for the corrupt witnesses that mock justice."[241] It illustrates a common motif in the book of Proverbs that "a man reaps what he sows" (cf., Gal 6:7). Longman writes of this verse, "There is a natural fit between punishment and fools."[242] Apparently this verse addresses the cavalier attitude of the "corrupt witness" of the preceding verse who "mocks at justice." He eventually receives his comeuppance.

This theme of punishment serving as an object lesson first seen in Prov 19:25 is addressed again in 21:11, "When a mocker is punished, the simple gain wisdom; when a wise man is instructed, he gets knowledge." Delitzsch notes the connection between the two verses. He writes, "The mocker at religion and virtue is incorrigible, punishment avails him nothing, but yet

---

238. Garrett, *Proverbs*, 172.
239. Ibid., 173.
240. Kravitz and Olitzky, *Mishlei*, 193.
241. Waltke, *The Book of Proverbs, Chapters 15–31*, 125.
242. Longman, *Proverbs*, 373.

it is not lost; for as a warning example it teaches the simple, who might otherwise be easily drawn into the same frivolity."[243] This verse teaches that by the punishment of the mocker, the simple observe and gain instruction. Apparently the mocker learns nothing from his punishment. A common motif of wisdom literature is the conversion of the simple to increasing in wisdom.[244] The simple is basically naive, uneducated, and ignorant, but he is not irredeemable. He is capable of observing and learning thereby increasing in wisdom. On the other hand, as Garrett suggests, "The mocker . . . is incorrigibly evil."[245]

The translation of Prov 21:11 is complex and difficult to render in a pithy, proverb form.[246] It is also difficult to determine if the subject is the same in both colas. Alter's translation is perhaps more helpful than that of the NIV in that he sets up the proverb as antithetical parallelism rather than synonymous: "When the scoffer is punished, the dupe gets wisdom, but when a wise man is taught, he gains knowledge."[247] The contrast is more easily seen in that the simple actually needs to see the fate of the mocker in order gain wisdom, whereas the wise man gains knowledge through instruction alone.

The mocker is recognized by his pride and arrogance, especially as it is demonstrated through the vehicle of his obnoxious speech: "The proud and arrogant man–'Mocker' is his name; he behaves with overweening pride" (Prov 21:24). This proverb uncovers what is at the root of the mocker's problem; it is pride. At first glance, this description appears to be a tautology. Why does he behave with overweening pride? It is because he is proud and arrogant. This verse is another one that is difficult to translate in a way that makes sense. One cannot define the word 'proud' as 'one who demonstrates pride'. Toy explains that the verse must be taken as providing a definition of the word *scoffer* (or mocker).[248] He thus takes verse 24 as a formal definition, but he errs in dating this verse after the Babylonian exile. He writes, "If this interpretation be correct, it appears to point to the existence of a precise, philosophical form of instruction in the schools, and to the distinct recognition of a class of arrogant disregarders of moral law, both

---

243. Delitzsch, *Proverbs*, 70.
244. Murphy, *Proverbs*, 159.
245. Garrett, *Proverbs*, 181.
246. Longman, *Proverbs*, 393.
247. Alter, *The Wisdom Books*, 283.
248. Toy, *Proverbs*, 408.

of which facts suit the time when the Jews came under Greek influence."[249] It is not necessary to date this verse well after the time of Solomon if this "definition" approach to the verse be taken. For example, Longman, a conservative commentator, writes, "The proverb defines what makes a mocker a mocker: pride. Pride causes people to look at others and make fun of them. Specifically, when they themselves are criticized, rather than taking an inward look and transforming for the better, they defend themselves by ridiculing those who are pointing out their weaknesses."[250] Clifford suggests that this verse, rather than being tautologous, actually "aims at intensification of experience" in defining a scoffer's (mocker) typical activity.[251] Such intensification can also be seen in Prov 6:12–19. Peterson's translation aptly captures this intensification: "You know their names–Brash, Impudent, Blasphemer–intemperate hotheads, every one."[252] Such a person was perhaps in the mind of Asaph when he wrote, "They scoff, and speak with malice; in their arrogance they threaten oppression. Their mouths lay claim to heaven, and their tongues take possession of the earth" (Ps 73:8–9).

The final two verses pertaining to mockers deal with the negative influence that they can exert on the quality of life in society, Prov 22:10, "Drive out the mocker, and out goes strife; quarrels and insults are ended," and Prov 29:8, "Mockers stir up a city, but wise men turn away anger." The former verse uses synonymous parallelism to list three things that getting rid of a mocker will do. It will eliminate strife, quarrels, and insults. The latter verse indicates the range of damage that a mocker can cause. He can "stir up a city." Therefore, it is preferable to expel him for the sake of peace and concord. An old Rabbinic proverb states, "When a fool leaves the room it seems as though a wise man entered."[253] Sometimes it is necessary to remove a troublemaker. Often he lacks moral and religious principles. Kidner in his commentary on this verse suggests, "Disagreement and bad blood sometimes arise not from the facts of a situation but from a person with a wrong attitude, who makes mischief. That is to say, what an institution sometimes needs is not reforms, but the expulsion of a member."[254] Longman expands upon this point of view thus:

249. Ibid.
250. Longman, *Proverbs*, 397.
251. Clifford, *Proverbs*, 193.
252. Peterson, *The Message of Leadership*, 114.
253. As cited by Alden, *Proverbs*, 161.
254. Kidner, *Proverbs*, 148.

Fights are not abstract entities; they arise from specific individuals. Mockers are those who pick fights. They respond to criticism in a defensive manner. In general, they are self-protective people who respond to any perceived assault with a counterattack. Thus, the solution to a situation of conflict may be to get rid of the troublemaker. In other words, this proverb says that it is often not the situation but rather the people involved in a situation who cause problems. Sometimes it is necessary to remove a difficult individual to preserve the harmony of a community.[255]

When such persons are expelled, harmony is restored.

In Prov 29:8 there is a contrast drawn by using antithetical parallelism between the mocker who stirs up a city in line one and the wise man who serves as a peacemaker in line two. The mocker has the potential to influence many and wield a wide path of destruction. Line one can actually be translated "blow" as in fan the flames on a city. Cohen's translation reflects this nuance: "Scornful men set a city in a blaze."[256] So does Alter's translation: "Scoffing men fan the flames of a city."[257] Clifford describes the possible wordplay here: "As the scoffers exhale their lies, they are actually fanning the flame of popular anger."[258] On the other hand, the wise man is the voice of quiet reason who acts as a peacemaker to turn away anger from the city. The mocker is associated with impulsive, passionate, incendiary behavior, whereas the wise man with a calm bearing is the voice of reason. He is forever putting out the fires that the mocker leaves in his wake.

Perverse Talk

Perverse talk is the final category of the improper use of the tongue that will be considered in this chapter. It can be defined as speech that is "deviating from what is considered right or acceptable; perverted; wicked; persisting in error or fault; stubbornly contrary; obstinately disobedient or difficult; intractable."[259] Prohibitions against this type of speech abound in the book of Proverbs, not just in the "Sayings" sections; for example, "Wisdom will save you from the ways of wicked men, from men whose words are

---

255. Longman, *Proverbs*, 406–7.
256. Cohen, *Proverbs*, 194.
257. Alter, *The Wisdom Books*, 319.
258. Clifford, *Proverbs*, 251.
259. *Webster's New World Dictionary*, 1093.

perverse" (Prov 2:12); and, "Put away perversity from your mouth; keep corrupt talk far from your lips" (Prov 4:24). In the Warnings Against Folly in Prov 6:1–19, the young man is warned by his father about this type of scoundrel in verse 12, "A scoundrel and villain, who goes about with a corrupt mouth." Finally, perverse talk is prominent in the catalogue of sins that God hates: "To fear the Lord is to hate evil; I hate pride and arrogance, evil behavior and perverse speech" (Prov 8:12); in other words, perverse speech is behavior that is incompatible with one who says that he fears the Lord.

In the "Sayings" sections (10:1—31:9), there are at least eleven verses that condemn this behavior. For example, Prov 10:31–32 notes, "From the mouth of the righteous comes the fruit of wisdom, but a perverse tongue will be silenced. The lips of the righteous know what finds favor, but the mouth of the wicked only what is perverse." These two verses follow an obvious A-B-A-B pattern in which the mouth (lips) of the righteous are contrasted using antithetical parallelism with the tongue (mouth) of the wicked. However, it is also possible to see a chiasmus here if only the following are considered: A (mouth)–B (tongue)–B (lips)–A (mouth). In any case, the clear contrast that is being made is between the proper and decorous speech of the righteous and the perverse speech of the wicked. Alden's observation that verse 31 is not truly antithetical is interesting, but hardly compelling. While conceding that the "lips of the righteous" and the "mouth of the wicked" are indeed opposite, he writes that ". . . the verbs are not parallel unless the verse means righteous men will continue to speak wisdom while wicked ones will be stopped."[260] Toy, on the other hand, argues that ". . . the antithesis is implicit. . . . Instead of saying that the tongue of the wicked *utters folly* or *falsehood* . . . the verse, looking forward to the consequences, declares that it shall be *cut off*; the proverb in full form would be: the righteous speaks wisdom, obeys God, and lives–the wicked speaks folly, disobeys, and dies. It is a repetition of the familiar idea of precise compensation in this life."[261]

The image in verse 31 is that of a fruit tree that brings forth fruit. The mouth of the righteous brings forth a bountiful harvest of wisdom, whereas the perverse tongue is pruned because its fruit is unacceptable. Jesus developed this metaphor in the Sermon on the Mount (cf. Matt. 7:15–20). Garrett remarks that the disciplinary action of cutting out the tongue is metaphorical in that the Old Testament Law does not impose

---

260. Alden, *Proverbs*, 90.
261. Toy, *Proverbs*, 218.

such a penalty.[262] Conversely, Longman argues that "the literal meaning of the verb makes perfect and vivid sense."[263] It seems likely that the metaphorical approach to this punishment is the better option. This is probably an example of hyperbole, and the cutting off of the tongue should not be taken literally. As Plaut concludes, "A man can talk perversity for a while, but the time comes when no one cares to listen to him any more and his tongue is as if it were cut off."[264] Thus, he is effectively silenced as if his tongue were severed.

Verse 32 teaches that a person is known by the type of speech that emanates from his mouth. Cohen observes that "... a man's speech is the reflection of his character and therefore his character reveals itself in his speech. Seneca, the Roman philosopher of the first century C.E. observed, 'Speech is the index of the mind.'"[265]

In Prov 16:27–28, "a perverse man" is mentioned in parallel with "a scoundrel," as the passage reads, "A scoundrel plots evil, and his speech is like a scorching fire. A perverse man stirs up dissension, and a gossip separates close friends." Taking verses 27–30 as a thematic unity as Garrett argues, then the scoundrel (verse 27) and the perverse man (verse 28) are also parallel with the "violent man" and the one who "is plotting perversity" of verses 29–30, "A violent man entices his neighbor and leads him down a path that is not good. He who winks with his eyes is plotting perversity." Although perverse speech is not explicitly mentioned, if the scoundrel, perverse man, violent man, and plotter of perversity can be taken synonymously, then this person's speech is "like a scorching fire," "stirs up dissension," separates close friends through gossip, and purses his lips "bent on evil." He "plots evil," "entices his neighbor and leads him down a path that is not good," and "plots perversity."

The individual in verse 27 "plots evil." Literally, he "digs up evil" in the sense of metaphorically digging a pit to trap the unwary.[266] The NIV captures the correct nuance that Solomon intended to convey. The same root is found in Lev 13:23, 28 for "a skin inflammation."[267] Alter's translation captures the destructive nature of this person's words: "A worthless man is

262. Garrett, *Proverbs*, 123.
263. Longman, *Proverbs*, 244.
264. Plaut, *Proverbs*, 133.
265. Cohen, *Proverbs*, 64.
266. Alter, *Proverbs*, 265; Cohen, *Proverbs*, 109.
267. Cohen, *Proverbs*, 109.

a furnace of evil, and on his lips like burning fire."[268] His words burn like a fire or a serious skin inflammation. They are destructive to the person who is the object of his wrath.

In verse 28, this "perverse man" uses his perverse speech to stir up dissension probably through the medium of vicious gossip. Gossip as a topic for discussion, and this verse in particular, have been dealt with in great detail earlier in this chapter. The intent of this person is explained further in verse 30 in that he is "plotting perversity." Longman explains the result of such behavior: "Evil folly produces social divisions. The perverse are those who turn things upside down and around, and so produce conflict. The gossips of the second colon should be understood as a subcategory or specification of the perverse, and through their loose and misleading tongues, they end up even separating those who beforehand were 'intimate associates.'"[269]

A subcategory of synthetic parallelism, comparison type, is used in Prov 19:1: "Better a poor man whose walk is blameless than a fool whose lips are perverse." In this verse a contrast is drawn between an honest and godly poor man and a dishonest fool. According to most commentators, the implication is that this fool is rich—some translators even supply the descriptor "rich," even though it is not found in the Hebrew text. For example, Peterson's translation does just that: "Better to be poor and honest than a rich person no one can trust."[270] Cohen, however, sees a different thrust in this verse, as he argues, "Here the point is: better is a poor man who is contented to remain poor and retain his integrity, than a person who tries to escape from poverty by resorting to a dishonest life; because the latter is a fool to imagine that by evil methods he can truly prosper. Either he will be found out and suffer punishment, or God will thwart his plans."[271] Alden agrees with Cohen in maintaining that the contrast is not between rich and poor, but "between honest poor men and dishonest foolish ones."[272] Thus, this proverb is teaching relative values. While few would argue for the benefits of poverty or that poverty is superior to possessing wealth, this verse teaches that ethical principles are superior to material possessions.

---

268. Alter, *Proverbs*, 265.
269. Longman, *Proverbs*, 337.
270. Peterson, *The Message of Leadership*, 108.
271. Cohen, *Proverbs*, 124.
272. Alden, *Proverbs*, 142.

Longman argues that this verse teaches that "folly is an ethical concept" and that fools are not only stupid, they are evil.[273]

In Prov 19:28 the corrupt witness who "mocks at justice" is paired with the "mouth of the wicked" that "gulps down evil," using synonymous parallelism: "A corrupt witness mocks at justice and the mouth of the wicked gulps down evil." The mocker, as a general topic for discussion, and this verse in particular have already been examined in detail previously in this chapter. This verse condemns mockery, false witness particularly in a court of law, and perverse speech which "gulps down evil." There is an apparent play on words in the Hebrew language here which is difficult to render adequately. The false witness of this verse "devoureth iniquity" or "feeds on" on it. It is his meat and drink. His perverse words attempt to pervert justice. Alter captures this nuance perfectly, "A worthless witness scoffs justice, and the mouth of the wicked swallows crime."[274]

Summary

This chapter has outlined the second of two courses of action that the tongue can take: The Proper Use of the Tongue and the Improper Use of the Tongue. The Proper Use of the Tongue includes Imparting Wisdom and Knowledge, Encouragement, Protection, Nurture, Healing, Telling the Truth, Pleasant Speech, Praise, Advice, Confessing Sin, Discretion, and Rebuke. The Improper Use of the Tongue is the other side of the coin and includes Lying, Gossip, Slander, Quarreling, Speaking Rashly, Boasting, Flattery, Mockery, Perverse Talk, and Foolish Talk. The godly leader should engage in the former and forsake the latter. What a person says does matter. One's words are an index to the heart.

---

273. Longman, *Proverbs*, 365.
274. Alter, *The Wisdom Books*, 277.

Chapter Six

Summary and Conclusions

ANDREW HILL AND JOHN Walton comment on the place of the book of Proverbs in the life of the Hebrew nation. They write, "The retribution principle expressed in the blessing and curses of the Pentateuchal covenant formulas resurfaces in the wisdom literature of the Old Testament. The expectation of reward for the nation's conformity to the law of God is logically applied to the individual Hebrew 'God-fearer' in the proverbial wisdom."[1] Furthermore, the proverbs are by their very nature generalized statements and principles that are not to be taken as legal prescriptions. As Hill and Walton continue, "The truisms of Proverbs are not absolute promises, but general principles based on careful observation of the human experience."[2] In other words, as Grant Osborne observes, they are not intended "to establish codes by which God works."[3]

Summary

This book has attempted to examine the book of Proverbs in order to derive principles that would benefit any person, not just Christian believers, in the broad areas of priorities, making plans, and the judicious use of the tongue. However, the overall thrust of this paper has been to apply those principles to Christian leaders either in church or para-church ministries. Further, this paper has endeavored to demonstrate and prove the following thesis: *A*

---

1. Hill and Walton, *A Survey of the Old Testament*, 290.
2. Ibid.
3. Osborne, *The Hermeneutical Spiral*, 195.

Summary and Conclusions

godly leader orders his priorities, plans, and tongue by the wisdom contained in the Proverbs.

In attempting to prove the Thesis, three broad areas of investigation were examined all from the perspective of the book of Proverbs: (1) The Leader's Priorities, (2) The Leader's Plans, and (3) The Leader's Tongue.

Under The Leader's Priorities, two major categories were examined: (1) Relationship to God, and (2) Relationship to Family. Under Relationship to Family, two subcategories were examined in some depth: (1) Husband and Wife, and (2) Parents and Children. It was determined that the first priority for any believer is his relationship to God. Then comes his relationship to his family with the relationship to his spouse being of primary importance after his relationship to God. Then in order of importance comes his children.

Under The Leader's Plans, two major categories were examined: (1) Partnership with God, and (2) Partnership with Others. Plans are futile unless made with the blessing of and under the guidance of God. The godly leader also consults other godly counselors to get their input. He never makes decisions by himself in a vacuum.

Under The Leader's Tongue, two major categories were examined comprising two separate chapters: (1) The Proper Use of the Tongue, and (2) The Improper Use of the Tongue.

Under the chapter heading, The Proper Use of the Tongue, twelve categories of positive speech were examined: (1) Imparting Knowledge and Wisdom, (2) Encouragement, (3) Protection, (4) Nurture, (5) Healing, (6) Telling the Truth, (7) Pleasant Speech, (8) Praise, (9) Advice, (10) Confessing Sin, (11) Discretion, and (12) Rebuke. All of the proverbs pertaining to the use of the tongue or speech from the Proverbs of Solomon, the Sayings of the Wise, and of Agur, Son of Jakeh (Prov 10:1—30:33) were classified and categorized in charts for easy reference. It was demonstrated that there is much material about the use of the tongue in the book of Proverbs that is of a positive nature. Their use is to be commended.

Under the chapter heading, The Improper Use of the Tongue, ten areas of speech that are considered to be negative uses were examined: (1) Lying, (2) Gossip, (3) Foolish Talk, (4) Slander, (5) Quarreling, (6) Speaking Rashly, (7) Boasting, (8) Flattery, (9) Mockery, and (10) Perverse Talk. These uses of the tongue are forbidden and are characteristic of the fool. They can be classified as sin and thus should not be part of the godly leader's speech patterns.

Conclusions

Effective leadership is not a skill that one stumbles upon and godly leadership does not happen by accident. It is developed and nurtured by the aspiring leader who would attempt to follow the epitome of godly leadership, Jesus Christ. A person does not become an effective, godly leader overnight, nor does he achieve it apart from following a plan for success and concerted effort. A plan grounded in Scripture is essential for the Christian leader. Christian character and leadership skills do not just happen. Andy Stanley writes of character and its relationship to leadership: "Understand that character is not essential to leadership, but character is what sets you apart as a leader worth following. Talent and determination determine your potential; character determines your legacy."[4]

The book of Proverbs is not a particularly long book. In terms of length, it stands sixteenth out of the thirty-nine books of the Old Testament. Yet within its thirty-one brief chapters, it offers a cornucopia of practical godly advice. In fact, it provides the reader with a manual for pursuing the life of godly wisdom. Moreover, it has much to say that is of value for the aspiring Christian leader. Whether he is seeking to lead in a church, para-church, or business setting, the aspiring godly leader would do well to follow the advice of Solomon to whom the authorship of the bulk of Proverbs is attributed.

The material pertaining to leadership in the book of Proverbs appears to be endless and could be the subject of a book, or even many books. Much remains to be written about the subject of leadership from Proverbs. For example, I am particularly interested in two topics: (1) the character of leadership, and (2) the practice or pattern of leadership. But those are topics yet to be mined from this sacred book of wisdom. This study is but a humble beginning that lays something of a foundation for a theology of leadership from the Proverbs. This book has strictly limited itself to an examination of how the godly leader orders his life with respect to three topics developed in the Proverbs. They are priorities, plans, and the use of the tongue. *A godly leader orders his priorities, plans, and tongue by the wisdom contained in the Proverbs.* His priorities are God first and family second. His plans are formulated first in partnership with God and then with others. He knows how to use his tongue properly and how not to use it improperly. Such is the path of wisdom. Any other way is the path of foolishness and folly. The godly leader should always follow the path of wisdom.

4. Stanley, *The Next Generation Leader*, 159.

Appendix 1

Classification of the Proverbs of Solomon, the Sayings of the Wise and of Agur, Son of Jakeh Pertaining to the Tongue by Chapter

VERSE	CLASSIFICATION	QUOTATION
10:6	General admonition	"Violence overwhelms the mouth of the wicked"
10:8	Foolish Talk	"A chattering fool comes to ruin"
10:10	Foolish Talk	"A chattering fool comes to ruin"
10:11	General admonition	"The mouth of the righteous is a fountain of life, but violence overwhelms the mouth of the wicked."
10:13	General admonition	"Wisdom is found on the lips of the discerning"
10:14	Foolish Talk	"The mouth of a fool invites ruin"
10:18	Lying Slander	"He who conceals his hatred has lying lips, and whoever spreads slander is a fool."
10:19	Loquaciousness	"When words are many, sin is not absent, but he who holds his tongue is wise."
10:20	General admonition	"The tongue of the righteous is choice silver"
10:21	Nourishment	"The lips of the righteous nourish many"
10:31	General admonition Perverse Talk	"The mouth of the righteous brings forth wisdom, but a perverse tongue will be cut out."
10:32	General admonition Perverse talk	"The lips of the righteous know what is fitting, but the mouth of the wicked only what is perverse."

Appendix 1

VERSE	CLASSIFICATION	QUOTATION
11:9	Gossip	"With his mouth the godless destroys his neighbor"
11:11	Perverse talk	"but by the mouth of the wicked it is destroyed"
11:12	Slander Discretion	"A man who lacks judgment derides his neighbor, but a man of understanding holds his tongue."
11:13	Gossip Discretion	"A gossip betrays a confidence, but a trustworthy man keeps a secret."
12:5	Deceit	"But the advice of the wicked is deceitful."
12:6	Protection	"The words of the wicked lie in wait for blood, but the speech of the upright rescues them."
12:8	Praise	"A man is praised according to his wisdom"
12:13	General admonition	"An evil man is trapped by his sinful talk"
12:14	General admonition	"From the fruit of his lips a man is filled with good things"
12:16	Discretion	"A fool shows his annoyance at once, but a prudent man overlooks an insult."
12:17	Honesty Lying	"A truthful witness gives honest testimony, but a false witness tells lies."
12:18	Reckless speech Healing	"Reckless words pierce like a sword, but the tongue of the wise bring healing."
12:19	Honesty Lying	"Truthful lips endure forever, but a lying tongue lasts only a moment."
12:22	Lying Honesty	"The Lord detests lying lips, but he delights in men who are truthful."
12:23	Discretion Foolish talk	"A prudent man keeps his knowledge to himself, but the heart of fools blurt out folly."
12:25	Encouragement	"But a kind word cheers him up."
13:1	Mocking	"But a mocker does not listen to rebuke."
13:2	General admonition	"From the fruit of his lips a man enjoys good things"
13:3	Discretion Reckless speech	"He who guards his lips guards his life, but he who speaks rashly will come to ruin."
13:10	Quarreling	"Pride only breeds quarrels"
14:3	Foolish talk General admonition	"A fool's talk brings a rod to his back, but the lips of the wise protect them."

Classification Pertaining to the Tongue by Chapter

VERSE	CLASSIFICATION	QUOTATION
14:5	Honesty Lying	"A truthful witness does not deceive, but a false witness pours out lies."
14:6	Mockery	"The mocker seeks wisdom and finds none"
14:7	Foolish talk	"Stay away from a foolish man, for you will not find knowledge on his lips."
14:9	Mockery	"Fools mock at making amends for sin"
14:23	General admonition	"All hard work brings a profit, but mere talk only leads to poverty."
14:25	Honesty Lying	"A truthful witness saves lives, but a false witness is deceitful."
15:1	Discretion Angry words	"A gentle answer turns away wrath, but a harsh word stirs up anger."
15:2	Knowledge Foolish talk	"The tongue of the wise commends knowledge, but the mouth of the fool gushes folly."
15:4	Healing Lying	"The tongue that brings healing is a tree of life, but a deceitful tongue crushes the spirit."
15:7	Instruction	"The lips of the wise spread knowledge"
15:12	Mockery	"A mocker resents correction; he will not consult the wise."
15:14	Foolish talk	"But the mouth of a fool feeds on folly."
15:18	Quarreling Discretion	"A hot-tempered man stirs up dissension, but a patient man calms a quarrel."
15:23	Discretion	"A man finds joy in giving an apt reply— and how good is a timely word."
15:28	Perverse talk	"But the mouth of the wicked gushes evil."
15:30	Healing	"A cheerful look brings joy to the heart, and good news gives health to the bones."
16:1	General admonition	"But from the Lord comes the reply of the tongue."
16:10	General admonition	"The lips of a king speak as an oracle, and his mouth should not betray justice."
16:13	Honesty	"Kings take pleasure in honest lips; they value a man who speaks the truth."
16:21	Instruction	"And pleasant words promote instruction."
16:23	Instruction	"A wise man's heart guides his mouth, and his lips promote instruction."

Appendix 1

VERSE	CLASSIFICATION	QUOTATION
16:24	Pleasant Speech Healing	"Pleasant words are a honeycomb, sweet to the soul and healing to the bones."
16:27	Perverse talk	"His speech is like a scorching fire."
16:28	Perverse talk Gossip	"A perverse man stirs up dissension, and a gossip separates close friends."
16:30	General admonition	"He who purses his lips is bent on evil."
17:4	Lying	"A wicked man listens to evil lips; a liar pays attention to a malicious tongue."
17:5	Mockery	"He who mocks the poor shows contempt for their maker."
17:7	Arrogant speech Lying	"Arrogant lips are unsuited to a fool– how much worse lying lips to a ruler!"
17:9	Gossip	"But whoever repeats the matter separates close friends."
17:10	Rebuke	"A rebuke impresses a man of discernment."
17:14	Quarreling	"Starting a quarrel is like breaching a dam."
17:19	Quarreling	"He who loves a quarrel loves sin."
17:20	Lying	"He whose tongue is deceitful falls into trouble."
17:27	Restraint in speech	"A man of knowledge uses words with restraint."
17:28	Restraint in speech	"Even a fool is thought wise if he keeps silent, and discerning if he holds his tongue."
18:2	Arrogant speech	"A fool finds no pleasure in understanding but delights in airing his own opinions."
18:4	General admonition	"The words of a man's mouth are deep waters, but the fountain of wisdom is a bubbling brook."
18:6	Foolish talk	"A fool's lips bring him strife, and his mouth invites a beating."
18:7	Foolish talk	"A fool's mouth is his undoing, and his lips are a snare to his soul."
18:8	Gossip	"The words of a gossip are like choice morsels; they go down to a man's inmost parts."
18:13	Reckless speech	"He who answers before listening– that is his folly and his shame."

Classification Pertaining to the Tongue by Chapter

VERSE	CLASSIFICATION	QUOTATION
18:20	General admonition	"From the fruit of his mouth a man's stomach is filled; with the harvest from his lips he is satisfied."
18:21	General admonition	"The tongue has the power of life and death, and those who love it will eat its fruit."
18:23	Pleading Harsh speech	"A poor man pleads for mercy, but a rich man answers harshly."
19:1	Perverse talk	"Better a poor man whose walk is blameless than a fool whose lips are perverse."
19:5	Slander (Perjury) Lying	"A false witness will not go unpunished, and he who pours out lies will not go free."
19:9	Slander (Perjury) Lying	"A false witness will not go unpunished, and he who pours out lies will perish."
19:13	Quarreling	"And a quarrelsome wife is like a constant dripping."
19:25	Mockery Rebuke	"Flog a mocker, and the simple will learn prudence, rebuke a discerning man, and he will gain knowledge."
19:28	Mockery Perverse talk	"A corrupt witness mocks at justice, and the mouth of the wicked gulps down evil."
19:29	Mockery	"Penalties are prepared for mockers."
20:3	Quarreling	"It is to every man's honor to avoid strife, but every fool is quick to quarrel."
20:14	Lying Boasting	"'It's no good, it's no good!' says the buyer; then off he goes and boasts about his purchase."
20:15	Instruction	"But lips that speak knowledge are a rare jewel."
20:19	Gossip	"A gossip betrays a confidence; so avoid a man who talks too much."
20:20	Cursing	"If a man curses his father or mother, his lamp will be snuffed out in pitch darkness."
20:22	Reckless speech	"Do not say, 'I'll pay you back for this wrong!' Wait for the Lord, and he will deliver you."
20:25	Reckless speech	"It is a trap for a man to dedicate something rashly and only later to consider his vows."
21:6	Lying	"A fortune made by a lying tongue is a fleeting vapor and a deadly snare."

Appendix 1

VERSE	CLASSIFICATION	QUOTATION
21:9	Quarreling	"Better to live on a corner of the roof than share a house with a quarrelsome wife."
21:11	Mockery	"When a mocker is punished, the simple gain wisdom."
21:19	Quarreling	"Better to live in a desert than with a quarrelsome and ill-tempered woman."
21:23	Restraint in speech	"He who guards his mouth and his tongue keeps himself from calamity."
21:24	Mockery	"The proud and arrogant man-Mocker is his name; he behaves with overweening pride."
21:28	Slander (Perjury)	"A false witness will perish, and whoever listens to him will be destroyed forever."
22:10	Mockery Quarreling	"Drive out the mocker, and out goes strife; quarrels and insults are ended."
22:11	Pleasant speech	"He who loves a pure heart and whose speech is gracious will have the king for his friend."
22:12	General admonition	"The eyes of the Lord keep watch over knowledge, but he frustrates the words of the unfaithful."
22:13	Lying	"The sluggard says, 'There is a lion outside!' or, ' I will be murdered in the streets!'"
22:14	General admonition	"The mouth of an adulteress is a deep pit; he who is under the Lord's wrath will fall into it."
22:18	Instruction	"For it is pleasing when you keep them in your heart, and have them ready on your lips."
22:21	Instruction	"Teaching you true and reliable words, so that you can give sound answers to him who sent you."
23:9	Mockery	"Do not speak to a fool, for he will scorn the wisdom of your words."
23:12	Instruction	"Apply your heart to instruction and your ears to words of knowledge."
23:16	Truthfulness	"My inmost being will rejoice when your lips speak what is right."
24:2	Perverse talk	"For their hearts plot violence, and their lips talk about making trouble."

Classification Pertaining to the Tongue by Chapter

VERSE	CLASSIFICATION	QUOTATION
24:7	Embarrassed silence	"Wisdom is too high for a fool; In the assembly at the gate he has nothing to say."
24:9	Mockery	"The schemes of folly are sin, And men despise a mocker."
24:26	Truthfulness	"An honest answer is like a kiss on the lips."
24:28	Slander Lying	"Do not testify against your neighbor without cause, or use your lips to deceive."
24:29	General admonition	"Do not say, 'I'll do to him as he has done to me; I'll pay that man back for what he did.'"
25:6	Boasting	"Do not exalt yourself in the king's presence, and do not claim a place among great men."
25:9	Gossip	"Do not betray another man's confidence."
25:11	Encouragement	"A word aptly spoken is like apples of gold in settings of silver."
25:12	Rebuke	"Like an earring of gold or an ornament of fine gold, is a wise man's rebuke to a listening ear."
25:14	Boasting	"Like clouds and wind without rain is a man who boasts of gifts he does not give."
25:15	Persuasion	"And a gentle tongue can break a bone."
25:18	Slander (perjury)	"Like a club or a sword or a sharp arrow is the man who gives false testimony against his neighbor."
25:20	Encouragement	"Like one who takes away a garment on a cold day or like vinegar poured on soda is one who sings songs to a heavy heart."
25:23	Slander	"As a north wind brings rain, so a sly tongue brings angry looks."
25:24	Quarreling	"Better to live on a corner of the roof than share a house with a quarrelsome wife."
26:2	Perverse talk	"Like a fluttering sparrow or a darting swallow, an undeserved curse does not come to rest."
26:4	Foolish talk	"Do not answer a fool according to his folly, or you will be like him yourself."

Appendix 1

VERSE	CLASSIFICATION	QUOTATION
26:5	Discretion	"Answer a fool according to his folly, or he will be wise in his own eyes."
26:7	Foolish talk	"Like a lame man's legs that hang limp is a proverb in the mouth of a fool."
26:9	Foolish talk	"Like an archer who wounds at random is he who hires a fool or any passer-by."
26:17	Quarreling	"Like one who seizes a dog by the ears is a passer-by who meddles in a quarrel not his own."
26:18-19	Lying / Foolish talk	"Like a madman shooting firebrands or deadly arrows is a man who deceives his neighbor and says, 'I was only joking!'"
26:20	Gossip / Quarreling	"Without wood a fire goes out; without gossip a quarrel dies down."
26:21	Quarreling	"As charcoal to embers and as wood to fire, so is a quarrelsome man for kindling strife."
26:22	Gossip	"The words of a gossip are like choice morsels; they go down to a man's inmost parts."
26:23	Perverse talk	"Like a coating of glaze over earthenware are fervent lips with an evil heart."
26:24	Deceit	"A malicious man disguises himself with his lips, but in his heart he harbors deceit."
26:25	Deceit	"Though his speech is charming, do not believe him, for seven abominations fill his heart."
26:28	Lying / Flattery	"A lying tongue hates those it hurts, and a flattering mouth works ruin."
27:1	Boasting	"Do not boast about tomorrow, for you do not know what a day may bring forth."
27:2	Boasting	"Let another praise you, and not your own mouth; someone else, and not your own lips."
27:9	Encouragement / Advice	"Perfume and incense bring joy to the heart, and the pleasantness of one's friend springs from his earnest counsel."
27:11	Encouragement	"Be wise, my son, and bring joy to my heart; then I can answer anyone who treats me with contempt."

Classification Pertaining to the Tongue by Chapter

VERSE	CLASSIFICATION	QUOTATION
27:14	Flattery	"If a man loudly blesses his neighbor early in the morning, it will be taken as a curse."
27:15-16	Quarreling	"A quarrelsome wife is like a constant dripping on a rainy day; restraining her is like restraining the wind or grasping oil with the hand."
28:4	General admonition	"Those who forsake the law praise the wicked."
28:13	Confessing sin	"He who conceals his sins does not prosper, but whoever confesses and renounces them finds mercy."
28:23	Rebuke Flattery	"He who rebukes a man will in the end gain more favor than he who has a flattering tongue."
29:5	Flattery	"Whoever flatters his neighbor is spreading a net for his feet."
29:6	General admonition	"An evil man is snared by his own sin, but a righteous one can sing and be glad."
29:8	Mockery	"Mockers stir up a city."
29:9	Angry talk and scoffing	"If a wise man goes to court with a fool, the fool rages and scoffs, and there is no peace."
29:11	Angry talk	"A fool gives full vent to his anger."
29:20	Reckless speech	"Do you see a man who speaks in haste? There is more hope for a fool than for him."
29:22	Quarreling	"An angry man stirs up dissension."
29:24	Failure to testify	"The accomplice of a thief is his own enemy; he is put under oath and dare not testify."
30:8	Lying	"Keep falsehood and lies far from me."
30:10	Slander Cursing	"Do not slander a servant to his master, or he will curse you, and you will pay for it."
30:11	Cursing	"There are those who curse their fathers and do not bless their mother."
30:20	Lying	"This is the way of an adulteress: she eats and wipes her mouth and says, 'I've done nothing wrong.'"
30:32	Boasting	"If you have played the fool and exalted yourself, or if you have planned evil clap your hand over your mouth!"
30:33	Quarreling	"For as churning the milk produces butter, and as twisting the nose produces blood, so stirring up anger produces strife."

Appendix 2

Classification of the Proverbs of Solomon, the Sayings of the Wise and of Agur, Son of Jakeh Pertaining to the Tongue by Category

FOOLISH TALK	LYING
10:8	10:18
10:10	12:17
10:14	12:19
12:23	12:22
14:3	14:5
14:7	14:25
15:2	15:4
15:14	17:4
18:6	17:7
18:7	17:20
22:13	19:5
24:28	19:9
26:4	20:14
26:7	20:16
26:9	26:18-19
26:18-19	26:28
	30:8
	30:20

Classification Pertaining to the Tongue by Category

GOSSIP	SLANDER
11:9	10:18
11:13	11:12
16:28	19:5
17:9	19:9
18:8	21:28
20:19	24:28
25:19	25:18
26:20	25:23
26:22	30:10

PROTECTION	HEALING
12:6	12:18
	15:4
	15:30
	16:24

PERVERSE TALK	RECKLESS SPEECH
10:31	12:18
10:32	13:3
11:11	18:13
15:28	20:22
16:27	20:25
16:28	29:20
19:1	
19:28	
24:2	
26:2	
26:23	

Appendix 2

MOCKERY	QUARRELING
13:1	13:10
14:6	15:18
14:9	17:14
15:12	17:19
17:5	19:13
19:25	20:3
19:28	21:9
19:29	21:19
21:11	22:10
21:24	25:24
22:10	26:17
24:9	26:20
29:8	26:21
	27:15-16
	29:22
	30:33

BOASTING	FLATTERY
20:14	26:28
25:6	27:14
25:14	28:23
27:1	29:5
27:2	
30:2	

INSTRUCTION	RESTRAINT IN SPEECH
15:2	17:27
15:7	17:28
16:21	21:23
16:23	
20:15	
22:18	
22:21	
23:12	

Classification Pertaining to the Tongue by Category

DISCRETION	ENCOURAGEMENT
11:12	12:25
11:13	25:11
12:16	25:20
12:23	27:9
13:3	27:11
15:1	
15:18	
15:23	
26:4	
26:5	

HONESTY	DECEIT
12:17	12:5
12:19	26:24
12:22	26:25
14:5	
14:25	
16:13	
23:16	
24:26	

REBUKE	CURSING
17:10	20:20
19:25	26:2
25:12	30:10
28:23	30:11

LOQUACIOUSNESS	PRAISE
10:19	12:8

NOURISHMENT	PLEADING
10:21	18:23

Appendix 2

HARSH SPEECH	PLEASANT SPEECH
18:23	16:24
	22:11

PERSUASION	EMBARRASSED SILENCE
25:15	24:7

ADVICE	CONFESSING SIN
27:9	28:13

ANGRY TALK	FAILURE TO TESTIFY
29:9	29:24
29:11	

GENERAL ADMONITION (difficult to classify)	
10:6	16:10
10:11	16:30
10:13	18:4
10:20	18:20
10:31	18:21
10:32	22:12
12:13	22:14
12:14	23:9
13:2	24:29
14:3	26:9
14:23	28:4
16:1	29:6

ARROGANT SPEECH	
17:7	18:2

Appendix 3

Table 2.1
Characteristics of Admired Leaders

Percentage of Respondents Selecting Each Characteristic

Appendix 3

Characteristics	2007 ed.	2002 ed.	1995 ed.	1987 ed.
Honest	89	88	88	83
Forward-looking	71	71	75	62
Inspiring	69	65	68	58
Competent	68	66	63	67
Intelligent	48	47	40	43
Fair-minded	39	42	49	40
Straightforward	36	34	33	34
Broad-minded	35	40	40	37
Supportive	35	35	41	32
Dependable	34	33	32	33
Cooperative	25	28	28	25
Courageous	25	20	29	27
Determined	25	24	17	17
Caring	22	20	23	26
Imaginative	17	23	28	34
Mature	15	17	13	23
Ambitious	16	21	13	21
Loyal	18	14	11	11
Self-controlled	10	8	5	13
Independent	4	6	5	10

Note: These percentages represent respondents from six continents: Africa, North America, South America, Asia, Europe, and Australia. The majority of respondents are from the United States. Since we asked people to select seven characteristics, the total adds up to more than 100 percent.

Appendix 4

Table 2.2
Cross-Cultural Comparisons of the Characteristics of Admired Leaders

Percentage of Respondents Selecting Each Characteristic

Country	Honest	Forward-Looking	Inspiring	Competent
Australia	93	83	73	59
Canada	88	88	73	60
Japan	67	83	51	61
Korea	74	82	55	62
Malaysia	95	78	60	62
Mexico	85	82	71	62
New Zealand	86	86	71	68
Singapore	72	76	69	76
Sweden, Denmark	84	86	90	53
United States	89	71	69	68

Bibliography

Aitken, Kenneth T. *Proverbs*. In The Daily Study Bible Series. John C. L. Gibson, Old Testament editor. Louisville, Ky.: Westminster John Knox, 1986.

Alden, Robert L. *Proverbs: A Commentary on an Ancient Book of Timeless Advice.* Grand Rapids: Baker Book House, 1983.

Allis, Oswald T. *The Old Testament: Its Claims and Its Critics.* Phillipsburg, N.J.: The Presbyterian and Reformed, 1972.

Alter, Robert. *The Wisdom Books*. New York: W. W. Norton and Company, 2010.

Anders, Max. *Proverbs. Holman Old Testament Commentary.* Edited by Max Anders. Nashville: Holman Reference, 2005.

Anderson, Leith. *Leadership That Works: Hope and Direction for Church and Parachurch Leaders in Today's Complex World.* Minneapolis: Bethany House, 1999.

Archer, Gleason. *A Survey of Old Testament Introduction.* 2nd ed. Chicago: Moody Press, 2007.

Armerding, Hudson T. *The Heart of Godly Leadership*. Wheaton: Crossway Books, 1992.

Arnot, William. *Studies in Proverbs*. London: T. Nelson, 1884; Reprint ed., Grand Rapids: Kregel Publications, 1978.

Atkinson, David. *The Message of Proverbs: Wisdom for Life*. In The Bible Speaks Today Series. J. A. Motyer, Old Testament Series Editor. Downers Grove: InterVarsity, 1996.

Barabas, Steven. "Balaam." Pages 121–22 in *The New International Dictionary of the Bible: Pictorial Edition*. Edited by J.D. Douglas and Merrill C. Tenney. Grand Rapids: Regency Reference Library, 1987.

Barna, George. *Leaders on Leadership*. Ventura, Calif.: Regal Books, 1997.

Barker, Kenneth L. ed. *Zondervan NIV Study Bible*. Grand Rapids: Zondervan, 2002.

Bartlett, John. *Familiar Quotations*. 15th edition. Edited by Emily Morison Beck. Boston: Little, Brown and Company, 1980.

Bennis, Warren, and Burt Nanus. *Leaders: Strategies for Taking Charge.* New York: HarperBusiness Essentials, 2003.

Blackaby, Henry, and Richard Blackaby. *Spiritual Leadership*. Nashville: Broadman and Holman, 2001.

Blanchard, Ken. *The Secret: What Great Leaders Know and Do.* 2nd edition. San Francisco: Berrett-Koehler, 2009.

———, and Mark Miller. *Great Leaders Grow: Becoming a Leader for Life.* San Francisco: Berrett-Koehler, 2012.

Blanchard, Ken, and Phil Hodges. *Lead Like Jesus*. Nashville: W. Publishing Group, 2005.

Bibliography

Booth, Wayne C., Gregory G. Colomb, and Joseph M. Williams. *The Craft of Research.* 3rd Edition. Chicago: The University of Chicago Press, 2008.

Bostrom, Lennart. *The God of the Sages: The Portrayal of God in the Book of the Proverbs.* Coniectanea Biblica Old Testament Series 29. Stockholm: Almqvist & Wiksell International, 1990.

Bridges, Charles. *A Commentary on Proverbs.* Reprint ed., Carlisle, Pa.: The Banner of Truth Trust, 1968.

Bright, John. *A History of Israel.* 3rd ed. Philadelphia: Westminster Press, 1981.

Brown, Francis, Driver, S. R., and Briggs, Charles A. *A Hebrew and English Lexicon of the Old Testament.* Reprint ed. Oxford: Clarendon Press, 1953.

Brownback, Paul. *The Danger of Self Love: Re-Examining a Popular Myth.* Chicago: Moody Press, 1982.

Bullock, C. Hassell. *An Introduction to the Old Testament Poetic Books.* Revised and expanded. Chicago: Moody Press, 1988.

Burkett, Larry. *Business by the Book.* Nashville: Thomas Nelson, 1998.

Chambers, Oswald. *Christian Disciplines.* Fort Washington, Pa.: Christian Literature Crusade, 1985.

———. *My Utmost For His Highest.* Edited by James Reimann. Uhrichsville, Ohio: Discovery House, 1992.

Clark, Irene L. *Writing the Successful Thesis and Dissertation.* Upper Saddle, N.J.: Prentice Hall, 2007.

Clifford, Richard J. *The Book of Proverbs and Our Search for Wisdom.* Milwaukee: Marquette University Press, 1995.

———. *Proverbs.* Vol. 11 in The Old Testament Library. Edited by James L. Mays, Carol A. Newsom, and David L. Petersen. 29 vols. Louisville: Westminster John Knox, 1999.

Cohen, A. *Proverbs. Soncino Books of the Bible.* Edited by A. Cohen. London: Soncino Press, 1946.

Coley, Kenneth S. *The Helmsman: Leading with Courage and Wisdom.* Colorado Springs: Purposeful Design Publications, 2006.

Collins, Jim. *Good to Great: Why Some Companies Make the Leap . . . and Others Don't.* New York: Harper Business, 2001.

Coogan, Michael D., ed. *The New Oxford Annotated Apocrypha.* 4th edition. New York: Oxford University Press, 2010.

Covey, Stephen M. R. *The Speed of Trust.* New York: Free Press, 2006.

Cox, Danny. *Leadership When the Heat's On.* New York: McGraw-Hill, 2003.

Crenshaw, James L. *Old Testament Wisdom: An Introduction.* Third edition. Louisville, Ky.: Westminster John Knox, 2010.

Dahood, Mitchell. *Proverbs and Northwest Semitic Philology.* Scripta Pontificii Instituti Biblici. Roma: Pontificum Institutum Biblicum, 1963.

daSilva, David A. *Introducing the Apocrypha.* Grand Rapids: Baker Academic, 2002.

Dayton, Edward R., and Ted W. Engstrom. *The Art of Management for Christian Leaders.* Waco: Word Books, 1976.

———. *Strategy for Leadership.* Old Tappan, N.J.: Fleming H. Revell, 1979.

Delitzsch, F. *Proverbs, Ecclesiastes, Song of Solomon.* Vol. 6 in *Commentary on the Old Testament.* Edited by C. F. Keil, and F. Delitzsch. 10 vols. Reprint edition. Grand Rapids: Eerdmans, 1975.

Douglas, J. D. *The New International Dictionary of the Bible.* Revising editor, J. D. Douglas. General editor, Merrill C. Tenney. Grand Rapids: Zondervan, 1987.

Bibliography

Drakeford, John W. *Humor in Preaching. The Craft of Preaching.* Grand Rapids: Ministry Resources Library, 1986.
Drane, John. *Introducing the Old Testament.* San Francisco: Harper & Row, 1987.
Draper, James T. *Proverbs: The Secret of Beautiful Living.* Wheaton: Tyndale House, 1977.
Eissfeldt, Otto. *The Old Testament: An Introduction.* Translated by P. R. Ackroyd. New York: Harper & Row, 1965.
Engstrom, Ted W. *The Making of a Christian Leader.* Grand Rapids: Zondervan, 1976.
Estes, Daniel J. *Handbook on the Wisdom Books and Psalms.* Grand Rapids: Baker Academic, 2005.
Fee, Gordon D., and Douglas Stuart. *How To Read the Bible For All Its Worth.* Grand Rapids: Zondervan, 1982.
Fisher, James L. *Positive Power: Your Path to a Higher Leadership Profile.* Provo, Utah: Executive Excellence Publishing, 2002.
Friedman, Hershey H. "Humor in the Hebrew Bible." *Humor: International Journal of Humor Research* 13:3 (Sept 2000): 258–85.
Friesen, Garry. *Decision Making & the Will of God: A Biblical Alternative to the Traditional View.* Portland, Oreg.: Multnomah Press, 1980.
———. *Proverbs 10–31. The Anchor Yale Bible.* Edited by William Foxwell Albright and David Noel Freedman. New Haven: Yale University Press, 2009.
Ford, Leighton. *Transforming Leadership.* Downers Grove: InterVarsity, 1991.
Foster, Richard J. *Celebration of Discipline.* New York: Harper & Row, 1978.
Fox, Michael V. *Proverbs 1–9.* Vol. 18A in The Anchor Yale Bible. Edited by William Foxwell Albright and David Noel Freedman. 44 vols. New Haven: Yale University Press, 2006.
Fulmer, Robert M. *The New Management.* Fourth edition. New York: Macmillan, 1988.
Gangel, Kenneth O. *Feeding & Leading: A Practical Handbook on Administration in Churches and Christian Organizations.* Wheaton: Victor Books, 1989.
———. *Team Leadership in Christian Ministry.* Chicago: Moody Press, 1997.
Garrett, Duane A. *Proverbs, Ecclesiastes, Song of Songs.* Vol. 14 in The New American Commentary Series. Edited by E. Ray Clendenen. 38 vols. Nashville: Broadman Press, 1993.
Getz, Gene A. *Elders and Leaders: God's Plan for Leading the Church.* Chicago: Moody Press, 2003.
Giuliani, Rudolph W. *Leadership.* New York: Miramax Books, 2002.
Goldberg, Louis. *Savoring the Wisdom of Proverbs.* Chicago: Moody Press, 1990.
Gross, Bertram M. *Organizations and Their Managing.* New York: The Free Press, 1968.
Harrington, Daniel J. "Introduction to Sirach." Page 133 in *The New Oxford Annotated Apocrypha.* Edited by Michael D. Coogan. 4th edition. New York: Oxford University Press, 2010.
Harris, R. Laird. "Book of Proverbs." Pages 830–31 in *The New International Dictionary of the Bible.* Revising editor J. D. Douglas. General editor, Merrill C. Tenney. Grand Rapids: Zondervan, 1987.
———, Gleason L. Archer, Jr., and Bruce K Waltke. *Theological Wordbook of the Old Testament.* 2 vols. Chicago: Moody Press, 1980.
Harrison, R. K. *Introduction to the Old Testament.* Grand Rapids: Eerdmans, 1969.
Hill, Andrew E., and John H. Walton. *A Survey of the Old Testament.* Grand Rapids: Zondervan, 1991.
Holman Topical Concordance. Philadelphia: A. J. Holman, 1973.

Bibliography

Holy Bible, English Standard Version Containing the Old and New Testaments. Wheaton: Crossway Bibles, 2001.

Holy Bible, Revised Standard Version Containing the Old and New Testaments. New York: Thomas Nelson & Sons, 1952.

House, H. Wayne, and Kenneth M. Durham. *Living Wisely in a Foolish World: A Contemporary Look at the Wisdom of Proverbs*. Grand Rapids: Kregel, 1992.

Hubbard, David. *Proverbs*. Vol. 15 in *The Communicator's Commentary*. Edited by Lloyd J. Oglivie. 35 vols. Waco, Tex.: Word, 1989.

Hummel, Horace D. *The Word Becoming Flesh*. St. Louis: Concordia, 1979.

Hybells, B *Axiom: Powerful Leadership Proverbs*. Grand Rapids: Zondervan, 2008.

Jacobs, T. O. *Leadership and Exchange in Formal Organizations*. Alexandria, Va.: Human Resources Research Organization, 1971.

Jinkins, Michael, and Deborah Bradshaw Jinkins. *The Character of Leadership*. San Francisco: Jossey-Bass, 1998.

Kahle, Paul, ed. *Biblia Hebraica Stuttgartensia*. Stuttgart: Deutsche Bibelgesellschaft, 1983.

Kaiser Jr., Walter C., and Moises Silva. *Introduction to Biblical Hermeneutics*. Revised and Expanded Edition. Grand Rapids: Zondervan, 2007.

Keen, Peter G. W. *Shaping the Future: Business Design Through Information Technology*. Boston: Harvard Business School, 1991.

Kidner, Derek. *The Proverbs*. Vol. 17 in the Tyndale Old Testament Commentaries. Edited by D. J. Wiseman. 28 vols. Downers Grove: InterVarsity, 1964.

Kilinski, Kenneth K., and Jerry C. Wofford. *Organization and Leadership in the Local Church*. Grand Rapids: Zondervan, 1973.

Klein, William W., Craig L. Blomberg, and Robert L. Hubbard, Jr. *Introduction to Biblical Interpretation*. Nashville: W. Publishing Group, 1993.

Knowles, Elizabeth, ed. *The Oxford Dictionary of Twentieth Century Quotations*. New York: Oxford University Press, 1998.

Kotter, John. *Our Iceberg Is Melting*. New York: St. Martin's, 2005.

Kouzes, James M., and Barry Z. Posner. *Christian Reflections on the Leadership Challenge*. San Francisco: Jossey-Bass, 2004.

———. *The Leadership Challenge*. 4th edition. San Francisco: John Wiley & Sons, Inc., 2007.

Kravitz, Leonard S., and Kerry M. Olitzky. *Mishlei: A Modern Commentary on Proverbs*. New York: Uahc Press, 2002.

Köstenberger, Andreas J., and Richard D. Patterson. *Biblical Interpretation: Exploring the Hermeneutical Triad of History, Literature, and Theology*. Grand Rapids: Kregel Academic & Professional, 2011.

Larsen, Paul E. *Wise Up & Live: Wisdom from Proverbs*. Glendale, Calif.: G/L Publications, 1974.

LaSor, William Sanford, David Allan Hubbard, and Frederic William Bush. *Old Testament Survey: The Message, Form, and Background of the Old Testament*. Grand Rapids: Eerdmans, 1982.

Lawson, George. *Exposition of Proverbs*. Edinburgh: W. Oliphant, 1829; Reprint ed. Grand Rapids: Kregel, 1980.

Leedy, Paul D., and Jeanne Elis Ormrod. *Practical Research: Planning and Design*. 7th Edition. Upper Saddle River, N.J.: Merrill Prentice Hall, 2001.

Likert, Rensis. *New Patterns of Management*. New York: McGraw-Hill, 1961.

Longman III, Tremper, and Raymond B. Dilliard. *An Introduction to the Old Testament*. 2nd ed. Grand Rapids: Zondervan, 2006.

———. *Proverbs.* Vol. 6 in the *Baker Commentary Series on the Old Testament Wisdom and Psalms.* Edited by Tremper Longman III. 8 vols. Grand Rapids: Baker Academic, 2006.
Mandelkern, Solomon. *Veteris Testamenti Concordantiae Hebraicae Atque Chaldaicae.* 2 vol. Graz, Austria: Akademische Druck-u. Verlagsanstalt, 1975.
Manyika, Noah. *The Challenge of Leadership.* Charlotte: Uplink, 2004.
Maxwell, John C. *Developing the Leader Within You.* Nashville: Thomas Nelson, 1993.
———. *Leadership 101.* Nashville: Thomas Nelson, 2002.
———. *The 21 Indispensable Qualities of a Leader.* Nashville: Thomas Nelson, 1999.
McKane, William. *Proverbs: A New Approach.* Vol. 10 in *The Old Testament Library.* Edited by Peter Ackroyd, James Barr, John Bright, and G. Ernest Wright. 15 vols. Philadelphia: The Westminster Press, 1970.
McQuilkin, Robertson. *Understanding and Applying the Bible.* Revised and Expanded. Chicago: Moody Press, 2009.
McIntosh, Gary L., and Samuel D. Rima, Sr. *Overcoming the Dark Side of Leadership.* Grand Rapids: Baker, 1997.
Merrill, Eugene H. *An Historical Survey of the Old Testament.* Grand Rapids: Baker, 1966.
Michael, Larry J. *Spurgeon on Leadership.* Grand Rapids: Kregel Academic & Professional, 2003.
Miller, Kathy Collard. *The Useful Proverbs.* Grand Rapids: Word, 1997.
Mouser, Jr., William E. *Walking in Wisdom: Studying the Proverbs of Solomon.* Downers Grove: InterVarsity, 1983.
Murphy, Roland. *Proverbs.* Vol. 22 in Word Biblical Commentary. Edited by Bruce Metzger, David A. Hubbard, and Glenn W. Barker. 58 vols. Nashville: Thomas Nelson, 1998.
Myra, Harold, ed. *Leaders: Learning Leadership from Some of Christianity's Best. The Leadership Library.* Waco: Word, 1987.
Neusner, Jacob, ed. and trans. *The Babylonian Talmud: A Translation and Commentary.* 22 vols. Peabody, Mass.: Hendrickson, 2005.
New International Version. Grand Rapids: Zondervan, 1978.
Oakley, Ed, and Doug Krug. *Enlightened Leadership: Getting to the Heart of Change.* New York: Simon & Schuster, 1991.
Osborne, Grant R. *The Hermeneutical Spiral: A Comprehensive Introduction to Biblical Interpretation.* Downer's Grove: InterVarsity, 1991.
Oesterley, W. O. E. *The Teaching of Amen-Em-Ope and The Book of Proverbs.* Whitefish, Minn.: Kessinger Publications, n.d.
Perowne, T. T. *The Proverbs.* Vol. 21 in The Cambridge Bible for Schools and Colleges. Edited by A. F. Kirkpatrick. 58 vols. Cambridge: The University Press, 1899.
Peterson, Eugene H., and Andy Southern. *The Message of Leadership.* Colorado Springs: Navpress, 2005.
Plaut, W. Gunther. *Book of Proverbs. The Jewish Commentary for Bible Readers.* New York: Union of American Hebrew Congregations, 1961.
Pollard, C. William. *The Soul of the Firm.* New York: Delta One Leadership Institute, 1996.
Poole, Matthew. *Psalms-Malachi.* Vol. 2 in *A Commentary on the Holy Bible.* 3 vols. Reprint ed.; McLean, Va.: MacDonald, n.d.
Powers, Bruce P. *Christian Leadership.* Nashville: Broadman, 1979.
Richards, James B. *Leadership That Builds People: Developing the Heart of a Leader.* Huntsville, Ala.: Impact International Publications, 1993.

Bibliography

Richards, Lawrence O., and Clyde Hoeldtke. *A Theology of Church Leadership*. Grand Rapids: Zondervan, 1980.
Ryken, Leland. *How To Read The Bible As Literature*. Grand Rapids: Zondervan, 1984.
Sanders, J. Oswald. *Dynamic Spiritual Leadership: Leading Like Paul*. Grand Rapids: Discovery House, 1999.
Schultz, Samuel J. *The Old Testament Speaks*. Second edition. New York: Harper & Row, 1970.
Scott, R. B. Y. *Proverbs Ecclesiastes. The Anchor Bible*. Edited by William Foxwell Albright and David Noel Freedman. New York: The Anchor Bible Doubleday, 1965.
———. *The Way of Wisdom in the Old Testament*. New York: Macmillan, 1971.
Shakespeare, William. *Othello. Oxford School Shakespeare*. Edited by Roma G Toronto: Oxford University Press, 1989.
Skehan, Patrick W. *Studies in Israelite Poetry and Wisdom*. The Catholic Biblical Quarterly-Monograph Series 1. Washington, D.C.: Catholic Biblical Association of America, 1971.
Smith, James E. *The Wisdom Literature and Psalms*. Joplin, Mo.: College Press, 1996.
Stanley, Andy. *The Next Generation Leader*. Sisters, Oreg.: Multnomah, 2003.
Stein, Robert H. *A Basic Guide to Interpreting the Bible*. 2nd edition. Grand Rapids: Baker Academic, 2011.
Stott, John. *Basic Christian Leadership: Biblical Models of Church, Gospel, and Ministry*. Downers Grove: InterVarsity Press, 2002.
Strauch, Alexander. *Biblical Eldership: An Urgent Call to Restore Biblical Church Leadership*. Revised and Expanded. Colorado Springs: Lewis and Roth, 1995.
Strong, James. *Strong's Exhaustive Concordance*. Nashville: Manna Publishers, n.d.
Tenney, Merrill C., and Steven Barabas, eds. *The Zondervan Pictorial Encyclopedia of the Bible*. 5 vols. Grand Rapids: Zondervan, 1975.
Thomas, David. *Book of Proverbs*. London: R. D. Dickinson, 1885; Reprint ed. Grand Rapids: Kregel, 1982.
Thomas, I. D. E. *The Golden Treasury of Puritan Quotations*. Chicago: Moody Press, 1975.
Thomas, Robert L. *Evangelical Hermeneutics: The New Versus the Old*. Grand Rapids: Kregel Academic & Professional, 2002.
Toy, Crawford H. *A Critical and Exegetical Commentary on the Book of Proverbs*. Vol. 13 in The International Critical Commentary on the Holy Scriptures of the Old and New Testaments. Edited by Samuel Rolles Driver, Alfred Plummer, and Charles Augustus Briggs. 53 vols. Edinburgh: T. & T. Clark, 1899.
Treier, Daniel J. *Proverbs and Ecclesiastes. Brazos Theological Commentary on the Bible*. Edited R. R. Reno. Grand Rapids: Brazos Press, 2011.
Turabian, Kate L. *A Manual for Writers of Research Papers, Theses, and Dissertations*. 7th Edition. Chicago: The University of Chicago Press, 2007.
Turner, Charles W. *Studies in Proverbs*. Grand Rapids: Baker Book House, 1976.
Unger, Merrill F. *Introductory Guide to the Old Testament*. Grand Rapids: Zondervan, 1951.
Unnamed. "Slander." Page 949 in *The New International Dictionary of the Bible*. Revising editor J. D. Douglas; General editor Merrill C. Tenney. Grand Rapids: Zondervan, 1987.
Van Leeuwen, Raymond. *Context and Meaning in Proverbs 25–27*. SBL Dissertation Series 96. Atlanta: Scholars Press, 1988.

Bibliography

———. "Proverbs." Pages 17–265 in vol. 5 of *The New Interpreter's Bible*. Edited by L. E. Keck. 12 vols. Nashville: Abingdon, 1997.

Von Rad, Gerhard. *Wisdom in Israel*. Nashville: Abingdon Press, 1972.

Virkler, Henry A. *Hermeneutics: Principles and Processes of Biblical Interpretation*. Grand Rapids: Baker Books, 1981.

Vyhmeister, Nancy Jean. *Your Guide to Writing Quality Research Paper for Students of Religion and Theology*. 2nd edition. Grand Rapids: Zondervan, 2008.

Wadsworth, Barry J. *Piaget's Theory of Cognitive Development*. New York: Longman, 1971.

Waltke, Bruce K. *The Book of Proverbs Chapters 1–15*. Vol. 11 in *The New International Commentary on the Old Testament*. Edited by R. K. Harrison and Robert L. Hubbard. 22 vols. Grand Rapids: Eerdmans, 2004.

———. *The Book of Proverbs Chapters 15–31*. Vol. 12 in *The New International Commentary on the Old Testament*. Edited by R. K. Harrison and Robert L. Hubbard. 22 vols. Grand Rapids: Eerdmans, 2005.

Wansbrough, ed., Henry. *New Jerusalem Bible*. New York: Darton, Longman, & Todd Limited and Doubleday, 1985.

Wardlaw, Ralph. *Lectures on The Book of Proverbs*. 3 vols. London: A. Fullerton & Co., 1861; Reprint ed., Minneapolis: Klock & Klock, 1981.

Webster's New World Dictionary of the American Language, College Edition. New York: The World Publishing Company, 1962.

Weeks, Stuart. *Instruction and Imagery in Proverbs 1–9*. New York: Oxford University Press, 2007.

Whybray, R. N. *The Book of Proverbs*. Vol. 24 in *The Cambridge Bible Commentary on the English Bible*. Edited by P. R. Ackroyd, A. R. C. Leaney, and J. W. Packer. 56 vols. Cambridge: University Press, 1972.

———. *Wisdom in Proverbs: The Concept of Wisdom in Proverbs 1–9*. Studies in Biblical Theology First Series 45. Eugene, Oreg.: Wipf & Stock, 1965.

Wiersbe, Warren W. *Be Skillful: God's Guidebook to Wise Living*. Colorado Springs: David C. Cook, 1995.

Wilkes, C. Gene. *Jesus on Leadership: Becoming a Servant Leader*. Nashville: Life Way Press, 1996.

Williams, James G. *Those Who Ponder Proverbs: Aphoristic Thinking and Biblical Literature*. Bible and Literature Series. Edited by David M. Gunn. Sheffield: Almond Press, 1981.

Witmer, Timothy Z. *The Shepherd Leader*. Phillipsburg, N.J.: P&R, 2010.

Wood, Leon. *A Survey of Israel's History*. Grand Rapids: Zondervan, 1970.

Woolfe, Lorin. *Leadership Secrets From The Bible*. New York: MJF Books, 2002.

Wright, J. Robert, ed. *Proverbs, Ecclesiastes, Song of Solomon*. Vol. 9 of *Ancient Christian Commentary on Scripture, Old Testament*. General Editor, Thomas C. Oden. 15 vols. Downers Grove: InterVarsity, 2005.

Yoder, Sanford Calvin. *Poetry of the Old Testament*. Scottdale, Pa.: Herald Press, 1948.

Young, Edward J. *An Introduction to the Old Testament*. Revised edition. Grand Rapids: Eerdmans, 1960.

Zigarelli, Michael. *Management by Proverbs*. Otsego, Mich.: PageFree Publishing, 2004.

Zuck, Roy B. *Basic Bible Interpretation*. Wheaton: Victor Books, 1991.

———, ed. *Learning From the Sages: Selected Studies on the Book of Proverbs*. Eugene, Oreg.: Wipf and Stock, 1995.

Ancient Writings Index

AMENEMOPE

24.9	12, 117
IX. xi.	13–14, 85

OLD TESTAMENT

Genesis

21:6	113

Exodus

20:15	81

Leviticus

13:23	28, 123

Numbers

22	26
22–24	67

Judges

8:1–3	62–63
12:1–6	63

1 Samuel

17:1–58	24

1 Kings

1–19	26
3:1–15	6
4:29–34	6
21	82

2 Kings

19:20–36	24

Nehemiah

4:1	113

Job

41:5	80

Psalms

1:9–16	44–45
12	117
15:1–4	84
19:10	53
23	43
23:2	43
23:5	44
24:4	80
32:1–4	58
35	117
37:13	80
58	117
59	117
69	117
70	117
73	117
73:8–9	120
83	117
104:26	80
109	117
119:11	36
137	117

Ancient Writings Index

Psalms (cont.)

140	117
147:1	55

Proverbs

1:5	26
1:7	9, 12–13, 56
1:8	15
1:9	66
2:12	121–122
3:5–7	13–14
3:11–12	18
3:13–15	35–36
3:22	66
3:30	89
4:9	66
4:24	122
5–7	108
5:1–2	59
5:1–5	15–16
5:13	33
5:15	17
5:15–18	16
5:21–23	18
6:1–19	122
6:6–11	117
6:12	122
6:12–19	120
6:16–19	70
6:17	83
6:19	83
8:7	70
8:12	59, 122
8:30	80
9:13	77
10:1	36, 114
10:1–22:17	31–32
10:1–31:9	122
10:4–5	117
10:6–11	76–77
10:7–10	76–77
10:8	76–77
10:10	76–77
10:13	59
10:18	71, 83–84
10:21	42–43, 44
10:31	52, 122–123
10:31–32	122
10:32	52, 123
11:9	60
11:9–13	60
11:10–11	60
11:12	60
11:12–13	59–60
11:12a	60
11:12b	60
11:13	60, 74–75
11:13a	60
11:13b	60
11:14	28
11:16	60–61
11:20	52
12:5–7	42
12:6	41–42
12:8	55–56
12:15	26, 27
12:16	46, 51, 99, 100
12:16–18	51
12:16–19	46, 99–100
12:16–22	50–51, 99
12:17	46, 49–50, 51
12:17–22	49
12:18	45, 46–47, 49, 50, 51, 99, 100
12:19	46, 49, 50, 51
12:19–22	51, 100
12:20	46, 49, 51, 52
12:21	46, 49, 51, 52
12:22	46, 49, 51, 52–53, 70
12:23	60, 61–62, 77
12:25	38, 118
13:1	26, 111, 113–114
13:3	62, 99, 100–101
13:3b	62
13:5	52
13:10	27, 90–91
13:13–14	26
13:24	20
14:3	31
14:5	53, 82
14:6	115
14:9	57, 115–116
14:9a	115
14:25	53, 82
15:1	63, 86

Ancient Writings Index

Reference	Pages
15:2	33–34, 77
15:4	45, 47
15:7	33, 34
15:12	114
15:18	64, 84, 85, 86, 89, 99, 101
15:19	23, 47, 62
15:21	23, 33
15:22	26, 64
15:23	54, 64
15:26	54
15:30	45, 47–48
16–22	102
16:1–5	24–25
16:3	29
16:9	25
16:13	52
16:19–22	46
16:21	35
16:23	34–35
16:24	45, 48, 53–54
16:25	23, 34–35
16:27	123–124
16:27–28	123
16:27–30	123
16:28	74, 123, 124
16:29–30	123
16:30	124
17:5	116–117
17:10	65–66, 111
17:14	90, 91–92
17:19	90, 91, 92–93
17:19a	92
17:19b	93
17:20	71, 72
17:22	81
17:27	99, 101, 102–103
17:27 18:4	101
17:27–28	32, 101–102
17:28	99, 101, 102–103
17:28–18:3	101
18:1	101
18:2	101, 102
18:3	101
18:4	101, 102
18:5	78
18:6	69
18:6–7	78
18:7	69
18:8	74
18:13	26
18:22	14, 15
19:1	124
19:5	71
19:11–12	87
19:13	14–15, 93–94, 97
19:13a	94
19:13b	94
19:14	14, 15, 97
19:18	20
19:20	26, 29
19:21	25
19:25	65–66, 118–119
19:25–20:1	118
19:28	118, 125
19:29	118
20:1	118
20:2	87
20:3	84, 87
20:14	103, 104–105
20:15	35–36
20:18	28
20:19	74–75
20:23	52
21:5	27, 29
21:9	93, 94, 95–96
21:11	118–119
21:19	14–15, 93, 94–95, 96
21:23	32
21:24	119–120
21:30	24
21:31	24
22:6	19–20
22:11	53, 54–55
22:15	20
22:17	36, 37
22:17–18	33
22:17–21	36
22:17–24:22	32
22:17–24:34	85
22:18	36, 37
22:19	37
22:20	37
22:21	37
22:22–24:22	36
22:24	85
22:24–25	85

Ancient Writings Index

Proverbs (cont.)

23:12	37
24:6	106
25:1	6, 32
25:1–29:27	32
25:11	38, 39, 54
25:12	66
25:18	82
25:20	39
26	109
26:4–5	64–65
26:17	84, 87–88
26:17–28	79
26:18–19	78–80
26:20	74
26:20–21	84–85, 88–89
26:20–28	109
26:21	93
26:22	74
26:24	71
26:25	71
26:27	110, 113
26:27–28	112
26:28	109–110
27:1	105
27:1–2	103–104, 105
27:1–10	106
27:2	106–107
27:5	111
27:9	39–40, 57
27:11	40, 97
27:11–27	97
27:14	111
27:15	93, 94, 96–97
27:15–16	97
27:16	97–98
27:17	28
28:12–29:2	58
28:13	58
28:14	58–59
28:23	66–67, 109, 111–112
28:23a	67
28:23b	67
29:5–6	109, 112–113
29:8	120–121
29:15	20
29:17	21
29:19	103
29:22	89
30	6
30:32	104, 107–108
30:33	85, 89–90, 108
31	6, 97
31:10	15
31:11–23	97
31:28	56
31:30–31	56

Ecclesiastes

9:13–16	29
10:12–13	101

Song of Solomon

4:10–15	16

Jeremiah

29:11	23
36:23–24	26

Ezekial

16:25	100
35:11–15	116–117

Amos

	1, 70
	2, 70

Micah

7:5	92

NEW TESTAMENT

Matthew

5:38–39	61
6:34	105
7:15–20	122
12:33–35	54–55
12:34–36	72
15:18	55
16:8	81
23:24	81
24:17	96

Luke

5:19	96
5:27–39	81
6:45	33
12	81
14:7–11	107
14:28–32	23
15:25–37	117
15:27	117

John

1:47	81

Acts of the Apostles

10:9	96
15:19–21	67

2 Corinthians

10:1–18	104
11:16–33	104
12:1–10	104

Romans

1:29–30	75

Galatians

2:11–14	67
6:7	110, 118
6:7–8a	72

Ephesians

5:3–4	81

1 Timothy

3:4–5	18–19

2 Timothy

2:1–2	37

Hebrews

3:13	40
10:24–25	40

James

1:26	31
3:1–12	31
3:13–16	105–106

1 Peter

3:15	36

1 John

1:9	58

APOCRYPHA

Sirach

25:9	69
25:16	95
28:14–18	82–83
28:24–25	100

Subject Index

A-B-A-B pattern, in Proverbs 10:31–32, 122
Abimelech, 110
Abraham ibn Ezra, 41, 92, 112
adages
  on evil, 110
  on foolish talk, 77
adornment, wisdom as, 66
adulterous women, 16
advice, seeking and accepting, 25–29, 57
Agur, 6, 90, 107
Aitken, Kenneth, 113
alcoholic beverages, 118
Alden, Robert
  on author of Proverbs, 5–6
  on foolish talk, 78
  on fools, 65
  on the future, 106
  on gender differences in Proverbs about quarreling, 96
  on gossip, 74
  on healing speech, 45
  on hot-tempered men and patient men, 86
  on memorizing Scripture, 36
  on mockers, 115
  on Proverbs 10:8,10, 77
  on Proverbs 10:31, 122
  on Proverbs 14:9, 116
  on Proverbs 15:30, 47–48
  on Proverbs 17:19, 92–93
  on Proverbs 19:1, 124
  on Proverbs 20:14, 104
  on Proverbs 21:30, 24
  on Proverbs 25:20, 39
  on Proverbs 26:18–19, 79
  Proverbs 27:9, translation of, 40
  on Proverbs 30:32, 108
  on Proverbs 30:33, 90
  on quarrelsome individuals, 96
  on sexual fidelity, metaphor for, 16–17
  on sinning, 71
  on slander, 83
  on speaking, timing of, 64
  on spiritual maturity, 114
  on teachers, words of, 35
  on trusting the Lord, 14
  on wise people, fools and, 66
Alter, Robert
  Proverbs 10:21, translation of, 42
  Proverbs 12:6, translation of, 41
  Proverbs 14:9, translation of, 115
  Proverbs 15:2, translation of, 33
  Proverbs 15:30, translation of, 47
  Proverbs 16:27, translation of, 123–124
  Proverbs 17:19b, translation of, 93
  on Proverbs 19:28, 125
  Proverbs 21:11, translation of, 119
  Proverbs 27:16, translation of, 97–98
  Proverbs 28:13, translation of, 58
  Proverbs 29:5, translation of, 112
  Proverbs 29:8, translation of, 121
  Proverbs 29:22, translation of, 89
Amenemope, 85–86
Amerding, Hudson, 103
anger, quarrels and, 89
answering fools, 64–65

Subject Index

anthithetic parallelism, 75
Antilegomena, Proverbs as, 64–65
antithetic parallelisms
   Proverbs 10:21, 43
   Proverbs 10:31, 122
   Proverbs 11:12, 60
   Proverbs 11:13, 60
   Proverbs 12:8, 55
   Proverbs 12:16, 60
   Proverbs 12:19, 50
   Proverbs 12:22, 70
   Proverbs 12:23, 61
   Proverbs 13:1, 113
   Proverbs 13:3, 62, 100
   Proverbs 13:10, 90–91
   Proverbs 15:4, 47
   Proverbs 15:18, 85, 89
   Proverbs 20:15, 35
   Proverbs 21:11, 119
   Proverbs 29, 112
   Proverbs 29:8, 121
   use of, 12–13
appearances, deceptive, 105
apt replies, 64
Arab proverbs, on intolerable living conditions, 93
Archer, Gleason, 86
arguments. *See* quarreling
Arnot, William, 13, 15, 68, 77
arrogance, boasting and, 105
Asaph, 117, 120
'awa (bend, twist), 55
Axiom: Powerful Leadership Proverbs (Hybels), 10

Balaam, 26, 67
Barabas, Steven, 67
bata (speaking rashly, thoughtlessly), 99
being upright, 115–116
Ben Sira. *See* Yeshua ben Eleazar ben Sira
Bennis, Warren, 17
Bible
   content on leadership, 1
   inerrancy, 5
   mockery, range of meanings, 113
Biblia Hebraica Stuttgartensia, 4
Blackaby, Henry, 10, 12, 17, 28, 73

Blackaby, Richard, 10, 12, 17, 28, 73
blasphemy, 116
boasting, 103–108
bones, fat in, 47–48
Book of Proverbs. *See* Proverbs, Book of
bootlickers, 111–112
Bridges, Charles, 14, 54, 66, 89, 103
Bright, John, 7
Brooks, Thomas, 72
Budge, E. A. Wallis, 85–86
building a high gate, 92–93
Burkett, Larry, 10
Business By the Book (Burkett), 10–11
busybodies, 87–88

canonicity discussions, 64–65
Caveat emptor (Let the buyer beware), 105
Chambers, Oswald, 12
character, 123, 128
chiasmus
   in Proverbs 10:31–32, 122
   in Proverbs 11:9–13, 60
   in Proverbs 12:19–22, 46, 51
   in Proverbs 18:6–7, 78
   of Proverbs 20:3 and surrounding verses, 87
Chicago Statement on Biblical Inerrancy, 5
children, 18–21, 20, 114
Chinese proverbs, on liars, 70
Clifford, Richard J.
   on confession of sin, 59
   on fools, children as, 114
   on Proverbs 12:19, 50
   on Proverbs 13:3b, 62
   Proverbs 17:19b, translation of, 93
   on Proverbs 21:24, 120
   on Proverbs 27:9, 40
   Proverbs 27:16, translation of, 97
   on Proverbs 28:23, 67
   on *puah*, meaning of, 49
   on scoffers, 121
Cohen, A.
   on advice, 57
   on fools vs. wise men, 47
   on the heart, 34
   on lying tongue, harm from, 109

Subject Index

on a man's speech, 123
on meddlers, 87–88
on mockery, 116
on pleasant words, 53
on Proverbs 19:1, 124
on Proverbs 20:15, 35
on Proverbs 22:11, 54
on Proverbs 25:11, 38
Proverbs 27:15, translation of, 97
on Proverbs 27:15, 96
Proverbs 29:8, translation of, 121
common sense, 56
confession of sin (in speech), 57–59
constructive criticism. *See* rebukes
contempt, expressing, 60
contradictions, 64–65
contrast, teaching by, 8
corporal punishment, 20, 21
corporate no-gossip policies, 75–76
counsel (advice), obtaining, 25–29
counselors, effective, 28
courtroom testimony, 49–50
criticism, constructive, 46
cutting out of the tongue, 122–123

dams, leaks in, 91
David (king), 26, 53, 55, 58, 84
Decalogue, on slander, 81
deceit, 109
delep (constant dripping), 93–94
delimitations of study, 4
Delitzsch, Franz
    on fools, 115–116
    on intolerable living conditions, 93
    on mockers, 118–119
    on Proverbs 12:18, 99
    Proverbs 14:9, translation of, 115
    on Proverbs 22:6, 19
    on Proverbs 27:1–10, 106
    on slander, 83–84
    on thoughtful speech, 50
Dillard, Raymond, 1, 6, 9
discerning men, rebuking of, 65–66
discipline, parental, 18–21
discretion in speech, 59–65
dishonesty in speech. *See* lying
divine justice, 9
divine sovereignty, 25

dogs, 88
Drakeford, John D., 80
Draper, James T., 31, 81, 86, 99, 108

Ecclesiastes, authorship of, 6
Edom, 116–117
education of children, 19–20
effective leadership, 126
Eissfeldt, Otto, 6
elders in the Church of Jesus Christ, 18–19
Eliezer ben Azariah, Rabbi, 66
emblematic parallelism, 88, 114
encouragement in speech, 38–40
The English Standard Version (ESV), 59
Ephraem the Syrian, 62
Ephraimites, 62–63
Estes, Daniel, 13, 16, 27, 29, 53
ESV (The English Standard Version), 59
evil men, flattery and, 113
Ezekiel, 116–117

false testimony, 82
false witness (slander), 71, 81–84
family
    discussion of, 14–22
    leaders' relationship to children, 18–21
    leaders' relationship to wife, 14–18
fat in the bones, 47–48
fatherly teachings, 97
fathers. *See* parents and children, relationship of
fear of the Lord, 12–13, 56
Fee, Gordon, 8–9
fidelity in marriage, 15–18
fighting, 120–121
flattery, 66–67, 108–113
flogging, 118
followers, leaders and, 5
Folly, 77
foolish sons, 93, 94
foolish talk, 76–81
fools
    answering, 64–65
    Arnot on, 77
    Cohen on, 34
    dishonest, 124

163

Subject Index

fools *(cont.)*
  flogging of, 65–66
  foolish talk, 76–81
  improper use of the tongue, 69
  Jewish frustration with, 65
  in the market, 104
  as mockers, 113–114, 115
  nourishment and, 44
  playing the fool, 107–108
  prudent men, comparison with, 60–61, 77
  quarreling and, 87
  silence of, 103
  sin, response to, 115
  as slanderers, 71
  wise men vs., 12–13, 33–34, 47, 66
  words of, 101
Ford, Leighton, 10
Fox, Michael V.
  on conflict, avoidance of, 100
  on the future, 105
  on hypocrites, 109
  Proverbs 15:30, translation of, 47
  on Proverbs 30:32, 108
  on reckless speech, 100
Franklin, Benjamin, 60
Friedman, Hershey H., 80
friendships, 111
Friesen, Gary, 27–28
fruit trees, metaphor of, 122
future, 105–106

galal (to roll), 110
Garrett, Duano
  on building a high gate, 93
  on busybodies, 88
  on concept of God in Proverbs, 59
  on confession of sin, 58
  on cutting out of the tongue, 122–123
  on discipline, 18, 20
  on discretion, 63
  on educating children, 19–20
  on infidelity, 16
  on jewelry, metaphors of, 66
  on mockers, 118, 119
  on Provebs 16:27–28, 123
  on Proverbs, 9
  on Proverbs 10:6–11, structure of, 76
  on Proverbs 11:9–13, structure of, 60
  on Proverbs 11:13, 60
  on Proverbs 12:5–7, structure of, 42
  on Proverbs 12:16–22, structure of, 46, 50–51, 99–100
  on Proverbs 15:23, 64
  on Proverbs 17:19, 91
  on Proverbs 17:27–28, structure of, 101
  on Proverbs 18:6–7, structure of, 78
  on Proverbs 19:25–20:1, structure of, 118
  on Proverbs 20:3, 87
  on Proverbs 21:9–19, structure of, 95
  on Proverbs 21:30, 24
  on Proverbs 22:10–11, 54
  on Proverbs 27:11–27, structure of, 97
  on Proverbs 28:23, 111
  on Proverbs 29:5–6, 112
  on Proverbs' emphasis on use of appropriate words, 101–102
  on quarreling, 86
  on quarrelsome wives, 94
  on seeking advice, 29
  on *sekel*, 55
  on Solomon's possible borrowings from Amenemope, 85
  on strife, 90
  on treasures, 35
  on wisdom literature, 9
  on wise men, 34–35
gender bias, 95–96
genetic epistemology, 19
Gersonides (Levi ben Gershom), 34, 41, 43, 114
Gideon, 62–63
Gileadites, 63
God
  concept of, in Proverbs, 59
  leader's relationship to, 12–14
  partnership with, 24–25
  planning and, 29
  playful spirit of, 80
  practices hateful to, 70
  sins hated by, 122
  trust in, 14
godly leaders, 4, 128

Subject Index

Goldberg, Louis, 21, 32
good words, 48
gossip and gossips, 60, 73–76, 88, 124
gracious speech, 54

halal (to praise), 105
Harrington, Daniel J., 95
Harris, R. Laird, 8
hatred, 109
healing speech, 45–48
heart, 33–34, 72
Hebrew sacrificial system, 115
Henry, Philip, 111
Hezekiah, King, 6, 7
high gates, building, meaning of, 92–93
Hildenbrandt, Ted, 76
Hill, Andrew, 126
Homily on Our Lord 22.3 (Ephraem the Syrian), 62
honesty, 48–53, 67, 71, 73, 111
  See also lying
honor-shame societies, 95
hot-tempered men, 85, 86, 89
Hubbard, David, 8
humility, 27, 62, 105, 107
humor, 80, 81
Humor in Preaching (Drakeford), 80
Humor: International Journal of Humor Research, 80
hunting instruments, 112
hurtful speech, 47
husband and wife, relationship of, 14–18
Hybels, Bill, 10, 18
hypocrites, 109

Iago (fict.), 82
ICBI (International Council on Biblical Inerrancy), 5
imparting knowledge and wisdom, 33–37
Imprecatory Psalms, 117
improper use of the tongue. *See* leader's speech (improper use of the tongue)
inclusios, 76, 95, 101, 118
individual self-discipline, 9

inerrancy, 5
insolence, 91
instruction, 26, 33–37
integrity, 17
intelligence, common sense vs., 56
International Council on Biblical Inerrancy (ICBI), 5

James (Apostle), 31, 105–106
Jehoiakim (king of Judah), 26
Jephthah, 63
Jeremiah (prophet), 23, 26
Jesus Christ
  on good vs. evil speech, 54–55
  humor, use of, 81
  as life's foundation, 21
  metaphor of fruit trees, 122
  Parable of the Good Samaritan, 117
  parable on self-praise, 107
  on planning, 23
  on tongue, connection with heart, 72
  on turning the other cheek, 61
Jethro, 118
jewelry. *See* adornment
John (Apostle), 58
Joseph, 55

kesil (fool), 13
Kidner, Derek
  on deceit, 109
  on fools, 13, 102
  on hot-tempered men, 89
  on individuals with wrong attitude, 120
  on Proverbs 20:15, 35
  on Proverbs 22:6, 19
  on Proverbs 22:17–21, 37
  on quarreling, 91
  on rashness, 62
  on sayings of Agur, 107
kind words (encouragement), 38–40
knowledge, value of, 33
knowledge and wisdom, imparting, 33–37
Köstenberger, Andreas, 10
Kouzes, James, 39, 72–73

Subject Index

Kravitz, Leonard
  on anger, 90
  on expressing contempt, 60
  on intelligence, 56
  on knowledge, 33–34
  Proverbs 12:6, translation of, 41
  on Proverbs 25:12, 66
  on quarreling, 87, 91
  on speaking, 64
  on unlearned masses, 43
  on women, status of, in Palestine, 96

Latin proverbs, 105
Law of God, King David on, 53
Lawson, George, 29, 110–111
leader's plans, 23–30
  God, partnership with, 24–25
  others, partnership with, 25–29
  summary, 30
leader's priorities, 12–22
  God, relationship to, 12–14
  husband and wife, 14–18
  parents and children, 18–21
  summary, 21–22
leader's speech (improper use of the tongue), 69–125
  boasting, 103–108
  flattery, 108–113
  foolish talk, 76–81
  gossip, 73–76
  lying, 69–73
  mockery, 113–121
  overview, 69
  perverse talk, 121–125
  quarreling, 84–98
  slander, 81–84
  speaking rashly, 99–103
  summary, 125
leader's speech (proper use of the tongue), 31–68
  advice, 57
  confession of sin, 57–59
  discretion, 59–65
  encouragement, 38–40
  healing, 45–48
  imparting knowledge and wisdom, 33–37
  nurture, 42–45
  overview, 31–33
  pleasant speech, 53–55
  praise, 55–56
  protection, 41–42
  rebuke, 65–67
  summary, 68
  telling the truth, 48–53
leadership, 4–5, 128
The Leadership Challenge (Kouzes and Posner), 73
leadership principles, derived from Proverbs, research on, 2, 10–11
leadership studies, 1, 4
Lemuel, sayings of, 6
Levi ben Gershom (Gersonides), 34, 41, 43, 114
liars, 53
lips, heart, connection with, 33–34
literary devices. *See* chiasmus; metonymies; parallelisms; similes; triplets; X + 1 formula
living conditions, intolerable, 93
Longman, Tremper, III
  on curring out of the tongue, 123
  on deceptive appearances, 105
  on discretion, 61
  on evil doers, truth and, 51
  on flattery, 110
  on fools, 116, 118
  on gender bias in Proverbs about quarreling, 96
  on gossip, 74
  on heart, connection with tongue, 72
  on insolence, 91
  on lying, 50, 71
  on mocker's pride, 120
  on mockery, 117
  on perverse men, 124
  on planning, 25
  on poverty, ridicule of, 117
  on Proverbs, authorship of, 6
  on Proverbs, content of, 9
  on Proverbs, popularity of, 1
  on Proverbs 10:21, 43
  on Proverbs 12:6, 41
  on Proverbs 12:11, 55
  on Proverbs 12:21, 51
  Proverbs 12:22, translation of, 70

Subject Index

on Proverbs 17:19, 91–92
Proverbs 17:19a, translation of, 92
on Proverbs 19:1, 125
on Proverbs 22:6, 19
on Proverbs 25:18, 82
on Proverbs 27:16, 97
Proverbs 29:5, translation of, 112
Proverbs 30:33, translation of, 90
on righteous men, vs. wicked, 52
on sexual intimacy, terminology for, 16
on speaking wisely, 38
on superscription to Proverbs, 5
on troublemakers, 120–121
long-range planning, 106
love thy neighbor, 117
lying, 69–73, 109–110
See also honesty

malicious intent, 78, 79, 80
Management by Proverbs (Zigarelli), 11
marketplace, bargaining in, 104–105
marriage, 14–18
material prosperity, 57–58
Maxwell, John, 10
McKane, William
  on flattery, recipient of, 113
  on fool's speech, 78
  on Proverbs 12:21, 52
  on Proverbs 12:22, 53
  on Proverbs 27:9, 57
  on rebukes, 111
  on self-praise, 107
meddlers, 87–88
men
  discerning, rebuking of, 65–66
  hot-tempered, 85, 86, 89
  patient, 64, 85, 86
  prudent, 60, 61–62, 77
  quarrelsome, 93
  righteous, 52, 113
  wicked, 17
  See also fools; wise men
The Message of Leadership (Peterson and Southern), 10
methodology of study, 3–4
metonymies, 50
Michael, Larry, 21–22

Midrash, 6
military training, 18
mits (churning, twisting), 89–90
mockery, 113–121
Murphy, Roland
  on anger, 61
  on author of Proverbs, 6
  on confession of sin, 59
  on fools, silence of, 102
  on gender bias in Proverbs about quarreling, 95–96
  on gossip, 74
  on loquaciousness, 99
  Proverbs 12:6, translation of, 41
  Proverbs 12:18, translation of, 99
  on Proverbs 13:3, 100–101
  on Proverbs 17:19, 92
  on Proverbs 20:14, 104
  on Proverbs 22:6, 20
  Proverbs 27:16, translation of, 97
  on Proverbs 29:5, 112
  on seeking advice, 27
  on self-judgment, 106
My Utmost For His Highest (Chambers), 12

Naboth, 82
Nanus, Burt, 17
negative feedback, 103
nets of flattery, 112–113
New International Version of the Bible
  gossip, verses mentioning, 73–74
  Micah 7:5, translation of, 92
  mits, translation of, 89–90
  Proverbs 12:6, translation of, 41
  on Proverbs 14:9a, 115
  Proverbs 15:30, translation of, 48
  on Proverbs 17:19, 92
  Proverbs 22:6, translation of, 20
  Proverbs 26:18–19, translaion of, 78
  translation philosophy, 98
The New Oxford Annotated Apocrypha, 4
nirgan (to murmur, whisper), 74
NIV Study Bible, on Proverbs 20:15, 36
no-gossip policies, 75–76
nurturing speech, 42–45

167

Subject Index

obesity, 47–48
Oesterley, W. O., 85
Old Testament, humor in, 80
Olitzky, Kerry
    on anger, 90
    on expressing contempt, 60
    on intelligence, 56
    on knowledge, value of, 33–34
    Proverbs 12:6, translation of, 41
    on Proverbs 25:12, 66
    on quarreling, 87, 91
    on speaking, 64
    on unlearned masses, 43
    on women, status of, in Palestine, 96
order, as center of wisdom thinking, 9
Osborne, Grant, 126
others, partnership with, 25–29

Parable of the Good Samaritan, 117
parables, 107
paradoxes, 65
parallelisms, 8, 92, 102
    See also antithetic parallelisms; emblematic parallelism; synonymous parallelism; synthetic parallelism
parents and children, relationship of, 18–21
partnership with God, 24–25
partnership with others, 25–29
pasaq (to part, open wide), 100
paternal teachings, 97
patient men, 64, 85, 86
Patterson, Richard, 10
Paul (Apostle)
    boasting by, 104
    on elders, qualifications for, 18–19
    on gossiping, 75
    on leaders, influence of, 37
    Peter, opposition to, 67
    on reaping what one sows, 110
    on sinning, 72
    on sins, 81
perjury, 82
persuasion, 62
perverse talk, 121–125
Peter (Apostle), 36, 67
Peterson, Eugene
    on leadership, difficulty of defining, 4–5
    The Message of Leadership, 10
    Proverbs 3:30, translation of, 89
    Proverbs 10:21, translation of, 42–43
    Proverbs 12:23, translation of, 61–62
    Proverbs 13:1, translation of, 114
    Proverbs 15:1, translation of, 86
    Proverbs 15:4, translation of, 47
    Proverbs 17:19b, translation of, 93
    Proverbs 19:1, translation of, 124
    Proverbs 20:15, translation of, 35
    Proverbs 21:24, translation of, 120
    Proverbs 27:1, translation of, 105
    Proverbs 27:9, translation of, 40, 57
    Proverbs 28:23, translation of, 111
    Proverbs 29:5, translation of, 112
    Proverbs 29:22, translation of, 89
    on sexual fidelity, 17
    on speech, power of, 31
Pharisees, 54–55
Piaget Jean, 19
piety, 24
plans. *See* leader's plans
Plaut, W. Gunther
    on contradictions in Proverbs, 64–65
    on mockery in mourning, 117
    on nourishment, 44
    on perverse talk, 123
    on Proverbs 22:11, 54
    on quarreling, 87
    on quarrelsome wives, 95
playing the fool, 107–108
pleasant speech, 45, 53–55
poor, ridicule of, 117
Posner, Barry, 39, 72–73
praise (in speech), 55–56
pride
    boasting and, 104, 108
    humility vs., 62
    mockery and, 114, 119
    seeking advice and, 27
    as source of quarrels, 91
priorities. *See* leader's priorities
proper use of the tongue. *See* leader's speech (proper use of the tongue)
Prosperity Gospel, 117
protective speech, 41–42

Subject Index

proverbs
  limitations of, 52
  See also Arab proverbs; Latin proverbs; Rabbinic proverbs
Proverbs, Book of
  anthithesis of, 13–14
  authorship, 5–7
  central purpose, 7–8
  content of, 8–9
  contradictions in, 64–65
  leadership principles derived from, research on, 2, 10–11
  main contrast in, 8
  place in life of Hebrew nation, 126
  speech, extent of mentions of, 31–32
  themes of, 9–10, 12–13
prudence, 61
prudent men, 60, 61–62, 77
puah (testifying), 49
punishment, 118–119

Qoheleth, 29
quarreling, 84–98
  dissension and, 89
  gossips and, 88–89
  pressing arguments, 90
  quarrelsome individuals, 93–98
  sources of, 85–88
  starting, 90–93
quarrelsome individuals, 93–98

ra'a (pasture, graze), 43
Rabbinic proverbs, 49, 104, 120
ragan (to murmur, whisper), 74, 88
rakil (talebearer, informer), 75
Rashi. See Solomon Yitzchak ben Isaac, Rabbi
rashness of speech, 62, 99–103
reaping what one sows, 118
rebukes, 46, 65–67, 111–112
reckless speech, 50, 99
Rehoboam (Solomon's son), 26, 29
reproofs, to children, 21
retribution and divine justice, 9
The Revised Standard Version (RSV), 59
rib (strife, dispute, quarrel), 84–85, 89

righteous men, 113
rimmah (deceive), 79
roofs, holes in, 93–94
RSV (The Revised Standard Version), 59
Ryken, Leland, 52, 65

Sayings of Agur son of Jakeh—an oracle (section of Proverbs), 6, 90, 107
Sayings of King Lemuel (section of Proverbs), 15
Sayings of the wise (section of Proverbs), 32, 37
scoffers. See mockery
Scott, Walter, 69
Scripture quotations, sources for, 3–4
sekel (wisdom), 55
self-judgment, 106
self-praise, 106–107
Seneca (Roman philosopher), 123
Sermon on the Mount, 122
sexual fidelity, 15–18
sexual intimacy, 16
shalah (to sow, spread), 74
sheep, 43
silence, 38, 60, 61, 102–103
similes, 57, 66, 82, 97
the simple, 119
sin and sinning, 57–59, 70–71, 72, 81, 115
  See also flattery; slander
Sira. See Yeshua ben Eleazar ben Sira
slander, 71, 81–84
Smith, James E., 28, 33, 42, 70, 82
Solomon (king)
  accomplishments, 7
  Amenemope, possible borrowings from, 85–86
  as author of Proverbs, 5–7
  David, contrast with, 26
  on discretion, 59
  on God, relationship with, 12–13
  knowledge, regard for, 34
  on speaking rashly, 99
  stress, understanding of, 38
  on wise men, 35
  on words of wise men vs. fools, 101

Subject Index

Solomon Yitzchak ben Isaac, Rabbi (Rashi)
  on Abimelech, 110
  on mockery in mourning, 117
  on Proverbs 17:14, 91
  on Proverbs 17:19, 92
  on Proverbs 18:6, 78
  on prudent people, 61
  on punishment as warning, 118
  as source for translations, 41
Song of Songs, 6
sons, foolish, 93, 94
Southern, Daniel, 4–5, 10, 17
speech and speaking
  encouragement in, 38–40
  imparting knowledge and wisdom, 33–37
  importance of, 62
  power of, 31, 99
  as reflection of character, 123
  speaking rashly, 99–103
  timing of, 64, 65
  See also leader's speech (improper use of the tongue); leader's speech (proper use of the tongue)
Spiritual Leadership (Blackaby and Blackaby), 10
spiritual maturity, 114
Stanley, Andy, 25, 128
stress, 38
structure of proverbs. *See* A-B-A-B pattern; chiasmus; literary devices; parallelisms; triplets (structural); X + 1 formula
Stuart, Douglas, 8–9, 52
superscription to Proverbs, 5–6
sword thrusts, 99
synonymous parallelism, 39–40, 89, 116, 120, 125
synthetic parallelism
  Proverbs 10:18, 83
  Proverbs 15:23, 64
  Proverbs 17:19, 91
  Proverbs 17:20, 72
  Proverbs 17:27–28, 102
  Proverbs 19:1, 124
  Proverbs 20:19, 75
  Proverbs 21:9, 94
  Proverbs 28:23, 66–67, 111

The Talmud, 48–49, 65, 83
Tarfon, Rabbi, 66
teachers, words of, 35
Teaching of Amenemope (Egyptian text), 36, 85–86, 117
telling the truth, 48–53
  See also lying
Thomas, David, 106, 112–113
thoughtful speech, 50
thoughtless reactions, 99
time, as factor in seeking advice, 27–28
tongue, 69, 72, 122–123
  See also leader's speech (improper use of the tongue); leader's speech (proper use of the tongue)
Toy, C. H.
  on antithetic parallelism in Proverbs 10:21, 43
  on antithetic parallelism in Proverbs 10:31, 122
  on author of Proverbs, 6
  on honesty in speech, 67
  on lying tongue, harm from, 109
  on mockers, 114
  on pleasant words, 53
  on Proverbs 10:18, 83
  on Proverbs 12:8, 55, 56
  Proverbs 14:9, translation of, 115
  on Proverbs 14:9, 115
  on Proverbs 15:4, 47
  on Proverbs 17:14, 91
  on Proverbs 17:19, 92
  on Proverbs 20:15, 35
  on Proverbs 21:24, dating of, 119–120
  on Proverbs 27:9, 40
  on Proverbs 28:23, 111
  translations by, 33
  on turning the other cheek, 61
tradition and the fathers, 9
Transforming Leadership (Ford), 10
triplets (structural), 79
troublemakers, 120–121
trust in God, 14
truthfulness, 48–53, 70
  See also lying

Subject Index

Turner, Charles, 45
turning the other cheek, 61

unsolicited advice, 26–27
uprightness, 115–116
use of the tongue. *See* leader's speech; leader's speech (improper use of the tongue); leader's speech (proper use of the tongue)

valor, 63
Van Leeuwen, R. C., 25, 79, 88, 106

Waltke, Bruce
    on contentious wives, 98
    on gossips, 88–89
    on healing speech, 47
    on kind words, 38
    on liars, 53
    on lying tongue, harm from, 109
    on nourishment, 44
    on pleasant words, 54
    on Proverbs 10:18, 83
    on Proverbs 12:18, 46
    on Proverbs 12:20–21, 52
    on Proverbs 15:30, 48
    on Proverbs 17:19, 92
    on Proverbs 17:27–28, 102
    on Proverbs 18:6–7, 78
    on Proverbs 19:28–29, 118
    on Proverbs 20:3, 87
    on Proverbs 25:20, 39
    on Proverbs 26:18–19, 79
    on Proverbs 27:1–10, 106
    on Proverbs 27:9, 57
    on Proverbs 28:23, 111
    on Proverbs 29:5–6, 112
    on Proverbs 30:32, 107–108
    on self-praise, 106–107
    on speaking, timing of, 64
    on speech, importance of, 62
    on telling the truth vs. lying, 49
    on thoughtful speech, 50
    on wise men, 34
Walton, John, 126
war, 28–29
Warnings Against Folly, 122

warped minds, 55–56
Watson, John, 55
wicked men, 17, 117
The Wife of Noble Character, 56
Williams, James, 9
wisdom
    as adornment, 66
    discretion, link to, 59, 62
    fear of the Lord and, 56
    and knowledge, imparting, 33–37
    warped minds vs., 55–56
wisdom literature, 9–10, 37, 38, 64, 119
The Wisdom of Amenemope (Egyptian text) ## d.p. as "Teaching of Amenemope," 36, 85–86, 117
wise men
    Alden on, 24
    fools vs., 12–13, 33–34, 47, 66
    method of gaining knowledge, 119
    mockers vs., 121
    wise sons, mockers vs., 113–114
    words of, 34–35, 101
wise sons, 113–114
wise utterance, 9
wives
    See also husband and wife
wives, quarrelsome, 93–97
women, 16, 96
Wood, Leon, 26
Woolfe, Lorin, 1
words, power of, 45, 46
workplaces, gossip in, 75

X + 1 formula, 70

yagareh (dissension), 89
yakah (correct, rebuke), 18
Yeshua ben Eleazar ben Sira (Sira, Ben Sira)
    on bad wives, 95
    on discretion, 61, 62
    on improper use of the tongue, 69
    on slander, 82–83
    on speaking rashly, 100
yhwh akah (Yahweh reproves), 18
Young, Edward J., 6–7

Subject Index

zadon (insolence), 91
Zigarelli, Michael
  on advice, 26–27
  on dishonesty in speech, 71
  on encouraging others, 39
  on gossip, 73
  Management by Proverbs, 11
  on negative feedback, delivering, 103
  on no-gossip policies, 75–76
  on planning, 23, 25
  on Proverbs, central purpose of, 7–8
  on Solomon, 7
  on words, power of, 46
Zuck, Roy, 71

www.ingramcontent.com/pod-product-compliance
Lightning Source LLC
Chambersburg PA
CBHW050806160426
43192CB00010B/1657